Shakespeare: The Sonnets

ANALYSING TEXTS

General Editor: Nicholas Marsh

Published

Chaucer: The Canterbury Tales   *Gail Ashton*
Aphra Behn: The Comedies   *Kate Aughterson*
Webster: The Tragedies   *Kate Aughterson*
John Keats   *John Blades*
Shakespeare: The Sonnets   *John Blades*
Wordsworth and Coleridge: Lyrical Ballads   *John Blades*
Shakespeare: The Comedies   *R. P. Draper*
Charlotte Brontë: The Novels   *Mike Edwards*
George Eliot: The Novels   *Mike Edwards*
E. M. Forster: The Novels   *Mike Edwards*
Jane Austen: The Novels   *Nicholas Marsh*
William Blake: The Poems   *Nicholas Marsh*
Emily Brontë: Wuthering Heights   *Nicholas Marsh*
Philip Larkin: The Poems   *Nicholas Marsh*
D. H. Lawrence: The Novels   *Nicholas Marsh*
Shakespeare: The Tragedies   *Nicholas Marsh*
Virginia Woolf: The Novels   *Nicholas Marsh*
John Donne: The Poems   *Joe Nutt*
Thomas Hardy: The Novels   *Norman Page*
Marlowe: The Plays   *Stevie Simkin*

Analysing Texts
Series Standing Order ISBN 0–333–73260–X
(outside North America only)

You can receive future titles in this series as they are published by placing a standing order.
Please contact your bookseller or, in the case of difficulty, write to us at the address below
with your name and address, the title of the series and the ISBN quoted above.

Customer Services Department, Palgrave Ltd
Houndmills, Basingstoke, Hampshire RG21 6XS, England

Shakespeare:
The Sonnets

JOHN BLADES

First published 2007 by
PALGRAVE MACMILLAN
Houndmills, Basingstoke, Hampshire RG21 6XS and
175 Fifth Avenue, New York, N.Y. 10010
Companies and representatives throughout the world

PALGRAVE MACMILLAN is the global academic imprint of the Palgrave
Macmillan division of St. Martin's Press, LLC and of Palgrave Macmillan Ltd.
Macmillan® is a registered trademark in the United States, United Kingdom
and other countries. Palgrave is a registered trademark in the European
Union and other countries.

ISBN-13: 978–1–4039–9240–6 hardback
ISBN-10: 1–4039–9240–1 hardback
ISBN-13: 978–1–4039–9241–3 paperback
ISBN-10: 1–4039–9241–X paperback

This book is printed on paper suitable for recycling and made from fully
managed and sustained forest sources. Logging, pulping and manufacturing
processes are expected to conform to the environmental regulations of the
country of origin.

A catalogue record for this book is available from the British Library.

A catalog record for this book is available from the Library of Congress.

10   9   8   7   6   5   4   3   2   1
16 15 14 13 12 11 10 09 08 07

Printed and bound in China

For Elaine Blades

Contents

General Editor's Preface

This series is dedicated to one clear belief: that we can all enjoy, understand and analyse literature for ourselves, provided we know how to do it. How can we build on close understanding of a short passage, and develop our insight into the whole work? What features do we expect to find in a text? Why do we study style in so much detail? In demystifying the study of literature, these are only some of the questions the *Analysing Texts* series addresses and answers.

The books in this series will not do all the work for you, but will provide you with the tools, and show you how to use them. Here, you will find samples of close, detailed analysis, with an explanation of the analytical techniques utilised. At the end of each chapter there are useful suggestions for further work you can do to practise, develop and hone the skills demonstrated and build confidence in your own analytical ability.

An author's individuality shows in the way they write: every work they produce bears the hallmark of that writer's personal 'style'. In the main part of each book we concentrate therefore on analysing the particular flavour and concerns of one author's work, and explain the features of their writing in connection with major themes. In Part 2 there are chapters about the author's life and work, assessing their contribution to developments in literature; and a sample of critics' views are summarised and discussed in comparison with each other. Some suggestions for further reading provide a bridge towards further critical research.

Analysing Texts is designed to stimulate and encourage your critical and analytic faculty, to develop your personal insight into the author's work and individual style, and to provide you with the skills and techniques to enjoy at first hand the excitement of discovering the richness of the text.

NICHOLAS MARSH

Introduction

In 1609 on the back of a grubby letter dated 19 June 1609 the renowned Elizabethan actor-manager and rival of Shakespeare Edward Alleyn hurriedly jotted down a note of his accounts. The list was brief and included sundry items, mostly to do with his clothing, but at the foot of the list he added tersely,

a book Shaksper Sonnetts – 5d

Alleyn probably bought his copy of the *Sonnets* in early summer of that year from the bookstall of John Wright or William Aspley at the sign of the Tiger's Head in St Paul's Churchyard. The book was first published some time after 20 May 1609, when it was registered for publication by Thomas Thorpe, a reputable publisher and son of a London innkeeper. On its second page the collection was dedicated enigmatically

TO . THE . ONLIE . BEGETTER . OF .
THESE . INSUING . SONNETS .
Mr W.H. . . .

From its first appearance *Shake-Speares Sonnets* has generated mystery and controversy. Not least among its mysteries has been the identity of that 'Mr W.H.' (who he?) and then the identity of the person who arranged the sonnets in the order we have them; did Shakespeare himself approve of and prepare these poems, seeing them through the press? The 1609 printing (the Quarto or simply '1609 Q', as it is often referred to) is riddled with printing errors – a point that has led many commentators to conclude that Mr. W.H. was not so much the inspiration of the sonnets as the procurer of the manuscripts, possibly obtained without the poet's knowledge or approval and rushed out to capitalise on Shakespeare's highly bankable reputation (the book appeared in the same period as the major tragedies).

Another important issue surrounding the *Sonnets* and one which has influenced the form of this study has been the question of whether they constitute a 'sonnet sequence'. Widely popular during the later Elizabethan period, a sonnet sequence represents a series of more or less continuous sonnets structured around shared themes, common situations, characters or narrative. Most sonneteers tried their hand at composing a sequence and notably successful were Sir Philip Sidney's *Astrophel and Stella* (1591) and Edmund Spenser's *Amoretti* (1595).

Does Shakespeare's *Sonnets* then represent a sonnet sequence? In the order in which we have the Sonnets there is nothing like a predetermined overall unity of design. The fact that they are numbered sequentially and are usually referred to as a body of work, 'the *Sonnets*', tends to portray the collection as more homogeneous and unified as a single enterprise than it actually is. But, compared with recognised sequences such as Sidney's or Spenser's, Shakespeare's collection is better described as a loose cycle of sonnets.

In the order in which we have the Sonnets any search for continuity is repeatedly frustrated. On the other hand, there are many pairs of sonnets that can be grouped into longer strings and there are links between sonnets in different parts of the collection. There are also connections between the sonnets on the level of their language, with recurring diction and imagery; for example, nature references, seasons and death, the body, legal and financial, family and metaphysics.

At the same time, within the 154 sonnets in the book there *are* three readily identifiable groups of poems that form what we might call micro-sequences. These are sonnets 1–17, the 'begetting' sonnets addressed to a young man; 78–86, the 'Rival Poet' group, addressed to a patron; and 127–52, the 'Dark Mistress' group, addressed to or about one or more women.

However, because I do not believe that the whole collection represents anything like a complete sequence, I have approached a discussion of the sonnets along thematic lines; so Part 1 of the book is concerned with a detailed examination of individual sonnets under five headings. Yet it is important to keep in mind that the poems I have selected in each of these chapters do not of course deal exclusively with single themes, and in my discussions I have tried to broaden and enrich the scope of the analysis by drawing in a range of other subjects that seem to be relevant at each point. The sonnets contain a rich multiplicity of themes, voices, figures, discourses and so on and it would be parochial to see them as anything less. My interpretations are not meant to be final or definitive and at the end of each chapter in Part 1 there are some suggestions for further research.

The discussion in Part 1 makes frequent reference to Shakespeare's use of rhetorical devices. The art of formal rhetoric represented a major element in Elizabethan education, and its principles and methods were deeply etched onto the memory of school pupils. It would have been dinned into Shakespeare too during his time at the King's New Grammar School in Stratford and, while his plays sometimes mock rhetoricians, formal rhetoric is still a major feature of the structures and persuasive strategies of the Sonnets. Contemporary readers would undoubtedly have expected to discover them and to savour a poet's rhetorical wit. Since in our own day the language occupies a more restricted percentage of the school timetable, modern readers may find the Glossary and Chapter 7 useful here.

Part 2 sets out to supply something of the important context for a broader discussion of Shakespeare's Sonnets. If you are new to the study of sonnets or the early modern period in literature then you may find it useful to begin your reading there. The reading list at the end includes books and articles that I have found most helpful as well as material intended to enrich and challenge your own ideas.

For the texts of the sonnets themselves I have leaned heavily on Katherine Duncan-Jones's Arden edition, cross-referenced against the editions of Stephen Booth and John Kerrigan. All references to Shakespeare's plays are taken from the Arden edition and references to his narrative verse come from Colin Burrow's edition of *The Complete Sonnets and Poems.* Books and articles are referred to by their author's or editor's name and year of publication – the full citation can be found in the Further Reading section.

My thanks go to the following, who gave help or support during the writing of this book: Phil Clayton, Giuseppe Cambise, Paul McLaughlin and Chris Piercy.

PART 1

ANALYSING SHAKESPEARE'S SONNETS

1

Love, or What You Will

No Poets verses yet did ever move,
  Whose Readers did not thinke he was in love
            (Ben Jonson, 'An Elegie' from *The Under-wood*)

Doubt that the stars are fire,
Doubt that the sun doth move,
Doubt truth to be a liar,
But never doubt I love.

                              (*Hamlet*, 2.2.115–18)

Towards the end of the twentieth century literary critics stopped falling in love. They still had amorous feelings towards one another, of course, but they became reluctant to talk about it in these terms. The chief reason for this was that in literary theory the idea of romantic love came to be regarded as subjectivist, mystifying and vague, not sufficiently materialistic. It ceased to be a viable concept.

Instead, critics pursued and endured relationships of *power* and *desire*. Both of these terms seem to have something more sinewy, more alienating about them that allows the critic to get behind the vague and often subjective uses of the word 'love', enabling him or her to understand the history and politics of sexual relations. 'Love is not love', as Shakespeare anticipates in sonnet 116. Yet 'love' has always been a powerful word and in the *Sonnets* Shakespeare uses it freely. So in this chapter (and subsequent chapters) I want to examine his different uses of the word and some of the many concepts resting behind it.

In this chapter we will be analysing in detail three of Shakespeare's sonnets in so far as they treat of the theme of love. Practically all of the sonnets are concerned with love in some of its polymorphic aspects and, by the same measure, each sonnet is concerned with many other things besides love, including themes of time and art, attitudes to women and to other men, Shakespeare's view of courtly ideals of love, notions of fidelity and deception, and so on.

At the end of the chapter there is a summary of the chief points that have emerged in the analysis. However, these should not be regarded as at all exhaustive and, hopefully, they should act as a spur to expanding and enriching your own interpretation. The chapter closes with a suggestion for further research. Use this research to explore and challenge the findings in the chapter and to develop your own lines of analysis. The discussions in this and the other chapters of Part 1 cast up a wide range of potential readings, so in no sense are my comments intended as final or definitive. We begin with sonnet 4.

Sonnet 4   'Unthrifty loveliness, why dost thou spend'

> Unthrifty loveliness, why dost thou spend,
> Upon thyself thy beauty's legacy?
> Nature's bequest gives nothing, but doth lend,
> And being frank, she lends to those are free: 4
> Then, beauteous niggard, why dost thou abuse,
> The bounteous largess given thee to give?
> Profitless usurer, why dost thou use
> So great a sum of sums yet canst not live?   8
> For having traffic with thyself alone,
> Thou of thyself thy sweet self dost deceive;
> Then how, when nature calls thee to be gone,
> What acceptable audit canst thou leave?   12
>   Thy unused beauty must be tombed with thee,
>   Which used lives th' executor to be.

A casual but engaged reading of sonnet 4 yields many of its key elements: the fact that its initial word is a negative at a key point in the poem seems important, and then there follows a series of questions from the speaker directly confronting the listener (and I think a listener is implied in the poem's conversational register).

What also strikes me is the large number of financial or legal terms (legacy, bequest, gives, lend, usurer, traffic, audit, executor) as well as the many references here to 'self'. Something else that registers clearly at this stage is the long /u/ sound, strongly marked, pulsing through the poem (but especially in lines 7, 13 and 14). This sets up the sound of 'you' as a parallel to the repetition of the word 'thy' in the poem reinforcing the themes of challenge and reproach in this sonnet.

The opening question directly challenges a young man for wasting the legacy of his inherited beauty, which does not, the speaker argues, belong to him. Beauty is lent to an individual to make use of, like a lump sum of money, to increase and to pass on to the next generation. But the young man ('Unthrifty') is wasting his capital, his beauteous looks, by indulging in self-admiration ('For having traffic with thyself alone') or by refusing to marry and beget children (line 12). If, the couplet concludes, he does not make profitable use of his beauty by getting a wife and then descendants, his beauty will merely die with him ('be tombed with thee').

The imagery of finance aptly matches the poem's theme of the transience of a limited stock of inherited beauty and the idea that in youth we are often lulled into believing we are immortal. Beauty can be cherished for itself but it also serves a valuable natural, sexual purpose. The speaker urges the youth out of a sense of love and he urges him to make love to others, to procreate, abandoning his current obsession with self, the self-love of line 9. This is a recurring theme of the opening suite of seventeen sonnets, what I have called the 'begetting' sonnets.

Although the opening word 'Unthrifty' is a provocative adjective it is immediately moderated by its noun, 'loveliness'. This combination sums up the relationship between the two men here and in the other begetting sonnets. The speaker would like to be quite forceful with the young man, shake him out of his complacency with a commanding word, but being socially inferior to him he must be deferential, watch his words, hence also 'beauteous niggard' (line 5). Not until line 7 does the speaker, perhaps out of frustration, take an unqualified risk by addressing him as 'Profitless usurer' – though he soon yields again, flattering the youth with 'thy sweet self' (line 10).

This tension of love and service between the two men is echoed in the tension between the themes of now and eternity. The older man who addresses the youth adopts a longer perspective on time from that of his protégé. The youth is preoccupied with present leisure and fun, strutting his endowed beauty narcissistically, or perhaps gratifying his good looks in brief and shallow sexual affairs. The older man tries to alert him to the longer vision: of his adult 'responsibilities' to his family, of passing on his ancestral inheritance, and even the greater time scale beyond death towards distant future generations. His experienced, objective eye moves with ready facility from the present to the inherited past and on to the far period ahead.

Although the sonnet opens with a question we get no sense of a reply. Instead, the speaker piles on the indictments like a provocation, reminding the young man of obligations, the counter to his free love. 'Legacy' in line 2 points at these and is reiterated in the following line with 'bequest'. The idea of accumulated wealth in these words plus 'largess' later is also literal in the sense that in addition to his natural looks the young man has inherited property in land and capital, and unless these are passed on through legitimate children they will be wasted, barren. Again it points both to predecessors and to descendants, stressing the view that he is simply one figure in a historical series.

Behind these ideas lurks the goddess Nature. She is the motive force in the individual life and in the chain of lives as well as the regulator of lives through death. She briefly confers our characteristics and properties, a person's good looks and the basis of physical attraction in nature. The word 'frank' in line 4 applied to nature is interesting because it seems to imply a range of attributes: that she is honest, brutally forthright, unrestrained, and open.

> And being frank, she lends to those are free.
>
> (4)

She lends to those she believes to be 'free'; that is she lends beauty on the assumption that the beneficiary will pass on such looks through procreation, the 'tender heir' of sonnet 1, and the 'fair child' of sonnet 2.

The young man is not free, however. His sin is self-love and this inhibits this free exchange of his legacy. This may simply be self-esteem, of course, respect for oneself (compare Leviticus 19:18). It may refer to narcissism, a preoccupation with himself or perhaps over-indulgent pride in his appearance (see sonnet 62:1). According to the Dauphin in *Henry V* there can even be some virtue in this:

> Self-love, my liege, is not so vile a sin
> As self-neglecting.
>
> (2.4.74–5)

But still a sin, even if we take the Dauphin's view.

And self-love may also refer to onanistic love, masturbation, as sonnet 129 may imply, 'The expense of spirit in a waste of shame'. Sonnet 10 claims he is 'beloved of many' yet he seems to repudiate this, being 'self-willed' in the words of sonnet 6 (with a bawdy pun on 'will' that rolls throughout the whole collection). The charge of onanism may explain why the speaker refers to his self-love as 'abuse' here in line 5 and as a deception in line 10. Yet the speaker censures him less from a moral than a practical point of view. As sonnet 6 more bluntly counsels, 'breed another thee'.

He must use his beauty to attract a 'happy mother' (sonnet 8:11). Instead, he is creating a dead end in his lineage before nature ravages his 'loveliness'. Nature here seems more of a moral presence even than the speaker, looming first bounteously then ruthlessly over human life. She appears almost as an ethical norm and the speaker tries to exploit this notion by suggesting that the young man's profitless fun-making is essentially unnatural.

At the beginning of line 5 the word 'Then' fulfils a number of functions. Structurally it works as a conjunction extending the argument of the opening quatrain. As an adverb it conveys the impression that the speaker is objective and rational (contrast the youth caught up in pleasurable distractions). Along with the other logical-sounding words in the sonnet ('For' and 'Then' in lines 9 and 11), it implies that the speaker is laying a carefully considered argument based on rhetorical principles leading to an undeniable conclusion, which in a way it does. The imagery of logical argument is another part of the speaker's aim of urging or persuading his protégé.

However, 'beauteous niggard' (5) is a daring move by the older man. At first it sounds like an insult, a positive and a negative held in tension. 'Beauteous' takes up the flattering metonymy of 'loveliness' from the first line but 'niggard' drives the poem in a new direction. In the opening line the youth is 'Unthrifty', a spendthrift of his beauty, but 'niggard' is paradoxically the opposite, a miser.

There is at least one solution to this conundrum. The young man is putting himself about, indulging extravagantly in pleasure and so is unthrifty, unstinting in his sexual diversions. But he is also niggardly in that he does not exercise his sex in the 'right' way, namely in the marriage bed and licit intercourse; in a word, he privileges fornication over procreation.

The older man too exerts a strong moral presence in the poem. He speaks like a father himself, one having gone before. Extending the imagery of financial commerce, interwoven with echoes from *The Merchant of Venice*, he now describes the youth as 'Profitless usurer', a lender who gets no return on his outgoings (7). Clearly he feels confident enough in his relationship to try a bolder reproval. Although Elizabethans considered usury a sinful un-Christian practice since it implied charging excessive interest on loans, Shakespeare's reference here can be better understood by glancing back at sonnet 6.

> That use is not forbidden usury
> Which happies those that pay the willing loan:
> That's for thyself to breed another thee.
>
> (6:5–7)

Usury is not a crime while both parties readily consent to it.

The first part of the sonnet is controlled by its three conspicuous questions, pausing slightly at the end of line 8, with a *volta*, the turning point in the poem. The first two quatrains of the poem, comprising the octave, also form a logical thematic unit in the sense that they present an account of the abundant beauty, material affluence and nobility inherited by the young man, even if he has wantonly dedicated himself to short-term pleasure, and so 'canst not live', at least not in the full sense implied in the latter part of the poem, the sestet.

Where the octave tends to dwell on the folly and profligacy of youth in light of his perceived responsibility, the sestet turns to the consequences of these. This change in focus is signalled by the preposition 'For' at the start of line 9 and the word makes a bridge between the two sections.

The poet/speaker now introduces the key theme of deception, which is also a major preoccupation of the *Sonnets* as a whole. Self-deception has emerged as both a cause and an effect of self-indulgence: self-love has baffled and diverted what should have been the youth's proper course:

> For having traffic with thyself alone,
> Thou of thyself thy sweet self dost deceive.
>
> (lines 9–10)

The confrontation implicit in these lines is meant to bring the young listener to his senses with a raw and unpalatable fact about his life. Again, this father figure is bold in making this charge but once more he attempts to soften the blow by interposing the phrase 'thy sweet self'. He has stressed the shallow, perfunctory lifestyle of his protégé and follows this up in lines 11 and 12 with another final direct challenge,

> Then how, when nature calls thee to be gone,
> What acceptable audit canst thou leave?

Suddenly the sonnet tries a different line and turns to the distant future. The intention seems to be to strike the young man, so blissfully unaware of the reality of his mortality, with a piercing disclosure on the finiteness of human existence.

As so often in the Sonnets, Shakespeare presents us with a double perspective. We see the abstracted immortal generations of the youth's family stretching back into the eternity of the past as well as forwards into posterity and an as yet unrealised potential. This is contrasted with the lease of the single life of an individual person, the young man, mortal, finite, subject to wrinkling time ('beauty's waste hath in the world an end' – 9:11).

The word 'audit' in line 12 is clearly crucial here, indicating that the youth will have to face an ultimate reckoning (the question that contains it acts as a sort of reckoning in itself). The audit, an inspection and an evaluation of his life, will be both religious and secular. He will have to face God's judgement on his life's actions but also face the verdict of those who continue to live on earth after him, reviewing how he invested or squandered his talents.

Line 13 balances hope and reality. The word 'unused' meshes into previous references to neglect in the poem but equally implies the idea of potential, something not yet exploited or employed to its full. Conversely, 'tombed' (short for 'entombed') is a chill reminder of death and therefore of the urgency of amending his life. Eventually, the final line comes down on the side of optimism by suggesting that if the man makes natural and proper use of his beauty by begetting an heir it will confer on him a stake in posterity, perpetuating his name, his looks and family wealth. Like an executor his heir will have survived him to carry out his will into the future, preserving his memory. In this narrow sense he will have actually cheated or transcended death, his beauty having become 'frank' and 'free', liberated from the constraints of mortality.

In the opening sequence of 17 sonnets Shakespeare's persona, the poet/speaker, applies a range of arguments to persuade the unthrifty young man to marry and have children. These include reproducing his beauty (sonnets 1–3), preserving the family estate (4 and 10), the possibility of cheating time's ravages (sonnet 6), the prospect of family life producing harmony (8), appeasing friends (9), procreation as a most natural thing to do (15 and 16), while its failure would mean the human race as a whole would cease (11). And in 17 and 18 he argues that while art may be able to perpetuate human traces, breeding does it much more effectively.

The argument that Shakespeare seems most fond of here is that of perpetuating the young man's beauty (see sonnets 1 to 5): procreation as the best defence ''gainst Time's scythe' (12:13). In sonnet 4 as elsewhere he adopts a humanistic emphasis in eschewing an explicitly religious course of action. Nature is the primary rationale for mankind on earth: 'she lends to those are free' (line 4). Because the man has himself come about through and exists within nature, there is an implied moral imperative for him to comply accordingly.

At the same time, the poet's prudent counsel about nature's bounteous generosity is only a starting point. His underlying strategy is really to tap into the young man's egoism, his self-serving pragmatism, and particularly his natural instinct for self-preservation. This is a hard-edged realism and thus bodes well of more success than an idealistic appeal would.

This self-love is the clearest expression of love in the poem. It may be spiritual narcissism, autoeroticism, self-indulgence, hedonism, or just a vague sort of time-wasting against which the sonnet is a wake-up call, a warning of the approach of adulthood.

The self-love of the young man is a recurring topic in the 1–17, 'begetting' or 'procreation' sequence of sonnets. As such it is often related with the topic of the man's locked-up potential so that the alarm call is also a call to bring forth the future, the other, and to set free the latent possibilities symbolised in the putative child, what sonnet 4 refers to as the 'unused'. In some other sonnets this otherness is referred to as a 'store'. For example, sonnet 14 hints that the potential is that of an artist,

> As truth and beauty shall together thrive
> If from thyself, to store thou wouldst convert.
>
> (14:11–12)

To the speaker, self-love implies not only vanity and profligacy but also reckless ingratitude in neglecting to pass on a 'copy' of himself. It hints too that the boy is spending his time and seed on idle fornication (there is more than a hint in this too of the wiser and older Shakespeare speaking from the point of view of his own youthful folly – he had in all probability been obliged to marry the pregnant Anne Hathaway). The young man substitutes love for lust, which is described in 129 as a woe, a dream, and ultimately hell. Yet the poet/speaker in sonnet 4 seems to stress not love but a biological desire, that if the lad must indulge his lust then he should at least vent it functionally in a marriage for the sake of his family.

Sonnet 4 is one of the poems in the sequence 1–17 addressed to a particular young man and urging him to marry. Although these early poems may have a homoerotic aspect to them the repeated plea is for the young man to procreate and get a male heir (i.e. as a heterosexual). The protégé's self-centred *eros*, or sexual love, contrasts with what appears to be the poet's *agape*, a selfless concern for another person (however, the speaker may be employed by the boy's father, and so his motives may ultimately be prudential).

Sonnet 129   'Th'expense of spirit in a waste of shame'

After a sonnet addressed by an older speaker to a young man we move to a sonnet addressed to the poet himself, but no less intensely. The poem is part of the sequence of sonnets 127–54 depicting his complex and uneasy relationship with a dark mistress (sometimes referred to as the 'dark lady'). This loosely connected sequence also re-addresses many of the issues and dichotomies from earlier sonnets, treated from a new perspective.

> Th'expense of spirit in a waste of shame
> Is lust in action, and till action, lust
> Is perjured, murd'rous, bloody, full of blame,
> Savage, extreme, rude, cruel, not to trust;   4
> Enjoyed no sooner but despised straight,
> Past reason hunted, and no sooner had,
> Past reason hated as a swallowed bait,
> On purpose laid to make the taker mad;   8
> Mad in pursuit and in possession so,
> Had, having, and in quest to have, extreme;
> A bliss in proof, and proved, a very woe;
> Before, a joy proposed, behind a dream.   12
>   All this the world well knows yet none knows well
>   To shun the heaven that leads men to this hell.

Like sonnet 4, 129 begins with a baldly provocative and intriguing statement that thrusts the reader directly into the poem. It is now the aftermath, the hollow malaise after sex. The opening vocabulary carries a heavy negative charge with strong hints of prurience: expense, waste, shame. However, the first line, even with its bold dramatic flourish, represents a moment of cool rationality from which the poem plunges headlong like a hectic in the blood, through its stressed and disrupted syntax until reaching a kind of calmness again in the aphoristic couplet.

The opening lines with the their hissing sibilants quickly impose a cloying effect on the indignant consciousness as the drama of line 1 pitches into the turmoil:

> Th'expense of spirit in a waste of shame
> Is lust in action, and till action
>
> (lines 1–2)

The present tense with which the poems begins misleads us into an idea that the poem is commenting on a concurrent event. Yet, here the present is the habitual present, referring also to the past and even ironically (as the final line indicates) to the future.

The present 'action' is the tumult of self-reproach that dominates the poem. Lust, given physical expression, released from mental control, is the surrender of the spirit, the dissipation of courage, resolve, vigour, morality and humour. It is a discharge into despondency, barrenness, a 'waste' or spending of shame, and the self-contempt of post-coital dejection.

Some readers have detected hints of the specific sexual act itself in a pun on 'waste (or waist) of shame'. Yet until this bursting lust finds an outlet in 'action' it is treacherous ('perjured'), violent, chancy, volatile, coarse and aggressive. Shakespeare's lists seems to emulate the recent pulse of lust itself even in the aftermath.

The first quatrain sees a movement from a series of nouns in the opening line to a swift tumble of adjectives in line 3. This switch to severe adjectives stresses the subjectivism of this part of the poem. The sheer weight of self-reviling adjectives piles up an almost visual sense of recrimination as the speaker struggles to rid himself of the festering panic of memory and unrelenting shame.

However, the poem is not in reality a random outflow of shame. Though it seems otherwise, it is in fact a highly organised portrayal of confusion. Note the shrewd balance of the phrasing in the second line and the anaphora in lines 2 and 3. And, the reversal of 'Is lust' at the end of the line to 'lust / Is' is another instance of highly organised writing that would not be possible for someone actually in the deep throes of despondency.

This device is one of many that skilfully disrupt the reader's initial ease and curiosity. We have already referred to the hissing and spitting /s/ sound that permeates the first two quatrains and the full effect of this is best felt by reading aloud – or try Ralph Fiennes's feisty recording of this sonnet in *When Love Speaks* (see Further Reading).

The opening quatrain has a rich variety of muscular consonant and vowel sounds exuding scorn and remorse. The rasping /er/ sound grunts murkily throughout, for example in 'sooner' (5 and 6), 'reason' (6 and 7), purpose (8), pursuit (9), and 'world' (13). Again, the final syllable of 'action' (2) is echoed in 'possession' (9) re-emerging at the end in 'shun' (14), and all three words are linked through the poem's moral theme of abstinence. The first four lines establish this theme but also initiate the dizzyingly complex miasma of sound through which the poem surges.

The second quatrain details the unstable, inevitable hazard of lust. Yet line 5 takes a new direction by a leap forward in time: 'Enjoyed no sooner'. The coolly ironic 'enjoyed' has strong sexual overtones in Elizabethan English as well as hinting at sexual exploitation. Although the speaker insists that sex offers release, the poem seems curiously uninterested in its enjoyment, the 'bliss' (11) or 'joy' (12), remaining embroiled in moral recrimination.

> Enjoyed no sooner but despised straight,
> Past reason hunted, and no sooner had,
> Past reason hated as a swallowed bait.

> (lines 5–7)

The object of lust – woman, man, autoerotic fantasy – is hunted relentlessly, hunted 'past reason'. The anaphora of lines 6 and 7 sketches out the intense grip of this fixation.

'Hunted' brilliantly fixes on the almost manic intensity of the pursuit. 'Past reason' in line 6 similarly conveys this madness that is beyond any reasonable limitation. But the same phrase in line 7 implies 'after reason', following reflection – the act and its madness become loathed since he now feels duped by his intemperance, led on as a victim who had been duped by

> 'a swallowed bait,
> On purpose laid to make the taker mad'.
>
> (line 8)

Lust is the poison chalice and the poet/speaker is the dupe, gulled by his own nature. In a brilliant *volte face* the hunter is seen in fact as the hunted.

The second quatrain is linked to the first thematically as well as structurally through the verb 'enjoyed', which is controlled by the repeated verb 'Is' at the start of lines 2 and 3 (line 2 seems to control most of the sonnet). The semi-colon in line 4 also prods the poem forward (the 1609 Quarto printing had only a comma here). Then the poem appears to come to a halt with the abrupt monosyllabic 'mad' in line 8 but by repeating this immediately at the start of line 9 the poet kick-starts the momentum (its dull thuddish pulse is heard again in the start of line 10). The word 'pursuit' is a slant rhyme with 'purpose' in the previous line, and thus extends the beat of the repeated /p/ sounds from the octave into the sestet: 'possession', 'proof', 'proved' and 'proposed'. 'Pursuit' and 'possession' are cognate with the words 'hunted' and 'had' in line 6, thereby repeating the idea of a gluttonous triumph.

One of the strongest impressions to emerge from this sonnet is that of a highly complex construction of repetitions and cross-references. For instance 'mad', as well as connecting lines 8 and 9, octave and sestet, also connects with 'Past reason' in lines 6 and 7 and with 'Savage' in line 4. Bestial passion overwhelms and deceives the reason so that the notion of a 'victim' becomes blurred and problematised. Sex is presented as a form of helpless addiction with only one satisfying, if ephemeral and fugitive, end for it.

Each of the stages of 'lust in action' is characterised by madness, suggested in the breathless lines 9 and 10,

> Mad in pursuit and in possession so,
> Had, having, and in quest to have, extreme.

Line 10 reverses the normal chronological order and its syntax emulates how the poet's mind is working retrospectively, tracing back the origins of this moment through its deterministic stages. 'Extreme' is repeated, too, from line 4 and here as there it reminds us that lust has no moderation in its savage frenzy.

In line 11 the chronology is briefly and mildly restored. Before sex, the anticipation of bliss and joy arouses him to test ('in proof') his expectations, but after it is 'proved' it becomes a real woe, and the promised bliss merely an illusion. (In the 1609 Quarto this word is actually printed as 'proud', offering alternative sexual connotations; for a trenchant discussion of the orthography of the poem see Graves and Riding, 1926.)

The speaker finds himself baffled and maddened by the experience. He has taken the 'swallowed bait' (7) hoping for the delight but all he gets is sadness and the feeling that the whole sexual experience has been a crude trick. He brilliantly adduces the different states of schizoid consciousness experienced in the course of sexual arousal together with the inevitability of the cycle repeating itself – in spite of his exasperation (contrast the unstable convulsions of desire in this poem with the more tranquil steadfastness of love in sonnet 116).

With all its repetitions and rephrasings the poem itself mimics this cycle. So, the couplet reiterates the inevitability expressed in lines 11 and 12. The full-stop at the end of line 12 brings to a momentous halt the hurly-burly brew of recollected passion and present recrimination. With the fury still reverberating beyond this line the poet now enforces a brake on his tormented mind as well as on the poem's hurtling metre. He makes explicit the truism that has lurked at the back of his seething introspection:

All this the world well knows...

Not surprisingly, line 13 strikes a note of mock seriousness. It is as insubstantial as the 'dream' itself. This point is validated by the rest of the couplet, a brief instant of lucidity for this poor addict, making him aware of the hell just suffered and the one to come, before inevitably he begins again to chase the illusory dragon of joy and heaven.

Significantly the poem ends instead on the word 'hell'. The word connects literally with 'possession' in line 9 since 'possession' can mean 'made mad by being under the control of devils'. On the other hand, more figuratively, 'hell' is also a piece of Elizabethan slang for the vagina (see sonnet 144 for more on this kind of hell, especially line 5 where it is linked with 'my female evil'). The idea of a private hell foregrounds the vital point that the speaker has fixed on a selfish hell of anguish rather than contemplated any prospect of fulfilment with a real lover.

In effect sonnet 129 has but two sentences. The first runs pell-mell from lines 1 to 12 and the second occupies the couplet. So, although it retains vestiges of the Petrarchan form, its structure really consists of three incorporated quatrains (the *douzaine*) plus an epigrammatic couplet.

Unlike sonnet 4 it is self-referential, not being addressed to or about anyone else. There is no 'I' or 'you' but it hovers in space, sustained by recrimination and anger (since all of the nouns are abstract the poem has a deceptively transcendent aura). On the other hand it does share with 4 a raw confrontational attitude, addressing real life. Moreover, although the style strives for impersonality its voice is far from detached and is embroiled in the dynamics of the moral subject.

This impersonal mode is very much in line with the poem's definitional approach towards sexual lust. Part of its turmoil arises from the poet's struggle to rationalise and define and so hold at bay the virulence in his sexuality (compare in this respect sonnet 94, with a similar style and purpose, and similar hurt). It is both an analysis and, in its maze of ambiguities, a direct attempt to express the confusion of the subject's mind especially as it appears to lose control in the second quatrain.

Sonnet 129 is the only one in which the word 'lust' appears. This is clearly the self-seeking physical desire of *eros*, contrasted with sonnet 4's *agape*, or selfless spiritual dedication. Yet in 129 lust is not a single idea but at least three. It is the blind driving force in carnality (line 2: inducing action) and it is also the vehicle of carnality (lines 6–7: the indulging or volition). And, further, the poet here intends 'lust' as the madness that both of these elements induce (as Helena notes

in *All's Well that Ends Well*, 'lust doth play / With what it loathes';
4.4.24–5).

Lust is singularly uncreative ('a waste') and rabidly self-centred.
The selfishness dwells behind both its motive and its subsequent
shameful remorse. It usurps the individual's reason or judgement
yet at the same time manipulates these by the very nature of its
intensity.

In this connection, lust is actually a metonymy for the self, for
ambition or even for volition. It is a signifier for the human suscept-
ibility to become wayward and unstable, 'not to trust', and it is
significant as a decisive driving force in some of Shakespeare's major
dramas, for instance in the characters of Macbeth, Cleopatra, Richard
III, and Angelo in *Measure for Measure*.

With its stress on indecorousness, lust and vanity, its allusions
to savagery and unreason, 129 (like other 'Dark Mistress' sonnets)
directly challenges the courtly ideals of Petrarchism. Yet there is a
distinction to be drawn here. Ironically, 129 exploits feelings of shame
to embrace indirectly one important strand of courtly ethos: namely
control of the selfish ego, the extreme and destructive id, through the
constraints of reason and decorum. *Venus and Adonis* distinguishes
lust from love:

> Call it not love, for love to heaven is fled,
> Since sweating lust on earth usurped his name.
>> (*Venus and Adonis*, lines 793–4)

Love is identified with spirit and heaven, lust with dull corporeal
earth. Courtly love is related with control and rationality, hence the
importance in 129 of the concepts of reason, judgement and moral
restraint encapsulated in the word 'shun'.

Sonnet 20   'A woman's face with Nature's own hand painted'

And so we reach the celebrated sonnet 20, famous or notorious,
depending on your point of view.

20

A woman's face with Nature's own hand painted,
Hast thou, the master mistress of my passion;
A woman's gentle heart, but not acquainted
With shifting change as is false women's fashion;   4
An eye more bright than theirs, less false in rolling,
Gilding the object whereupon it gazeth;
A man in hue, all hues in his controlling,
Which steals men's eyes and women's souls amazeth.   8
And for a woman wert thou first created,
Till Nature as she wrought thee fell a-doting,
And by addition me of thee defeated,
By adding one thing to my purpose nothing.   12
   But since she pricked thee out for women's pleasure,
   Mine be thy love, and thy love's use their treasure

In 1780 George Steevens denounced the sonnet unreservedly, declaring '[it is] impossible to read this fulsome panegyrick, addressed to a male object, without an equal admixture of disgust and indignation'. Edmond Malone's 1780 edition of the poems in *Supplement to the Edition of Shakespeare's Plays* (which had so excited Steevens's ire) was also touchy on the homoerotic potential of this and other sonnets, and added a footnote to this sonnet to mollify his readers,

> such addresses to men, however indelicate, were customary in our author's time, and neither imported criminality, nor were esteemed indecorous.

From the middle of the seventeenth century critics sought to defend the national bard from any potential 'scandal' implicit in homoerotic affections. Many of Steevens's contemporaries could remember, with some facetious scorn, that John Benson had converted several of Shakespeare's masculine pronouns to feminine to protect him against such a charge. Benson's *Poems Written by Wil Shake-speare. Gent.* (1640) had also regrouped the Sonnets, allocating them seemly titles that might direct the reader into seeing the love that dare not speak its name as an idealised Renaissance friendship or

Platonic affection (the censorious Benson assigned florid titles to his rearranged sonnets, and labelled number 20 coyly as 'The Exchange').

The Sonnets treat of a great range and complexity of loves and perspectives on love and there seems no reason why homo-erotic experiences should not be among them. On the question of Shakespeare's sexual orientation, Stanley Wells (2003) has offered an elegant apostrophe,

> If Shakespeare himself did not, in the fullest sense of the word, love a man, he certainly understood the feelings of those who do. (*Shakespeare: For all Time*, p. 327)

Whether Shakespeare's sexual orientation was homoerotic may not in itself be the important issue. Although many of the sonnets – and especially this one – are private, often confessional in tone and attitude, what I am primarily interested in here are the nuances in which it is expressed, whether to a man or a woman.

The poem starts out by cataloguing its subject's features (each controlled by the phrase 'Hast thou' in line 2). Although a young man, he has the face, heart and eye of a woman. That his face, the outward appearance, is painted implies some deception, especially the idea that women are by nature deceptive, and the rest of the octave consistently denigrates women (we have heard of such painting too, in *Hamlet* for instance, as a satire on woman, painted 'an inch thick'; 5.1.188). But the fact that the painting is by 'Nature's own hand' implies some authentication: here; it is not artificially cosmetic. In a woman this painting might have seemed a deception but since it is natural we must take it for what it is, at face value, though this is qualified and clarified at line 10. The antithesis here between natural and artificial is also significant for the distinction between sex (biolo-gically given) and gender (socially or personally defined). And there remains the thorny crux of sexuality.

The second line is a declaration that the subject of the poem is, enigmatically, 'master mistress' of his passion. Passion may simply mean emotions, but it can also refer to sexual desire and may even mean 'my infatuation', the 'ruling and driving force of my life'. The caesura before the mysterious oxymoron here draws attention to or perhaps rehearses the poet's deliberation on this conundrum of a man. Some editors capitalise and hyphenate the haunting phrase, though this unnecessarily limits its possibilities: the lover outdoes women as a mistress (his chief or master 'mistress'); a bisexual lover or at least a lover possessing the best of all possible worlds; both patron and partner; or, a compound of masculine and feminine elements, hermaphrodite . . . and so on.

In *Twelfth Night*, Orsino uses a similar phrase of Viola/Cesario. He draws attention to the sexual frisson generated in cross-dressing and sexual duality after Viola reveals her true identity as a woman, by proposing to her, that she would become 'Your master's mistress' (5.1.325). Given the velocity of this proposal Orsino must have fallen for Viola while she was still in the masculine guise of Cesario, as Olivia had. All of which is reminiscent of line 8 of sonnet 20, 'Which steals men's eyes and women's souls amazeth'. The sonnet as a whole might have been narrated by the lovelorn Orsino, as a satire on sexual idiom and gender roles.

The young man who is the subject of the poem has also the 'gentle heart' (3) of a woman. Metaphorically, 'gentle heart' takes up the theme of emotion from 'passion' in the previous line but perhaps at first adds compassion – until this is satirised by line 4. The word 'but' in line 3 introduces the same negative tone as 'painted' had in the opening line and all three of the compliments in the octave carry with them a corresponding misogynistic slight against women (compare sonnet 144:3, 'The better angel is a man right fair'). The thrust of the octave is to say that the young man surpasses woman in her own qualities while remaining free of her defects. However, 'not acquainted' (3) hides a bawdy pun which depends on the Chaucerian word 'quenyte', vagina or 'cunt': outwardly at least, the 'master mistress' has most of the interesting physical attributes of a woman except one, a point taken up again in the sestet ('acquainted' appears again in sonnet 88, with similar mood and meaning).

Here, in line 4, the young master has none of the fickle inconstancy or perfidy of women, a point struck home by the tautologies of the line,

With shifting change as is false women's fashion.

'Shifting change', 'false' and 'fashion' constitute a cluster pointing to capriciousness, the connection underlined through the alliteration (in sonnets 137 and 138, 'false' points up the theme of duplicity). 'Fashion' here implies that women are typically manipulative, yet the epithet 'false' may delimit this, improbably, to only those women who are false.

On the other hand the word 'theirs' in the following line perhaps undermines this (and further demarcates the young man from women). His eye is 'more bright', vital, alert, more likely to 'steal' eyes and hearts. But the eye is also an index of fidelity/infidelity so the young man's eye is less false in 'rolling'. John Kerrigan clarifies the word 'rolling' as 'roving' while David Crystal in *Shakespeare's Words* also advises 'flashing', which could imply that the 'bright' eye is more honest. In the following line, if 'Gilding' refers to the young man's eye then it may suggest he exalts what he gazes on, though if it refers again to the eye of 'false women' it extends the theme of deception introduced in 'painted' (1), and superficial flattery. In one contemporary theory of light and optics which Shakespeare commonly alludes to, the eye itself generates the light to see by, thus comparing the young man's eye to the sun (see sonnets 33 and 130 for different treatments of this idea; see too *Love's Labour's Lost*, 4.3.25–7, and *The Merry Wives of Windsor*, 1.3.57).

Then follows a most memorable line,

> A man in hue, all hues in his controlling.
>
> (line 7)

In Elizabethan English, 'hue' (or 'hew' as printed in the Quarto) could mean 'appearance' or 'beauty', in addition to 'colour' (i.e. 'complexion'; compare sonnet 67:5–6), intimating that outwardly too, although he is a man he can pull men's glances as well as reach down into and beguile the very souls of women. That this young man can draw the looks of other men (with a pun on 'who's') seems to imply that the poet is not exceptional in his rapture, but further, that sexual orientation is a very frail thing, subject to 'shifting change'.

In the 1609 Quarto printing 'Hews' is italicised, possibly suggesting a cryptic pun or allusion. Accordingly, the line has given rise to various speculative theories about the identity again of W.H., the 'onlie begetter' of 1609 Q. Beginning with Thomas Tyrwhitt in 1766 some readers (including Oscar Wilde) have seen in 'hues' a punning reference to William Hughes, a boy actor who played women's parts. And then the nineteenth-century novelist Samuel Butler conceived of 'hues/hews' as an allusion to one 'Willie Hughes', a naval rating and ship's cook. Yet caution is urged – none of these hypotheses has any convincing evidence to support them.

The idea of 'controlling', however, does fit in with other references in the poem to making or shaping, including 'master' (2), 'fashion' (4), 'created' (9), 'wrought' (10), 'pricked' (13) – and we should perhaps recall that the 1609 Quarto in line 7 had printed 'hew'. This is important from the point of view of Elizabethan humanism since it hints at the theme of the man's autonomous development, a prince in control of his own fortunes, especially in control of and steward of nature. Yet it is also ironic in that the poet/speaker is not able to control nature, either in the form of his sex or in his sexual leaning.

The octave thus refers to the day-to-day interaction of the poet with men and women. It employs four pairs of roughly isomorphic statements three of which extol the feminine virtues of the young man, and ends with both male and female as his conquests. The hyperbole of the octave is extended into the sestet by the heightened language in line 10. Thus the second part of the poem begins with the personification of Nature that opened it. On the other hand, the conceit in

> Till Nature as she wrought thee fell a-doting   (10)

is a little too precious (compare sonnets 11 and 19, which recount the myth of Nature as an artist fashioning humans from a pattern and assigning them *their* nature).

Shakespeare bridges the octave and the sestet with the conjunction 'And' in line 9, but then the sonnet takes a new and unexpected direction. The young man was created 'for' a woman. But is this 'for the pleasure of women' or perhaps created 'as a woman'? Both meanings are bodied here as one of the poem's many ambivalences. The line also hints at the biblical Edenic myth and Adam and Eve, 'first created for woman', the beginnings of nature, making the division of the sexes. But it is only hinted because Shakespeare speaks through a humanist-classical voice, replacing God with Nature.

That Nature is a female deity is, of course, not without its irony in a poem on sex and sexuality. She appears to inflict revenge on the 'woman' out of envy, by botching the job or playing a cruel joke. But, then, what would constitute the ideal woman? Or maybe, Pygmalion-like she falls in love, 'a-doting', enchanted with this ideal beauty in the act of fashioning 'it'. And yet, after all, not quite ideal – as lines 11 and 12 suggest. In the process of creating this female darling, Nature lapses and donates her a penis, 'by addition', and so thwarts the poet's ardent desires. This 'one thing' harks back to the 'object' in line 6, there gilded but here related to 'nothing': it is a thing of nought in that it contributes nothing to the poet's 'purpose' if he is a heterosexual man.

In the third quartet the rhymes are untypically irregular: 'created' (9) to rhyme with 'defeated' (11), and 'a-doting' (10) with 'nothing' (12), which may suggest that the manuscript could have intended 'no thing' at the end of line 12. This would then have suggested female genitalia and that the poet's 'purpose' was more inclined that way. However, 'she' is 'pricked out', fitted with a penis (line 13).

But, whatever – the young man is designed biologically at least for women's pleasure and ultimately the exercise of his genitals will be their treasure (14). If so, then by the same token the poet's love, in 'Mine be thy love', suggests his own sex is available for the young man. Some critics have also interpreted the line in financial terms again: women benefiting from the capital while the poet/speaker delights in the interest. But at the very least the young man can depend on the devotion of the poet.

Sonnet 20 boldly exploits a broad range of rhetorical tropes; most conspicuously, metaphor (lines 1, 2, 6 and 13) and an orthodox personification of nature as a classical goddess. In addition to the imagery of fabrication and sex there is a strong vein of 'deception' running through the first part of the poem (for instance, 'painted', 'shifting', 'false'), so that the young man himself appears as a type of deception. This too heightens the aura of uncertainty of feeling and of definition, all one with the touchiness of the subject, the ambivalence of the young man's sexuality and the contingency of the poet/speaker's own feelings.

In praising the young man, the poem employs the Renaissance device of the 'blazon' – cataloguing each of those physical parts in which the man surpasses women, albeit being 'pricked' rather than 'acquainted' (for more on 'blazon' see Chapter 6). However, the speaker is dismayed and the sestet unsettlingly adduces his despondency, the victim of nature's unkind swindle.

This dismay is enacted, and almost palpably so, in the dying away between the two main sections of the poem. It is equally discernible in the cadences of individual lines – each line of the poem is hypermetric, ending on one extra feminine or unstressed syllable, softening and disappointing each line ('By adding one thing'!).

The poet depicts the beautiful youth as quite passive, even precious in his poise, conspicuously free in having little will of his own since the poem stresses the drive and enterprise of others. This too adds materially to the speaker's exasperation but he comes to accept this reality in reluctant acquiescence.

The young man is a siren for both sexes, and as a 'master mistress', a misfit, an oxymoron, a lapse of 'doting' Nature. He defies the usual stereotyping and this, naturally, intensifies the thrill of his charm. Yet he himself does not appear to be attracted to men, will not share the dissatisfaction of the poet who predicts that he has been singled out 'for women's pleasure' via the addition of his 'treasure'.

As an extension of this the thwarted speaker comes across as ineffectual and impotent, since he is unable to reach the young man on the terms laid out here. He is a star-crossed, or at least Nature-crossed lover. If the young man is a sexual paradox then so too is the speaker. The ambiguities in the sonnet mirror the ambivalences of the subject: a man by sexual anatomy but by inclination attracted to this striking man with a woman's face etc. In truth Nature 'fell a-doting' when she made the *poet* a man too, 'pricked out for women's pleasure',

> By adding one thing to my purpose nothing'   (11)

(recall, too, that in sonnet 4, 'Nature's bequest gives nothing'). By the same token, although he impeaches women with 'shifting change' (4) and 'false in rolling' (5) the poet himself is shifty in his language, elliptical, equivocal and paradoxical. And the 'gilding' flattery of the octave looks over-painted, and perhaps masks his bitter envy of women.

Is the poet/speaker homosexual? On the terms of this poem the conclusion would probably be that he is not (though the ambiguity of the expression makes other interpretations available). He tries earnestly not to be so. In the octave he warms to his love's womanly qualities, his beauty, sensitivity and sparkling eyes. After the autoeroticism of the octave, the sestet expresses his great feeling of frustration and regret at this impasse imposed on the two of them,

> And by addition me of thee defeated,
> By adding one thing to my purpose nothing.

The young man is part-woman but not the part he would have liked and this may, ironically, be the source of the poet/speaker's misogyny. Nature's gaffe disqualifies him from carnality. Therefore he can love the young man only spiritually while women make 'love's use their treasure' (14). In private terms this sonnet is a denial rather than an avowal of sexual desire. It is of course another, if curious, variant on the unachievable woman which is the chief motivator in Petrarch's verse.

Alan Bray in *Homosexuality in Renaissance England* argues that 'To talk of an individual in this period as being or not being "a homosexual" is an anachronism and ruinously misleading' (p. 16). His grounds for this claim are that the nuances of key sexual terms in the Elizabethan period are often very different from ours; for example, 'homosexuality was classified under depravity as a general idea, not distinguished from sorcery and witchcraft'. 'No-one in England', he continues, 'in the sixteenth or seventeenth centuries would have thought himself as "gay" or "homosexual" for the simple reason that those categories of self-definition did not exist.' (In fact the term 'homosexual' did not appear in print until the final decade of the nineteenth century.) Which is not to say that some men did not have sexual desires aroused by other men.

Bruce R. Smith, in *Homosexual Desire in Shakespeare's England*, stresses the importance of distinguishing sexual practice from sexual feelings and desire. He interprets sonnet 20 as an expression of the strong sexual desire of one man for another, a version of pastoral seduction verse. He suggests that the phrase 'master mistress' can be unpacked as meaning a man who is a substitute for a wife – but in the end of the poem the speaker settles for something more akin to male bonding (see his chapter 7, 'The Secret Sharer'). Conversely, Margreta de Grazia's essay 'The Scandal of Shakespeare's Sonnets' contends that outrage and scandal (the term is ironic in her title) are really products of eighteenth-century criticism and that the Elizabethan assumptions about homosexuality were close to those of the Greeks: women were regarded as an inferior form of male and it was expected that a man's love for a woman was much to do with procreation (see sonnets 1–17), while loving another man was considered as the epitome of companionship (p. 42). Sonnet 20 may be seen to bear out this latter theme, especially given that the poem conflates the two sexes: male is marked out arbitrarily from female on the basis of a mere slip of a detail.

On the question of Shakespeare's sexuality, the sonnets offer no conclusive evidence and the modern critical opinion is that they are not inevitably biographical. We have noted how the language and punctuation of sonnet 20 are ambiguous on this question and the exact standing in the sixteenth century of words such as 'friend', 'love', 'lover' and 'mistress' may or may not imply sexual desire. The ambiguity of the language in this sonnet extends to Shakespeare's deployment of the second-person pronouns 'thou' and 'thee' here and throughout the Sonnets. In the plays, Shakespeare sometimes uses the older form 'thou' in the speech of an inferior addressing a superior (child to parents, servant to master/mistress) and 'you' in return (*Othello* and *King Lear* have good examples of this). 'Thou'/'thee' is the singular and more formal style but might be adopted to convey intimacy between equals of a lower class.

However, by the early modern period the distinction between 'thou' and 'you' had become very much blurred and Shakespeare applies them interchangeably. Often his choice may be on the grounds of euphony or syllabic quantity or to facilitate the use of a pun. The speaker's use of 'thou' in sonnet 20 sorts well with its intimate tone but, as Andrew Gurr concedes after some research ('You and Thou in Shakespeare's Sonnets'), there is no conclusive pattern in the Sonnets regarding the use of these personal pronouns; for example, in the 'begetting' sonnets most address their subject as 'thou' but numbers 13, 15, 16 and 17 address the young man as 'you', without any obvious reason. In fact, the apparent randomness of the usage has sometimes been used to support the view that the true order of the Sonnets has been disrupted.

Conclusions

Although we have analysed in detail only three of Shakespeare's sonnets I think a number of important points have clearly emerged. It is apparent that Shakespeare's treatment of love in the Sonnets is at least as complex as in the plays and it is richly multifarious both in terms of the range and intensity of modes of loving and in the ways they are imaginatively conceived. After studying only this handful of sonnets, it is impossible to underestimate the profound realities about Shakespeare's intimate experience of love and the deeper psychological connotations that the theme symbolises for the man as for the poet.

Shakespeare's treatment of love takes in a wide intervention of themes including rivalry, loneliness, suspicion, inconstancy, conventions of courtship, uncertainty, beauty and sexuality, together with issues of possession, deception and fidelity. And central, of course, is the relationship of language to all of these issues. A strong impression emerges of love as an unremitting dynamic, played out on a field of shifting identity, memory, flattery, power and desire. The sonnets repeatedly personify a nervous, uneasy balance between on the one hand the day-to-day reality of powerful feelings and on the other the deeper abstractions of love that have implications for the broader metaphysics of humanity as a whole. It somehow manages to be transcendent without losing sight of the painful realities of indecisive relationships.

So much of the *Sonnets* is a satirical deconstruction of the conventional Petrarchan literary model of love (see Chapter 6) and its exalted, quixotic and fanciful postures. The Sonnets demystify the idea of love as an arcane, heaven-ordained marvel. Instead, they are pervaded by the voice of an older and sophisticated, increasingly sceptical man, sardonic perhaps, but convinced of the inevitability of love even with all its proven anguish.

The vast majority of the Sonnets are sharply focused on the subject of love, especially on the mature realities of sexual experience and its intense emotional aftermath. Consistent with his revisionary attitude to courtly romance, Shakespeare invokes the traditional language of courtly love for the purpose of a range of explicitly uncourtly themes such as erotic love, troilism, sexuality and gender, homoeroticism, betrayal, duplicity, prostitution, and sexual politics.

The essence of love in the Sonnets is its anxiety. Accordingly they are often confessional in tone and claustral in attitude, having a highly private tenor. Even so we are likely to feel that their experiences are firmly objectified. At the heart of the speaker's anxiety lie issues of desire, commitment, control, mistrust, suspicion, human frailty, paranoia, frustration, jealousy. Many of the poems are powered by the universal questions about relationships: uncertainty about his lover's feelings and affections, the nature of his own feelings, commitment, the longing for exclusive rights over his lover, fidelity, and the veracity of his perceptions.

The poet/speaker's vexations are inevitably paralleled in Shakespeare's language and poetic technique. The themes of the Sonnets are mobilised by ambiguity and, consistent with themes of dissembling and deception, its language is in general terms epitomised by supersubtlety, duplicity, ellipsis, equivocation, evasion, unsettled and open syntax, and unstable punctuation. By the same token we should not overlook the role played in the creation of uncertainty by Shakespeare's cunning and deep-reaching ironies.

We have noted how Shakespeare subtly interrogates the sonnet's form, experimenting with variations on its internal shape and its voices, modifying metre and rhyme, extending individual sonnets to form broader conflated units and thus to invite intertextual readings.

Because themes of art and love come together so frequently in the sonnets we, like Shakespeare, are often forced to consider love in literary terms, to see the way love is itself controlled by language (and by the expectations of art, such as in Petrarchism). Shakespeare strives to resist these limits and the historic effect of past time in forming and controlling his perceptions of love but in the end even this becomes inevitably subsumed as a literary element.

Love in the sonnets is essentially unsatisfactory and unfulfilling. It is epitomised by large swings in fortune and emotion, and is more likely to end in tears and turmoil. And yet Shakespeare is likely to convince us that in spite of all these exasperating aspects leading all mankind to this hell, love is as crucial to life as physical nutrition and as inevitable,

> Thus do I pine and surfeit day by day,
> Or gluttoning on all, or all away.
>
> (Sonnet 75:13–14)

Further Research

Have a look in detail at sonnet 46 and its complement 47 and try to work out what devices Shakespeare uses to connect the two poems as a single, conflated sonnet. How does sonnet 47 develop and complete the ideas originated in 46? How do the eye and the heart in these poems differently perceive the young man who is their object (in this respect compare sonnet 148 too). What does Shakespeare say about the themes of freedom and constraint in these two poems and how does this bear on the theme of love there?

2

Time: to Posterity and Beyond

Make use of time, let not advantage slip:
Beauty within itself should not be wasted,
    Fair flowers that are not gathered in their prime
    Rot, and consume themselves in little time.
                    (*Venus and Adonis*, lines 129–32)

We have already come across the theme of change, changeability and shifting nature in Chapter 1, especially in terms of the notion of lovers' inconstancy, and we will return to this theme frequently. In Chapter 1 the prevailing idea, in the context of time and change, was that lovers are free to make deliberate changes in their preferences. In this chapter we may be more struck by seeing lovers within the complex of wider forces.

Ovid, a Roman poet exercising a pointed influence on Renaissance poets, depicts Time as an overwhelmingly destructive force to whose power all mortal life is subject.

Thou tyme, the eater up of things, and age of spiteful teen
Destroy all things. And when that long continuance hath them bit,
You leysurely by lingring death consume them every whit.
                    (Ovid, *Metamorphoses*, book XV, 234–6)

(Quotations from *Metamorphoses* are taken from Arthur Golding's 1567 translation, probably the version read by Shakespeare.)

Shakespeare takes up this strikingly awesome image of Time and applies it as a recurring motif in the poems as well as in the plays, for instance in *Love's Labour's Lost* where Navarre complains of the

> cormorant devouring Time   (1.1.4).

In Shakespeare's work as a whole, the theme of time is, of course, one of his most pervasive preoccupations. His views on the subject very much reflect those of his period and so before we begin to analyse some of the sonnets it will be useful to briefly introduce some of the ideas current in the late sixteenth and early seventeenth centuries.

Although Elizabethan philosophers held widely disparate views on the metaphysics of time, writers of the period were more congruent on the properties and effects of time. Their chief temporal concern was the theme of mutability: namely that mortal life on earth is epitomised by change and death. Fluellen in Shakespeare's *Henry V* links mutability with turning, inconstancy and variation (3.6.32–5), while in *Twelfth Night* Feste thinks of time and therefore life as a 'whirligig', a spinning top constantly on the move (5.1.375). The Sonnets too are vitally engaged with related topics such as cosmic change, the fickleness of fortune, the unpredictability of events, the inconstancy of lovers, and ageing.

The Sonnets are profoundly troubled with problems of time, change, death and eternity. They are rooted in the mutability of everyday life yet explore the possibility of sublimely transcending the natural and temporal in ways that ultimately make us still more conscious of time's effects on us. This juxtaposition of the sublime alongside the mundane is exemplified by Justice Shallow's famous reflection in reply to his country colleague in *Henry IV, part 2*:

> Death, as the Psalmist saith, is certain to all, all shall die. How a good yoke of bullocks at Stamford fair?   (3.2.36–8)

By seeking this escape from time and the mundane, Shakespeare's verse appears to commune with the essence of eternity itself in vivid and complex ways.

One of the most lucid and persuasive expositions of the phenomenon of mutability is Edmund Spenser's *Mutability Cantos*, published in 1609, the same year as Shakespeare's *Sonnets*. An allegory of time in its myriad aspects, Spenser's exquisite poem portrays change as a rebellious goddess attempting to seize sovereignty over the universe.

> What man that sees the ever-whirling wheel
> Of change, the which all mortal things doth sway,
> But that thereby doth find, and plainly feel,
> How MUTABILITY in them doth play
> Her cruel sports, to many men's decay.
>
> (Spenser, *Two Cantos of Mutability* (1609), Canto VI)

For Shakespeare as for Spenser, mutability is a curse which nevertheless unites all sublunary creation, and the Sonnets too are keenly about this 'plainly feel', the fact that the double edge of mutability is at the root of our greatest delight and deepest woe. Shakespeare's favourite, Ovid, describes it in Golding's version as

> No kind of thing keepes ay his shape and hew.
> For nature loving ever chaunge repayres one shape a new
> Uppon another, neyther dooth there perrish aught (trust mee)
> In all the world, but altring takes new shape.
>
> (Ovid, *Metamorphoses*, book XV, 252–7)

Here in two nutshells is Shakespeare's view of mutability. Time is relentless change, bringing about maturity and beauty, but the process that renews inevitably ends the individual or particular thing itself. One of Shakespeare's many interests in the Sonnets is a striving to come to terms with the awful paradox of this.

I will be analysing sonnets 5, 12, 60 and 116, to try to get a take on the wide range of ideas on the theme of time that Shakespeare treats in the collection.

Sonnet 5 'Those hours that with gentle work did frame'

After the austere financial imagery of sonnet 4, sonnet 5 comes as one of Shakespeare's most exquisite, richly loaded with verbal music, images and figures that shape the poem's form.

> Those hours that with gentle work did frame
> The lovely gaze where every eye doth dwell
> Will play the tyrants to the very same,
> And that unfair which fairly doth excel;   4
> For never-resting time leads summer on
> To hideous winter and confounds him there,
> Sap checked with frost and lusty leaves quite gone,
> Beauty o'er-snowed and bareness everywhere;   8
> Then were not summer's distillation left
> A liquid prisoner pent in walls of glass,
> Beauty's effect with beauty were bereft,
> Nor it nor no remembrance what it was.   12
> > But flowers distilled, though they with winter meet,
> > Leese but their show; their substance still lives sweet.

The first quatrain sets up in simple metaphorical terms the double view of time which is the core of the poem's metaphysics as well as its appeal. Time, 'Those hours' which have laboured carefully to create the young man's very popular good looks, will become the tyrant that will destroy ('unfair') them. The demonstrative, deictic pronoun at the very start of the poem is clearly intended to make an arresting effect on the young man, determining the relationship between the speaker and the subject as well as the distance between them (compare the start of line 9). It introduces a muddle of such pronouns and adverbs – 'those', 'that' (lines 1 and 4), 'there' (line 6), 'then' (line 9) – lending an assertive, prescriptive tone to the poem. It asserts that the older man speaks with authority, based on hard experience.

Although other poems in the 1–17 sequence emphasise the formative role of preceding family generations, here beauty is created in a matter of 'hours'. Ironically, though, the word 'hours' conjures up the painstaking labour of a craftsman – time working on a curiosity, such as a miniature painting or tapestry (implied in the words 'gentle' and 'frame'). Gentleness is also suggested in the quiet decorum of the opening two lines of the poem, in contrast with the traumatic actions of the second quatrain perpetrated by time, both artist and devastator. The play on the sounds – dwell/Will, every/very, unfair/fairly – seems to signify the tricksy caprice of time.

The poem begins quietly, working through 'gentle' and 'lovely'. 'Gaze' (part of a complex synecdoche in line 2) is both the young man's face or appearance on which his admirers linger ('dwell'), and his eyes, which meet and hold every other eye. Line 2's charm deepens the surprise which comes in the word 'tyrants' in line 3. The surprise is part of the poem's mild shock tactics based on Shakespeare's mature grasp of the reality of time ('prisoner' in line 10 is another such vivid if melodramatic personification).

'Tyrants' implies a cruel pitiless despot, carrying overtones of treachery – compare sonnet 16 where the speaker urges the young man to 'Make war upon this bloody tyrant time (16.2). This double knavery will eventually 'unfair' that fairness of the youth. Here 'unfair' is another of the poem's shocks, working as a transitive verb (to undo beauty) but also implying the injustice of the tyrant's duplicity. The oddness of the word's function gives the poem's calm one more jolt but, as if to soften and reassure, the quatrain comes to momentary rest on 'excel', a familiar Shakespearean hyperbole.

The early part of the poem is infused with imagery of time's action (frame, play, leads, leaves, confounds) while the later is concerned with that of attempts at holding it back (checked, left, pent, still). The poem itself mimics time's harsh continuity in having very few caesurae to slow it down (only in the first two lines and in the couplet).

Line 5 extends the motion begun in the initial quatrain, with a memorable image of its relentlessness. Yet, although the first quatrain attributed agency to Time personified, the phrase 'never-resting' in line 5 implies that time itself obeys some hidden, perhaps inner compulsion,

> For never-resting time leads summer on.

The word 'leads' here suggests that, in its tyrannical mode, time compels summer forward like some manic tormentor, rehearsing the idea in line 1, of forcing summer to fashion or 'frame' nature's beauty. As a verbal phrase , 'leads on' also carries with it the idea of deceiving. 'Hideous winter', with its connotations of repulsiveness and menace, contrasts with the earlier calm beauty, and its associations of 'gentle', 'lovely' and 'fairly'. The word 'and', appearing in the middle of each of lines 6, 7 and 8 (technically, in rhetoric this is polysyndeton), has the effect of drawing the reader forward in a corresponding movement. Summer is led allegorically on and then mugged in a frozen wasteland: 'Beauty o'er-snowed and bareness everywhere' (8). 'Confounds' implies confusion but also utter destruction.

In effect the second quatrain repeats the idea of the first (enunciated by the initial word 'For') but with more vividly emotional and menacing images. In particular, line 7 with its sexual allusions in 'Sap' (compare sonnet 15:7) and 'lusty leaves' (see sonnet 2:6) seems aptly formulated to unsettle and strike at the young man's prodigal dissipations, a trenchant as well as a timely warning (the metre becomes slightly irregular here too, in lines 7–9). 'Leaves' puns with 'gone', double-stressing the finality of beauty's ruin.

In a different context the remarkable image contained in 'o'ersnowed' might seem conventionally picturesque but here it again implies concealing and deceiving. For Elizabethans the snow was more likely to evoke horrors of devastation, the dread of food shortages, and death. And 'bareness everywhere' thus conveys total desolation while also suggesting 'barrenness' (8). It is important to stress at this point, too, that nature stands specifically for human life as well as for the mortal sphere in general.

In the opening lines of the poem the speaker's tone is both meticulously controlled and detached. His use of reasoned argument imposes calm. But in the second quatrain the voice becomes more pressing through the vivid and coercive image of time's destructiveness, warning the young man that time is the destroyer not only of beauty but also of sexual vigour. Yet, although the attitude of the speaker is counselling rather than didactic, the lyric as it stands is not addressed to anyone directly, having no personal pronoun (a rare characteristic in the Sonnets: see 129 for a similar impersonality). The poem seems averse to confrontation, and other elements support this idea, including its calm, the application of rational argument, modest sounds and regular rhythm instilling an unruffled propriety.

The adverb 'Then' (deixis again) arrests the cyclical action of the first two quatrains. Until this moment there is a strong forward thrust created by the paucity of caesurae, combined with suspended sentences and hanging clauses – such as in lines 2, 7 and 14.

'Then' is also a synonym for 'therefore' and as a discursive marker it connects and leads the discussion on towards a solution to time's problem. Where the previous eight lines used a self-assured indicative verb, this now changes in line 9 to the subjunctive mood, expressing the conditional, uncertainty,

> were not summer's distillation left.

If the essence or fragrance of summer's flower had not been concentrated and therefore preserved in alcohol or oil, the fundamental substance of beauty would have been lost. The outward show of beauty has now already faded with time. Thus we would otherwise now have neither the particular original object, the rose for example, nor its essential property captured in the glass bottle, the eternal soul or elemental idea of beauty:

> Beauty's effect with beauty were bereft.   (11)

Beauty's effect becomes imprisoned in 'walls of glass', preserving the sensory aspects of summer's growth, in the fragrance and perhaps the colour of the plant's fruit or blossom ('left' takes up the pun in 'leaves' in line 7 and transfers it towards 'Leese' in the final line).

What then can we make of all this? Shakespeare is addressing a profound and still controversial question in aesthetics. In short, does the beauty of an object exist really and only in the eye of the beholder (the subjective view: see sonnets 127 and 130); or is beauty an objective property inherent in the object itself (the objective view)? Put simply, if the former then not everyone will see the same object as beautiful; if the latter then everyone ought to agree on the object's beauty. Shakespeare in the sestet of the poem sets out a neo-platonist position: that beauty is a property which is temporarily bestowed on or lent to a mortal object, in this case the flower (see line 11 and compare sonnet 4:3) – as such it vanishes when the object perishes.

The neo-platonist view is that true or essential beauty exists as a fixed *substance* only in the immortal realm of heaven. Here on earth something of this *substance* is lent to some mortal objects as an outward and temporary *show* (see line 14). This show is subject to time, but in the poem, the substance or essence of beauty may be trapped, 'pent in walls of glass', and preserved while the flower is in full bloom.

The alliterative 'l' in these two lines evokes a fragility and sensuality of sound which parallels the theme of beauty's vulnerable delicacy. As a liquid, alcohol or oil, the distillation is a reasonably convincing analogue for immortality, but the negative associations of constraint in 'prisoner pent in walls' (line 10) qualify somewhat the appeal of the eternal life. The suspended, conditional sentence (beginning in line 9) leads us further on and into a first indication of the metaphysical argument of the poem: that the essential substance of beauty too would have been lost when the beautiful plant, blossom, fruit etc. had faded away. Neither the plant nor any reminder of its splendour would have survived. The treble negative in the elliptical line 12 looks like a quibble (or a printer's intervention) and is all one with the multitude of negatives or quasi-negatives in this poem (unfair, never, not; plus quasi-negatives: tyrants, hideous, checked, bareness, bereft, and so on).

After the intimidating images of mutability in the octave the sestet releases some of the poem's tension by hinting obscurely at curative action, before the couplet's timely portent,

> But flowers distilled, though they with winter meet,
> Leese but their show; their substance still lives sweet.

Just as the second quatrain repeated the idea of the first, the couplet now repeats the theme of lines 9–12. Time is cheated by distilling the essence of beauty and thus preserving 'Beauty's effect'. Flowers which have had their beautiful perfume purified and condensed 'Leese' (meaning 'lose' but also punning on 'lease'; see 18:4) only their outward show, their substance or essential nature enduring even over time, 'though they with winter meet' (line 13). Not only does it endure but it retains its unspoiled state ('still lives sweet'; line 14), the final word, 'sweet', linking up with those earlier adjectives 'gentle', 'lovely' and 'fairly', implying the former state. Read aloud, the word 'still' resonates through the sestet, reiterating the theme of immortality, resolving and bringing to a close the intricate action of verb tenses that plays throughout the poem.

The couplet is less epigrammatic than many of the other sonnets in the collection but it retains a proverbial feel in its reminder of 'more show than substance' (compare *Romeo and Juliet*, 3.2.77).

The ideas of Sonnet 5 are marshalled around its two vividly remarkable images of time and beauty: time as tyrant, and beauty as the 'liquid prisoner'. The image of beauty as a 'prisoner' under assault from time, and mutability battering its frail bastion, strengthens the idea of a despotic aggressor intent on rape, as he had bullied summer into ravishment.

Each of these two themes has a double aspect: time is creator and destroyer, while beauty is both show and substance. In effect, therefore, the poem is an allegory of time as a medieval despot laying siege to the damsel beauty, oppressed (from 'frame in line 1 to 'walls' in line 10) but resisting his ruinous onslaught. The poem's keen wit springs from the cogency of these two images, as well as preventing a lapse into a dry metaphysical debate on time.

The imagery of the poem falls into four main groups centred on ideas of time: action, confinement, loss, and in the middle lines of the sonnet, the elements of beauty's plant. These relate to the supple and surprising modes in which Shakespeare conceives the theme of time. Time is paradoxically both a moment ('hours' implies a series of these moments) and a continual flow ('never-resting'). Connected to these is the idea of time as eternity, the 'still lives' of the distilled flower preserved within 'glass walls' (though immortality can also mean the end of time, existing outside of it). Furthermore, as well as movement and stillness, time is here also memory, 'remembrance what it was'.

We have noted that time is both creative and destructive, and this is the crucial point of the poet/speaker's argument to the Young Man, his immediate audience. Time is represented as the dominant force in the productivity of nature (it makes beauty and 'leads summer on'). It is the co-conspirator with nature, the two together generating and controlling (even though tyrant time eventually turns against nature). Time is represented as an artist too, with the power to form and reshape. Thus the poem strikes a shrewd affinity between the poet and time, perhaps a rivalry, but by expressing his own awareness of this the poet assumes some power over Time.

In challenging and defying Time the speaker aims at self-empowerment, both figuratively in asserting the sovereignty of art and in a personal sense in taking charge of the young man's destiny.

In general, Shakespeare's metaphors dovetail eloquently with his metaphysical arguments. 'Walls of glass' may not quite convince as a bastion against time's blasts, but we are minded to go along with the useful image of a scent bottle. A more fundamental objection lies in the idea of time as an incessant force leading summer on to 'hideous' winter. If Shakespeare is to exploit his powerful 'seasons' metaphor then, we can reasonably wonder, why does 'never-resting time' lead only on to winter, since his figure also holds out the inevitable prospect of spring? (Time in the form of the seasons posits a cyclical motion.)

One answer lies in the turn between the octave and the sestet. After line 8 the speaker's attention switches from the movement of time to the metaphor of the flower. Thus he becomes less interested in the realistic course of time than in what happens to the beauty of the flower. Time is defeated and thematically comes to an end once the flower's beauty is distilled, and thus Shakespeare excludes the possibility of a recurring spring (and the sentimental ending that might have resulted).

Comparing time to an artist of course focuses on the human consequences of the theme and we should not lose sight of this amid all the metaphysics. The words 'remembrance' and 'gaze' also support this human dimension. Equally, the youth is linked with the loss of 'sap' and 'lusty' summer, his sex and sexuality (sonnet 1 describes him as the 'world's fresh ornament'). Shakespeare seeks to harrow the man with a threat of loss of beauty, popularity and virility, the things that he seems to value most and which are at the heart of his self-love. The summer is male (line 6) and so is aligned with the youth as intended reader of the poem, and the poet's specific reminder is that unless he acts to produce an heir he too will be led on and confounded, 'hideous' and barren.

As I have pointed out, this sonnet is not overtly addressed to a specific 'you', a point which some commentators have regarded as a weakness. Others have noted that in concentrating on the effects of time on beauty the poem does not sponsor any particular course of action. It does not say 'do that' or 'do this'. Is it all a bit vague, generalised, overly metaphorical? The poet's role is as a counsellor and in accordance with this he exercises a certain degree of courtly deference to the young man, mixed with courtly wit and prudent equivocation. He proffers *prudentia* to the man, practical wisdom. But what is he counselling and, though the couplet sounds aphoristic, what is its exact practical wisdom?

Shakespeare's point here is not, of course, *carpe diem* ('make the most of the present') nor is it *carpe florem* ('enjoy the moment'). The key is that sonnet 5 must be read with sonnet 6, its companion piece, forming a conflated sonnet. Taken out of the context of the 1–17 'begetting' sonnets this poem can seem vague and austerely philosophical, yet graphic and highly musical. It has little in common with sonnet 4 apart from the common epithet 'sweet' and the hint that beauty is but leased ('tombed' in 4:13 too perhaps anticipates something of the 'liquid prisoner pent' in sonnet 5).

Sonnet 6 is the companion to sonnet 5 in extending and completing it, making the familiar message clearer. Its opening word 'Then' takes up and has the same function as it has in 5:9, meaning 'therefore' but seizing and stressing the temporal urgency. Sonnet 6 discusses the imagery of the same seasons, urging the young man to preserve his own 'sweet' beauty by procreation, metaphorically the 'walls of glass' or 'vial' (phial), as an indemnity against death's ruinous clench,

> Then let not winter's ragged hand deface
> In thee thy summer, ere thou be distilled;
> Make sweet some vial . . .
>
> (sonnet 6:1–3)

Some critics such as Katharine M. Wilson have rightly judged sonnets 5 and 6 together as a 'single, logically complete', poem. Wilson opens up the sonnet to a much broader context, proposing that sonnet 6 'gathers up the image of distilling, unites it with images from sonnet 4 and gives a comic twist by granting [the young man] ten children' (Wilson, 1974, p. 155). Others, notably Helen Vendler, have preferred to see sonnet 5 as a separate, complete entity, resting on a proverb-like metaphor, and concluding with an eloquent silence (Vendler, 1997, p. 66).

Sonnet 12 'When I do count the clock that tells the time'

When I do count the clock that tells the time,
And see the brave day sunk in hideous night;
When I behold the violet past prime,
And sable curls all silvered o'er with white: 4
When lofty trees I see barren of leaves,
Which erst from heat did canopy the herd,
And summer's green all girded up in sheaves,
Borne on the bier with white and bristly beard: 8
Then of thy beauty do I question make,
That thou among the wastes of time must go,
Since sweets and beauties do themselves forsake,
And die as fast as they see others grow;   12
  And nothing 'gainst Time's scythe can make defence
  Save breed to brave him, when he takes thee hence.

The couplet of sonnet 5 offered us a sanguine consolation about immortality rooted in a metaphysical slant on beauty. Its argument is highly conceptual and its proof clever if plain, even ascetic. Sonnet 12, on the other hand, mixes gravitas with gravy. While maintaining the urgency and penetration of sonnet 5's message, sonnet 12 greatly enriches it with copious and picturesque imagery and association.

Nevertheless, the two poems share some important imagery and diction as well as ideas on time. Again there is white and snow, sweet, beauty and summer; winter was hideous, now night too is just as hideous, and Sonnet 5's 'lusty leaves quite gone' becomes in sonnet 12 'barren of leaves'. In the opening to sonnet 12 the poet/speaker counts out those hours that had earlier framed the young man's 'lovely gaze', delineated by the 'clock that tells the time'.

In addition to the new fertile imagery of sonnet 12 Shakespeare presents us with three versions of time. The first occupies the octave of the poem. The neutral clock of the opening line simply 'tells' the time as it ticks away. The syntax in this section lends a strong impression that change and death – *mutability* – simply happen: day is 'sunk' (line 2), the violet is 'past prime' (3), sable curls become 'silvered o'er' (4), while the lofty trees become 'barren of leaves' (5), and summer's green growth ends 'girded up in sheaves', to be 'Borne on the bier' (lines 7–8). Which is all very passive. Time is a natural, predictable and acceptable process of nature.

In the third quatrain, however, time and death take on a cogently different aspect.

> Since sweets and beauties do themselves forsake,
> And die as fast as they see others grow
>
> (11–12)

Here there is a strong sense in the word 'forsake' that the younger generation – the 'sweets and beauties' – actively seek self-sacrifice, in abandoning themselves. But this can mean both that they fritter away their lives in profligate self-love, or perhaps that, seeing the inevitability of the coming generation ('others grow'), they readily acquiesce and 'die as fast'.

Then, in the couplet, we encounter the speaker's third depiction of time and death. Time is again the callous tyrant, but now in the familiar guise of the reaper, a brusque and active executioner:

> And nothing 'gainst Time's scythe can make defence . . .
>
> (13)

By making time increasingly aggressive, the speaker tersely seeks to bring home to the 'fair youth' the urgency of his message. But the speaker himself is quite passive, a detached observer of nature who counts, sees and pronounces from the privilege of mature years.

He is well-versed in human life but also seems in tune with nature and its unremitting flux. The opening adverb, 'When', strikes the key solemn note after which the line, and the poem itself, ticks out the seconds in regular rhythm (this sonnet has the most regular metre of all the sonnets). The speaker counts while the clock 'tells'. As John Kerrigan suggests, the clock takes on a calculating life of its own (Kerrigan, 1986, p. 188) and the poem does have many anthropomorphic elements; for examples, see lines 7 and 8.

The day too is 'brave' (2), implying a courageous human-like resistance against the inevitable encroachment of awful night. 'Brave' suggests defiance, a point which is echoed in the final line, but here in line 2 it has a more wistful tone carrying nuances of colour and beauty. It anticipates the idea in lines 11–12 that even the beautiful are not immune to time's violations. 'Sunk' urges on us the notion of total and helpless destruction and is part of the poem's consciousness of height and depth (compare 'lofty' and 'girded up').

Line 3 repeats the poem's opening, establishing another internal rhythm: of 'When I / And' (lines 1 and 2, 3 and 4, 5 and 7). It reminds us of the solemn slow beat of a pendulum or a clock's escapement (the principle of the clock pendulum had been recently discovered by Galileo, in 1581). The violet is described as 'past prime', with strong temporal irony since 'prime' implies 'at its best', or maturity. 'Prime' means literally the first, primordial, and hence springtime (compare Italian *primavera*, 'first truth'), and the first part of the monastic day.

The violet is one of the earliest spring flowers (compare the 'forward violet' in sonnet 99:1) and so is associated here with youthfulness. Shakespeare uses the flower to suggest another interval of time, and the poem as a whole contains at least five different timescales. The 'clock' in line 1 reminds us of the 'hours' in sonnet 5, and line 2 has 'day' and 'night' denoting time as a series of relatively brief moments. Further, the violet suggests the seasons, a point reiterated in lines 7 and 8. This is followed in line 4 by the human span of time, time measured out by an individual life (see also line 7) and by generations of lives (in lines 10 and 12),

And sable curls all silvered o'er with white.

As the violet refers to youth, so silvered hair points to old age. Hair that had once been black and healthy has become silvery white, or grey, and that word 'all' hits at the thoroughness and absoluteness of time's action. As in sonnet 5, white is here associated with decline and death, and contrasts with the other vibrant colours of the octave, violet and green, and even sable (compare sonnet 2, lines 3–4, and *Hamlet*, 4.7.77–80).

In November 1817 John Keats wrote to his friend John Reynolds rhapsodising about Shakespeare's sonnets but he singled out the second quatrain of sonnet 12 as just too much, too lush in sound and association – though Keats himself often sought to 'load every rift with ore'.

> One of the three books I have with me is Shakespeare's Poems: I neer found so many beauties in the Sonnets – they seem to be full of fine things said unintentionally – in the intensity of working out conceits. Is this to be borne? hark ye!

He cited in evidence the second quatrain:

> When lofty trees I see barren of leaves,
> Which erst from heat did canopy the herd,
> And summer's green all girded up in sheaves,
> Borne on the bier with white and bristly beard.

The second quatrain opens, like the first, with the temporal adverb 'When'. It announces the start of a string of marvellously evocative and complex images. 'Lofty trees' in line 5 conjures up the visual scene but also conveys the vigour and strength of these noble mature trees, in the same breath emphasising the much greater potency of time in denuding them. The words 'lofty' with 'barren', in the same line, play with the idea of former sexual vigour and signify how wintry old age has become infertile, merely show (compare the effect of 'lusty' in sonnet 5:7).

The trees that had formerly sheltered the cattle or sheep from nature in the form of the solar heat are now themselves subject to nature's mutability. The effect is made deeper by the counterpoint of 'barren' and 'canopy'. The poem advances through a series of crucial antitheses: brave day/hideous night, sable/white, wastes/sweets. Note too the unpleasant opposition between these rich hints of summer and the nihilistic prospect of 'wastes', 'die' and 'nothing', intended of course to alarm the young man to whom the poem is addressed.

Lines 7 and 8 present a brilliantly intricate complex of image and idea,

> And summer's green all girded up in sheaves,
> Borne on the bier with white and bristly beard.

Paraphrase can hardly do it justice. The once-green summer crop, now a memory, bleached pale in the fierce ripening sunlight, has been harvested to be carted away, dead and bundled up. Again there is the antithesis of high and low, the crop is 'girded up' then laid on the bier. A 'bier' was originally a frame on which to lay farm crops, the word later becoming particularised as a funeral platform, and since it derives from the word 'to bear' it resonates punningly with 'Borne' (John Keats considered the pun and alliteration in line 8 a little too rich – though he himself uses a similarly transmuting figure in the middle stanza of *To Autumn*).

Yet, as the line moves forward the image subtly metamorphoses into a picture of a dead man with white and stubbly beard. The word 'white' echoes the old man's 'curls' in line 4, now seen as a premonition of his death, yet the sombreness of this idea is somewhat relieved by the (implied) idea of harvested seed representing the following season's seedcorn (its foison also contrasts with 'barren' and 'wastes'). Past, present and future converge on these lines but anticipate and stress the poem's homiletic message: you must breed in order to produce a future generation or submit to the 'wastes of time'.

So in the opening eight lines of the poem Shakespeare weaves together a tight complex of thematic strands and striking visual image. His diction works to conflate the worlds of man and nature, by choosing words and pictures which neatly cross between the two: 'brave', 'bier', and 'beard'. Man is not so much the Renaissance semi-divine figure of wisdom, infinite in reason, but simply another element of the natural world, alike mutable, being singularly obedient to the ineluctable change wrought by the seasons.

Perhaps inevitably, the lyric reverie of the octave is routed by the peremptory force of 'Then' at the start of line 9 (as in sonnet 5). It announces the third element in the sonnet's dialectic ('When ... When ... Then ... '), and advances a provisional conclusion to the poem, together with the prospect of action or remedy. The poetry becomes more rigorously focused, confrontational and business-like. The phrase 'of *thy* beauty' now firmly points the finger at the young man, as the poet/speaker ponders what will happen to his good looks. Chillingly realistic, there is only one, and inevitable, end

> ... thou among the wastes of time must go.
>
> (10)

That's hard. Note the heavy force of that word 'must'. Just as for Marlowe's Doctor Faustus the pleasures of earthly life are merely transient toys, delights to distract from the ultimate reality of its terminus.

The 'wastes of time' is another of the poem's brilliantly compact conceits. On the one hand it conjures up a place (the undiscovered bourn of hell) reserved for those who on earth squandered their time and opportunities. On the other, it implies an image of deserts of vast eternity, a sterile place, a metaphor for the emptiness underlying the young man's lifestyle of 'brave' but idle profligacy. In either case there is of course the inescapable idea of time's indifferent desolation.

With unfeigned irony the delights of life are reiterated in line 11, those 'sweets and beauties'. Helen Vendler has argued persuasively that rather than the tautology this phrase seems to be, it actually embodies an interesting distinction: 'sweetness' standing for inner virtue, and 'beauties' for outward show, each element thus designating different values (see sonnet 54; Vendler, p. 98) This distinction reminds us again of the dichotomy of substance/show in sonnet 5.

'Sweets' can denote happy moments, of course, such as those in the octave of the poem, or indeed it may refer to lovers. 'Forsake', as 'abandon', carries with it that idea of self-destruction we have discussed above but it can equally suggest that lovers lose themselves in each other. Since 'die' is a familiar Elizabethan euphemism for orgasm it hints too at procreation, that is to make 'others grow', the breeding referred to in the final line of the poem.

The couplet begins in hope and ends in doom, reversing the movement of the final line in sonnet 5. The word 'die' in line 12 brings the audience more explicitly to time's enormous truth: nothing is invincible against time's destruction. The only recourse is to breed (though, again, this is not an exact defence). The couplet reverses the chiming of 'When/And' repeated in the opening quatrain, and the words 'brave' and 'time' also refer back to the opening. 'And nothing' at the start of the couplet parallels the stark reality of 'And die' in line 12, introducing a prospect of seeming hopelessness which is held over to the next line, and to the word 'Save', extending salvation. The caesura in the final line enforces a pause, which hovers briefly before the death sentence in the end, 'when he takes thee hence'.

Time is here conventionally personified with a scythe, the harvester referencing back to lines 7 and 8. Scythe, however, also presents phallic possibilities. Similarly, the word 'nothing', while warning of the earlier threat of 'barren' and 'wastes', signifies again the female genitals and thus promotes the theme of procreation; see sonnet 136 (lines 11–12) as well as sonnet 20, and note Hamlet's bawdy repartee with Ophelia:

> *Hamlet*: Do you think I meant country matters?
> *Ophelia*: I think nothing, my lord.
> *Hamlet*: That's a fair thought to lie between maids' legs.
> *Ophelia*: What is, my lord?
> *Hamlet*: Nothing.
>
> (*Hamlet*, 3.2.115–19)

'Brave', reappearing from line 2, repeats the idea of defiance, with an implausible suggestion of 'cheating' time. Now, however, because it takes up the earlier theme of beauty, 'brave' may in fact involve the idea of reverencing the figure of Time through the beauty of an offspring. Yet, even though begetting an heir will certainly be delightful there is still the certainty of death in the end.

This sonnet portrays the young man as a mere cog in the great mechanism of time. He is no different from others in the final reality that our lives are such stuff as dreams are made on. In the concluding line, 'breed' too sounds mechanistic and ruthlessly biological, the culmination of a series of sexual nudges and innuendo, including 'lofty', 'die', 'nothing', and that phallic scythe.

The very beautiful and striking imagery of the octave section of the poem works to drive home the point to the young man that if the stunning beauties of nature are subject to cruel mutability then his own beauty and life are not secure from it. (John Kerrigan makes a convincing case that this sonnet's imagery and themes are 'heavily influenced' once again by book XV of Ovid's *Metamorphoses*; Kerrigan, pp. 187–8.)

In effect the poet himself imitates nature by sweetening our reading with lyrical beauties, holding off the inevitable truth. Once more, while beauty and sexual vigour are now at their prime as sources of pleasure and popularity, they and he will ultimately fade 'among the wastes of time'. Again, Shakespeare's thrust is less *carpe diem* than *sic transit gloria mundi*, thus fade the glories of nature set out by the poet in the metonymy of the first seven lines.

This is the mainspring of the poem and again is expressed loosely as a syllogism, a logical argument. In reality the 'when' clauses of the poem function as 'because': so the argument runs, (a) all natural beautiful entities are mutable and will die (lines 1–8); (b) you are both part of nature and beautiful (9 and 11); (c) you are therefore mutable and will inevitably die (10 and 12). Then Shakespeare adds an important codicil: accordingly you must 'brave' time by getting a beautiful child.

And yet, even beauty, though an essence or form, is no guarantee of immortality (for further evidence see, for example, sonnets 5 and 18). This is of course a very orthodox argument but the strength and originality of the poem rest in its sophisticated style and form. On one level there is vividness and economy in the images and figures of nature and in particular of summer. Yet, on another level there is the beautiful music of the sound patterning in, for instance, lines 4, 7–8, and 11.

The poem presents a complex interplay of sound as well as of theme. For example, consider the relationship of assonance and alliteration in line 14, which grows out of the lines preceding it.

> Save breed to brave him, when he takes thee hence.

The word 'brave' assimilates the sounds of 'save' and 'breed' as well as the long /ai/ sounds from the sestet ('wastes', 'gainst', 'make'). The /b/ and /r/ sounds are an echo of the end of line 8 (both lines containing an image of being carried away). The long /ee/ sound in 'breed' is prominent in the middle area of the sonnet ('see', 'heat', 'green', 'bier', 'sweets') and extends in line 14 through 'he' and 'thee', thus connecting Time and the young man through sound as well as sense. The two figures are framed within the adverbs of time and place, 'when' and 'hence', which seem to define the mortal existence as expressed in the octave. The final line has an exquisite symmetry as well as euphony, poised on the fulcrum of the caesura, driven quietly on by the steady iambic rhythm.

In effect this sonnet consists of one sentence only, protracted through suspended and conditional clauses embodying a series of supple movements. The poem's phlegmatic consciousness curls sinuously through these clauses and their caesurae, pressing forward until it pauses fleetingly at the main clause in lines 9 and 10, before driving unstoppably through a tumble of conjunctions to the conclusion.

The poem has a strong atmosphere of action and time and this derives in part from these movements. This effect is supported by teeming visual images together with a surfeit of imagery relating to actions: 'count', 'tells', 'sunk', 'canopy', 'girded up', 'grow', 'go', and so on, and although the speaker himself is relatively passive the poem seems to buzz with movement and energy. This matching of subject and style in the movements and action establishes the poem's 'decorum'.

In addition, the poem's motions draw together sound patterns such as the ticking of the iambic. The purling /er/ sound in the middle of the poem eventually gives way to /s/ and /z/ in the sestet (especially in lines 11 and 12), imitating the rhythmic swish and swing of Time's indomitable scythe, hesitating momentously in that ominous pause in the middle of line 14.

Everything imaged or discussed in this sonnet serves the theme of mutability and the poem is governed by the consciousness embedded in the sombre pun in line 8, that we are

> Borne on the bier . . . .

It is a profound if gloomy conceit, that our birth naturally entails our death. Samuel Beckett expresses a similar idea with stark candour in *Waiting for Godot*, in the words of Pozzo:

> They give birth astride a grave, the light gleams an instant, then it's night once more. (*Waiting for Godot*, Act 2)

The movement between the time of 'born(e)' and the time of 'bier', between birth and death, is depicted conventionally as a journey: life or the end of it, in line 10, is a journey towards and into timelessness,

> thou among the wastes of time must go.
>
> (line 10)

And, as line 12 indicates, it is a relatively 'fast' transit – not only are all things in nature mutable, but swiftly so. Thus the violet, the trees and the summer's green have all too short a lease, stressing the urgency of the poet's warning. The word 'defence' in line 14, in the context of 'fast' and 'Time's scythe', further implies that Time is not a simple passive figure but a cruelly vengeful presence.

Even the rhetorical figures participate in the poem's universe of time. We have already noted the anaphora of the octave, the repetition implying circularity. The hypotyposis in lines 2, 4, 6 and 7 (an expression of time past as though it were present to the speaker) is interesting since it arrays these scenes as ever-living moments, a type of epiphany,

> And summer's green all girded up in sheaves.
>
> (line 7)

And ironically the idea itself is ever-living. The speaker sees these images in memory but they are presented now as a constant reminder of the movement of time.

The examples in the octave, of earth's glories, are used as the main leverage for the moral of the poem. Ironically, although their purpose is to intensify the brevity and singularity of the individual life, they actually exemplify the concept of change, and with change, regeneration: the leaves will return to the lofty trees to canopy the herd from the newly hot sun. But not, ultimately, for the young man as himself: he must incorporate himself into nature's great cycle of change and regeneration, become obedient to time, and he may do this only by breeding.

Sonnet 60   'Like as the waves make towards the pebbled shore'

In sonnet 59 Shakespeare ponders whether, as some ancient Greek writers (such as Parmenides and Pythagoras) supposed, there is 'nothing new' in life and art. Are we deceived, he asks, in thinking that we are truly creative and original? In other words, is a cyclical view of time and change, the same things recurring anew, the correct view? If so, history would not be history in the usual sense since the past would be constantly present to us.

In sonnet 60 Shakespeare offers a sort of answer to this by offering a different paradigm of time, one in which its units, 'our minutes', proceed in 'sequent toil', or in a linear process.

> Like as the waves make towards the pebbled shore,
> So do our minutes hasten to their end,
> Each changing place with that which goes before,
> In sequent toil all forwards do contend.   4
> Nativity, once in the main of light,
> Crawls to maturity, wherewith being crowned,
> Crooked eclipses 'gainst his glory fight,
> And Time that gave doth now his gift confound.   8
> Time doth transfix the flourish set on youth,
> And delves the parallels in beauty's brow,
> Feeds on the rarities of nature's truth,
> And nothing stands but for his scythe to mow.   12
>   And yet to times in hope my verse shall stand
>   Praising thy worth, despite his cruel hand.

In the opening simile the word 'waves' ironically combines the ideas of both a cycle and a line: circular motion within itself but moving forwards in a line. Yet for us in our particular human life our minutes move in a straight line: just as sea waves head directly to the shore, inevitably and inexorably, so our lives advance towards their end.

It is a starkly bold statement of human mortality. Perhaps a little too realistic but intending to unsettle that possibility of deception so marked in sonnet 59. The 'end' to which our waves make is the 'pebbled shore' and pebbled because, unlike a rocky beach, pebbles demonstrate more readily the effects of time and a shifting current, as a pebbled beach itself is in continual motion, its components 'Each changing place' (3). But tracing the word 'pebble' to Shakespeare's plays also throws up other possible nuances; Coriolanus's 'pebbles on the hungry beach' (5.3.58–9) suggests triviality in contrast to the stars, while in *King Lear*, Edgar's 'unnumber'd idle pebble' (4.6.21) implies a barren existence, countless stones rolled round adventitiously and shifting to no obvious purpose.

Line 2 of sonnet 60 opens with a nimble pun on minutes and hour (and some critics here make much of the sonnet's number, 60). The imagery of motion continues with our allotted time hastening to its finish. Thus although line 6 suggests that infancy literally 'Crawls', our lives as a whole hasten by. In line 3, the word 'Each' soberly tells us that time embraces everyone, with no exception (a common view of the 'begetting' sonnets), and 'changing places' implies both human life in its generations and the mutability of mortal existence. But the line hints at something more complex since it proposes both a cyclical and a pulse pattern in time and change, unsettling the order and faintly hinting at chaos behind the flux, a whole set of processes at work and at war with each other (and note the poem's imagery of conflict, for example in line 4).

But given the decorum and syntax of these early lines the surface impression is one of the steady and unrelenting passage of time, and 'place' in line 3 conveys the idea of order. Each moment is replaced precisely by the next. The word 'all' in line 4 reinforces the inclusiveness introduced by 'Each' in the preceding line, each of Shakespeare's own words changing place with and modifying that which goes before. 'Forwards' here stresses the inclusiveness of time, too, there being only one direction. The imagery of conflict in 'toil' and 'contend' beautifully expresses both the busy press of daily lives and the quality of 'hasten' from line 2.

The first quatrain introduces Shakespeare's speculative take on time, incorporating both the familiar and the uncommon (though if sonnet 59 *is* correct he cannot claim to be wholly original). After the metaphysical or conceptual angle on mortal time the second quatrain adapts this to the human sphere, opening with an abstract metonymy for this in the word 'Nativity'. But the line is no less easy for the new direction and fires off some interesting ideas.

Once born, we crawl via the famous seven ages of man (*As You Like It*, 2.7.139–66), mewling and puking through to maturity, and then comes the decline of beauty and health. Let us cheat time and linger on line 5,

> Nativity, once in the main of light.

The line throws out a number of possibilities. Nativity refers not only to the period of infancy and to 'Crawls', of course, but also to the precise moment of our coming to this great stage (*As You Like It*, 2.7.165). The 'main of light' can mean the principal light, that is heaven, as God's light, signifying that we were once in heaven before falling to earth (one of the few suggestions of transcendence in the poem).

At the same time the word 'Nativity' together with the astrological reference to 'eclipses', below (7), introduces the idea of the zodiacal chart or horoscope (and perhaps the lines or 'parallels' in line 10 also point to this) and thus to the notion of a child's life as unknown but mapped out by time. The child is born into the 'main of light', on earth, entering the realm beneath the sun. Alternatively, the child before birth was 'once' in this realm of light, or heaven, compared to which the earth is now to him a realm of 'Crooked eclipses'.

Further, the word 'main' in the sense of 'sea' extends the metaphor of the waves from the opening line. Thus the 'light' can also mean that the newborn child is thrust onto a broad expanse (a boundless sea) of great potential (compare 'bud' in 1:11). Each of these substantive words resonates with its own dizzying possibilities. None more so than the temporal adverb 'once', implying 'no sooner than' or perhaps a single unique occasion, or 'formerly and more', each possibility extending and deepening the ideas around it.

For certain, though, after we are born Shakespeare portrays the infant in a world of constant motion: crawling, crowning, crooked, fighting, confounding. All of these stem from the 'sequent toil' in those primordial waves at the beginning whose protean sea is synonymous with flux. 'Crawls' evokes the movement of infancy but additionally, going back to the pebbles, a humbling stature, maybe satirising the ideal of human 'glory'. Nevertheless, 'maturity' is the crown and glory, zenith of human vigour and beauty (the equivalent to sonnet 5's 'summer' and 12's 'prime') – and even in its archaic sense 'glory' involves being blessed by the presence of God (and the eternal dimension of time).

The triangle of *cr-* words in these lines (*Crawls – crowned – Crooked*) embodies the major stations of adulthood, and then 'confound' points to the end of the mortal life. Such patterns of highly textured sounds help to bind together the middle section at a point where the previously regular rhythm begins to break up.

This group also has resonances of Richard III crook-back king, glorious sun of York eclipsed in pursuit of crown and glory:

King Richard: Myself myself confound!

(*Richard III*, 4.4.399)

(Compare sonnet 100, line 14: 'his scythe and crooked knife'.)

'Crooked' (7) implies bent old age but also a malignant moral will at work in the 'eclipses' that blight the glory of man's and woman's beauty. The idea of such a will is strengthened by the familiar personification of 'Time' in terms that remind us yet again of the perfidious tyrant of sonnet 5, bestowing the gift of beauty and then ravaging it,

And Time that gave doth now his gift confound.

(8)

The balance of this idea also recalls sonnet 4's theme that Nature merely lends and duly calls in the capital. The same hand that gave the gift of beauty (and of life) now takes it back.

At the end of the line, in a significant position, 'confound' rounds off the quatrain and also the crawls–crowned–crooked sequence with amazement or oblivion. As a metrical rhyme with contend (4) the word 'confound' resolves and releases the turmoil and struggle that suffuses the octave. The adverb 'now' in line 8 is the complement of 'once' in line 5.

'Confound' is an apt note for the middle of the sonnet for another reason. In its sense of 'perplex' it makes plain an important element in the poem, at the same time casting a glance back to sonnet 59:2, and 'how are our brains beguiled' (note also in line 9 here the word 'transfix' meaning 'to astonish'). Sonnet 60 not only verbalises the poet's perplexity at life's cynical game of cruelly bestowing and taking back, but the sonnet's unstable semantics and syntax too articulate a fitting discordancy.

The third quatrain follows directly on from the second; in other words, the form of sonnet 60 is, appropriately, a linear one, $12 + 2$ with no clear *volta* at line 9. (Philip Martin disagrees with this interpretation, arguing that the relations between the second and third quatrains are 'strained', with only a perfunctory connection between the two; Martin, p. 107.)

However, the 'gift' referred to at the end of the second quatrain is made more explicit by the start of the third. The opening word of line 9, 'Time', acts as a bridge with the previous line and then the gift is reified as the bloom of youth, epitomised as 'beauty's brow' in line 10.

Tyrant time 'doth transfix the flourish set on youth'. The word 'flourish' is another example of Shakespeare's brilliantly powerful economy of word both bursting with connotation and at the same time defying any easy gloss. A flourish is an ornamental affectation in a signature or work of art. Here it suggests the vigorous beauty of youth, while the phrase 'set on' suggests that it is only temporary. And the flourish of a signature might make us think of the final words of the poem, the 'cruel hand' that signs the death warrant. But, of course, 'flourish' can equally mean 'to thrive or prosper', a point which makes its transfixion or destruction deeply ironic. That it was Time itself that had first set the 'flourish' on the youth drives home the cynicism of the process.

'Transfix' here means to stab or slash, an idea reinforced by 'delves' in the following line, whose idea is cognate with the second line of sonnet 2:

> And dig deep trenches in thy beauty's field.

The 'parallels' referred to in line 10 are, of course, the wrinkles of those advancing years, the 'Crooked eclipses' (but the word also looks back to the 'waves' in the first line). Parallels are military trenches, an adjunct to the poem's imagery of conflict, while the contrast of 'delves' and 'brow' is part of the poem's antithesis of high and low (for example, sun v. sea, and crawls v. stand).

In Shakespeare, appetite is rarely a positive figure (in this context see sonnet 146 too; consider also *King Lear*, 5.3.24, and *The Rape of Lucrece*, line 1687). In the plays it is usually a reminder of bestiality. Thus in line 11 time 'Feeds' on the beauty of the young man or woman here like a parasite. The whole line is a beautiful example of Shakespeare's characteristically succinct nuancing:

> Feeds on the rarities of nature's truth.

'Rarities' brilliantly focuses together youth's exquisite glory (7) and unequalled 'worth' (14) yet also youth's brisk transience. However, I find 'nature's truth' less easy to gloss, but it involves the metaphysical ideas that on the one hand the stark reality of mortal (or natural) life is its mutability; while, on the other, the rarity or gem of nature is beauty, the flourish or bloom lent for a certain time on the 'brow' (beauty is nature's truth). But behind the phrase lies the unswerving awareness of time and nature in conflict.

The epitome of mutability is Time as the great devourer, and we have noted already Shakespeare's debt to Ovid's *Metamorphoses* for this (book XV, 234, refers to *tempus edax rerum*, time the devourer of matter). His borrowing is made explicit in sonnet 19:

> Devouring Time, blunt thou the lion's paws
> And make earth devour her own sweet brood.
>
> (lines 1–2)

In sonnet 60 the outcome of great devouring is a void, 'And nothing stands', and this phrase harks back to the harvested corn implied in sonnet 12. It also recalls the sexual pun of sonnet 20:12 and impotence in sonnet 5:7. 'Nothing' is a severe reminder too of nature's hard truth, the abyss of death, brought on by time the destroyer, while his scythe is another element in the poem's imagery of cutting (for instance, 'transfix', 'delves' and 'mow'). The word 'nothing' functions as an absolute or universal here, another reminder that no one is exempt from time's devouring jaws (note 'Each' and 'all' in lines 3 and 4).

The couplet begins conversationally with 'And yet'. This is the last in a series of 'And' clauses whose effect has been to draw attention to the relentlessness of time's onslaught and its consequences. In contrast to the start of the couplets of sonnets 5 and 12, 'And yet' turns the mood suddenly brighter, holding out some promise against the continual downward movement of the poem. However, this is just as swiftly hesitated by the uncertainty of the phrase 'in hope'. Yet, though we have recently been told that 'nothing stands', there now lingers the possibility that 'my verse shall stand' in spite of time's 'cruel hand'. The change in perspective, to the future, draws the focus beyond the sonnet's immediate moment, bringing a feeling, but just a feeling, of aesthetic closure.

Only now, in the final line of the poem, does the speaker address the friend, male or female, directly. This is typical of that movement from the general to the particular commonly found in Shakespeare's sonnets. And yet while apparently holding out the prospect of cheating time, the hope turns out to be both ironic and egoistic in origin. You and I will die but my verse will survive (perhaps this is Shakespeare's own 'cruel hand' busying about its unkind work). 'Cruel' significantly closes the group of *cr-* words of time begun in line 6.

Again it is self-referential verse: poetry about poetry. The promise about praising the reader is a bit of a feint, an artistic deception.

The poet does not actually praise his/her worth (loyalty or beauty) or make clear what their 'rarities' are. Art will, however, prevail. After the destruction of youth (9), beauty (10) and knowledge (11), 'my verse shall stand'.

The ending is unusually cadential, negative and chill. There is hope and yet no hope. The couplet looks and feels like an after-thought, a practical rather than a momentous ending to the poem. Unlike the 1–17 'begetting' poems it offers no action or even realistic perspective, no freshness or crisply pert epigram. And this after all perhaps deepens the sense of its despair.

Sonnet 60 comes near the start of a suite of sonnets connected by the theme of time (sonnets 59–77), chiefly concerning its destructiveness and the comparison of the present age with past eras. It is addressed to a friend, male or female, though, as we have noted, the personal address does not appear until the vocative pronoun in the final line. This may or may not be the same friend as in the 1–17 group but the speaker here lacks the obvious deference of that group. While this pronoun 'thy' may be simply a rhetorical device it does furnish a relatively austere poem with some token of intimacy.

What is to cheat time now is not the begetting of an heir, nor love, nor natural beauty or memory, but art, 'my verse', which will, hopefully, through its own beauty, become immune to time's desolation.

Not surprisingly there is no real suggestion of transcendence (except perhaps in the symbolism of 'sea' or the 'main of light'). In this sonnet time is chiefly human time: 'our minutes' (2), and they are 'sequent', unstopping, each pushed on by new ones following on. In the opening line, 'waves' may also suggest generations of lives too, moving on in a cycle. As we have seen, the cycle of an individual life is set out in the second quatrain, beginning with 'Nativity', then flourishing youth, crawling to glory in maturity, which is eventually overshadowed by crooked old age.

For humankind time is a parcelling out in units of a life (compare John Donne's 'hours, days, months, which are the rags of time'; 'The Sun Rising', line 10). We think of moments, whether in the minutes and hours or in the stages of the growing person, leading to the cruel scythe. In fact the personification of Time and his scythe naturally emphasises this human horizon. Conversely, natural time is characterised by the concept of mutability (and in this context the word 'changing' in line 3 is the key term). This compels entities not to a final discrete end but to relentless changes of state, and thus all things remain in perpetual flux, becoming rather than being. Which is another aspect of that 'nature's truth' referred to in line 11. More on this below.

In the human apprehension of time its effects are usually too intensely subjective and critical to take a neutral standpoint. Thus 'cruel' (14) and 'Feeds on' (11) reveal more about its victim's feelings than about time the reaper. Once again there is a double view. Time cultivates the growing infant, raises it to maturity, the crowning glory, but then ravages and ruins this crown,

> And Time that gave doth now his gift confound.
>
> (line 8)

At war with nature, time destroys nature's splendour and it is no consolation to know that as a species we continue like waves. In fact, the truth that we change places with the next generation actually hammers home our mortality. If the ending is grimly realistic then at least Shakespeare attempts to make us the less deceived; this is as good as it gets, and even Homer nods.

Metaphysically, change just happens. As in the 'begetting' group of sonnets Shakespeare offers no causes, only mystery and his acceptance of that mystery. With the ingenuousness of the ancients he resignedly puts it down to the amoral figure of Time, the reaper, and those inscrutable 'Crooked eclipses'.

The dominant temporal imagery of the poem clusters into a convergent set: time, motion, and conflict. All relate to the theme of mutability, the idea that all life on earth and indeed all existence is subject to change and is in a state of inexorable flux. Extending this view leads to the idea that the earth is a quite unstable location, with its atoms, elements, animals, people, and states at war, unable to stand,

> In sequent toil all forwards do contend.
>
> (line 4)

The poem imparts a strong impression of this side of the temporal theme. Not only are things in motion, subject to time, but also they are in Heraclitean conflict with each other. Above all, Time itself seems to be in contention with human life, bringing individuals on, to lead them through the stages of life and then discarding them with a sharp slash of his blade: 'nothing stands' except for his scythe but equally nothing stands still.

The style of sonnet 60 seems to concur with all this and finds expression in discord. The first quatrain sets up the sense of constant motion; then the *cr-* words introduce a grating, discomposing tone just at the moment when the iambic rhythm becomes disrupted in the second quatrain; the third quatrain with its series of present tenses insists that the absurd process of life and ruin is unending. The picture is horridly cruel, perversely so, and the couplet, where we customarily hope to find understanding or at least solace, gives back nothing but a sadistic laugh of egoistic conceit ('to mow' also means 'to make a contemptuous grin'). But even this is only tentative, 'in hope', a vague muttering vow about praising 'thy worth' some time or other.

Sonnet 116 'Let me not to the marriage of true minds'

> Let me not to the marriage of true minds
> Admit impediments; love is not love
> Which alters when it alteration finds,
> Or bends with the remover to remove.   4
> O no, it is an ever-fixed mark
> That looks on tempests and is never shaken;
> It is the star to every wandering bark,
> Whose worth's unknown, although his height be taken.   8
> Love's not Time's fool, though rosy lips and cheeks
> Within his bending sickle's compass come;
> Love alters not with his brief hours and weeks,
> But bears it out even to the edge of doom.   12
>   If this be error and upon me proved,
>   I never writ, nor no man ever loved.

Love is as constant as the northern star and, astonishingly, even time itself seems to defer to its steadfastness in this brilliantly provocative lyric. Nevertheless, as if to emphasise this steadfastness, sonnet 116 begins with a slight hesitancy, a request, 'Let me ... '. Its courtesy, however, soon yields to a more resolute tone in the famous words recalling the Solemnisation of Matrimony from the Book of Common Prayer,

> I require and charge you (as you will answer at the dreadful day of judgement, when the secrets of all hearts shall be disclosed) that if either of you do know of any impediment, why ye shall not be lawfully joined together in matrimony, that ye do now confess it.

This duality, of constancy and transience, is something which pervades the whole poem and has led some critics to see this marriage reference as a parody. The very opening word, 'Let', embodies two opposites: 'allow' and 'obstruct', and these two meanings unfold in line 2 as 'Admit impediments'.

By the same token, the poem opens with a positive that quickly becomes qualified as a negative. The effect of the opening is to unsettle the reader, a pivotal characteristic of the rest of the poem. So the opening line and a half can mean: 'I will never stand in the way of true lovers so if you have another lover then I will leave'; or, 'our love is so perfect or valuable I will never grow tired of you, even if you change'. Each reading inevitably affects the way the rest of the poem is interpreted.

The nature of the intended audience is not clear. But that there is an audience seems apparent from the opening line and line 5, and from the general discursive nature of the syntax. 'Minds' is a surprising word here, however, where we might have expected 'hearts', and seems to imply that (true) love is a matter of spiritual disposition or that the poem will proceed by intellectual debate, as it does. In any case it envisages love as transcending the mortal and physical domain.

After the mild imperative in the opening lines the poem proceeds through a series of extended sentences, again a feature of the poem's discursive cast. The nature of (my) love is independent of what my partner does or thinks, and what you call 'love' is only love if it does not change (lines 2–4). Each of these ideas, of altering and bending, is taken up later in the poem, respectively, in lines 5–8 and 9–12.

So we have once again the idea of mutability, only now love cannot change. If it does (as in sonnet 20's 'With shifting change as is false women's fashion'), then what you called or thought was love is not so. It would not match up to the absolute conditions of the speaker's strict definition and we would need to apply a different term for such a lesser attachment: affection, desire, lust, infatuation and so on.

To meet the stringent terms of the speaker's definition, love is not something that can alter. It cannot bend either (4). The meaning of line 4 is not very clear in its detail, though the gist is apparent. 'Bending' shares the same semantic field as 'altering' and mutability and, taken together with the later reference to 'sickle', the word points to mortality and the idea of yielding to change. Thus both words strike at the heart of the problem of time for humans: 'alters' relates to change and 'bends' to death (this point is made more explicit by line 10).

'O no,' at the start of the second quatrain, reinforces the strong orational style of the poem, mirroring the verbal opening to the first. It is as though a charge has been made against Love, and Shakespeare is here speaking as counsel for the defence. The style continues to be highly self-assured.

While the first quatrain opens with abstract nouns the second now switches to concrete, conveying a sense of durability. Thus Love is an 'ever-fixed mark'; it is like a rock out at sea, a fixed point around which the seas and tempests of time war and howl. If it were not for this sea-mark, shipping (represented in the synecdoche of the 'bark' or barquentine) would drift without purpose or direction. Philip Martin notes how the imagery here bursts open the perspectives of the poem: 'while it suggests certain stable points, [it] combines to create a sense of great height, immensities of space and darkness' (Martin, p. 96). This space is deployed to suggest the vulnerability of the wandering bark set against the vast universe and the inevitability of its 'doom'.

Love too seems to soar above the scene. It is personified through the phrase 'looks on' (6), and the poem also depicts love as towering, monumental and invulnerable. A dispassionate observer, it is 'never shaken'. Shakespeare uses the same image in *Othello* when the Moor talks of his death in similarly absolute terms:

> Here is my journey's end, here is my butt
> And very sea-mark of my utmost sail.
>
> (*Othello*, 5.2.268–9)

A sea-mark is a fixed point by which navigators take their bearings, and in this way love invests the speaker's life with meaning or purpose. And that word 'ever' (lines 5 and 14) underlines the eternity of love (another absolute, like 'never' and 'every' in lines 6 and 7).

In line 7 Shakespeare applies a second extended metaphor, seeing love as a star, specifically the North or lode-star. That he is referring to love is borne out by the pronoun 'his', personifying love as a child as in sonnet 115:13, that is, Cupid (see also 126:1, 'lovely boy').

The height or declination of the star can be assessed objectively or scientifically by navigators and surveyors but it remains a mystery, since the exact operation by which the lode-star or lode-stone seems to attract the compass needle is puzzling (Robert Burton, in his *The Anatomy of Melancholy* of 1621, posited a theory that there was a pile of strong magnetic rock at the north pole; Burton, p. 119). Hence its 'worth's unknown'. At the same time, its 'worth's unknown' is especially relevant too in the sense that love is a mystery in its operation and thus its true worth is never appreciated.

We have been here before. Sure enough, Shakespeare may once again be proposing a Platonist view of love: that love in its perfect or ideal sense only really exists (and as an ideal) in a supernatural realm, beyond mortal existence, in the same way that the fixed stars exist in a higher sphere from our earthly zone. In this way people may fall in love but never *understand* the true, almost mystical nature of love (for a comparable use of nautical images see sonnet 80, and in particular line 5).

The third quatrain extends the poem's study of time by turning towards more overtly human applications. Line 9 draws out the theme that Love is inviolable to time, the otherwise supreme power,

> Love's not Time's fool, though rosy lips and cheeks
> Within his bending sickle's compass come.
>
> (lines 9–10)

Love is not the plaything or toy of mocking Time, not subject to its whim or domination, an idea that Shakespeare also deploys in *1 Henry IV*,

> But thoughts, the slaves of life, and life, time's fool.   (5.4.80)

(See also sonnet 124:13.)

'Rosy lips and cheeks' is a touchingly elegiac metonymy for youth and mortal beauty, and the diminutive 'rosy' is both a poignant familiarity and a hint of the flower, conventional metaphor of mortal beauty. What's more, 'roses' as flowers prepares for the fuller significance of the 'bending sickle'.

The sickle is literally the reaper's instrument and a reminder of the scythe in previous sonnets. Its modifier, 'bending', opens up a wide array of potential meanings, especially as it may be either transitive or intransitive. As an intransitive verb or adjective it describes both the curve of the tool and the action of the reaper stooping to mow down the standing crop (compare 60:12, 'And nothing stands but for his scythe to mow'). But as a transitive verb it also refers to the action of Time forcing the 'crop' (metaphorically, mortal life itself) to yield and crumple before its power. We humans fall within its compass, the scope or bend of its attentions. 'Compass' additionally extends the marine imagery from the second quatrain.

As often happens in a Shakespeare sonnet the third quatrain holds before us an earlier theme as a prelude to the couplet's dense amalgam. In repeating the word 'alters', line 11 reiterates the theme of lines 2 and 3, but now with stronger moral force: 'Love alters not' but 'bears it out'. It now seems as if Love does not merely withstand but is obligated to do so (the first line of the poem also has that same tone of duty about it). It is the duty and fact of love to endure, altering not as other things do within the human span of allotted time, our 'brief hours and weeks'.

'Brief' is the heavy fact of human plight, our allotted time is as nothing compared with the eternities of love, beauty and art. Love 'bears it out' implies that love continues or survives us, of course. Moreover, as M. M. Mahood points out, it can mean 'steers a course', broadening the octave's 'powerful navigation image' (Mahood, p. 94). The phrase suggests 'proves' or 'corroborates' and thus it anticipates the legal connotations in the couplet.

This sense is reiterated at the end of the beautifully sonorous line 12,

> Love alters not with his brief hours and weeks,
> But bears it out even to the edge of doom.
>
> (11–12)

It has unmistakable echoes of Macbeth's 'to the crack of doom' (*Macbeth*, 4.1.117). The word 'Doomsday' refers to the specific day of judgement ('doom' derives from Old English *dom*, or judgement) but doomsday is also the end of time, eternity, and in this context the reference here ties in with the opening of the poem.

The sonnet opened with resonances of the marriage service and likewise ends with them because at the solemnisation of a Christian marriage a couple would be reminded that their union would be tried 'at the dreadful day of judgement' (see the above quotation from the Book of Common Prayer). Doom, coming at the end of the line, seems apposite but in that location its sense of 'annihilation' resounds uncomfortably into the caesura which looms before the couplet.

In spite of its many certainties in imagery and theme I find this an elusive poem. Philip Martin calls it 'a poem without a flaw' (Martin, p. 96) while J. B. Leishman acclaims it as 'immortal ... literally and metaphorically incomparable' and doubts if 'any medieval or Renaissance poet' even approaches Shakespeare's treatment of the theme of 'Love as the Defier of Time' (Leishman, p. 105).

The theme is by now a familiar one: the conflict between mortal mankind on one side and, on the other, time together with its effects. But now, sonnet 116 goes further by saying that Love lies outside of time and, unlike nature, is impervious to its erosive effects. The sonnet is driven by this theme via its two principal metaphors: love as a sea-mark and as the lode-star. Thus the poem adds Love to those other entities, of Beauty (sonnet 5) and Art (60), that are impervious to Time's deadly power.

The poem begins and ends with the impression of hesitancy ('Let me . . . If . . .'). These introduce an unsettling note of existential uncertainty, the same note implicit in lines 7 ('wandering') and 13 ('error'). However, this is eventually dispelled by the forthrightness of the narrative voice in asserting his statements on the theme. These carry much greater force too when seen in the context of sonnet 115, to which this is a reply. Sonnet 116 takes up 115's question of the absoluteness of love but where 115 appears to accept that love may be mutable, 116 rejects this unconditionally.

As many readers have noted, sonnet 116 talks in terms of love as the 'marriage of two *minds*,' rather than hearts, or perhaps affections. To be sure, this implies that love here is less a matter of emotion than of disposition or even intellect, and this is important for the theme of love in a broader perspective, as we will see below. It exalts and elevates Love out of the mortal sphere and into the spiritual.

Clearly the poem's awareness of sonnet 115's themes does much to broaden its own horizons while drawing in other consciousnesses, and to intensify its own colours. The vocative address in the first line and then the exclamation in line 5 are orational devices which betray the poem's consciousness of itself, and of others beyond its fourteen lines. Other presences in the sonnet include us, the present readers, plus the speaker's lover, as well as a possible rival lover. The 'impediment' to true minds may be the speaker himself, standing in the way of his lover's new affair; alternatively, it may be that the speaker has a potential new lover, a potential impediment to the existing love. This complexity of the 'Other', which imbues the poem with some of its essential tension, naturally depends on how we construe the 'two minds' in line 1.

However we interpret this, the speaker's voice is remarkably calm and assuring throughout. If we accept the possibility that the speaker himself is the 'impediment' then he sounds serene, resigned, even stoical about what is effectively a separation. This tone derives from the series of five simple but solid statements between lines 2 and 12. These are framed by a muted imperative at the start, and a complex conditional statement at the end. The extensions to the main statement make for a fairly loose structure and this supports the discursive tenor of the piece (unlike sonnets 115 and 117 there is no strong emotional intensity). Each quatrain begins with a negative, as though the speaker were resolutely refuting his (absent) rival's claims or opinions. The poem is both an essay on defining love and a dialogue. It is, however, a dialogue with one side of the debate missing (the opening to line 5 is an example of *epanorthosis*, a rhetorical figure which involves a reply to counter or correct a previous statement, here off-stage).

To support the relaxed, casual tone, the poem employs half-rhymes for lines 10 and 12 and eye-rhymes for 2 and 4, and 13 and 14, making the whole sound less contrived. The opening words have a soft, imploring tone. The principal vowel sound is /o/ and the foremost consonant /r/ and these together buzz through the poem, converging in the final line with its conspicuous /o/ and /r/ sounds. So prevalent is the /o/ sound that the sonnet noticeably begins to sigh.

On earth all things can be seen as subject to mutability: nature views this neutrally, simply as change, altered states. For us humans, on the other hand, seeing it more personally, change is maturity, decline and death, alas. In sonnet 116, this theme of mutability is epitomised by lines 3 and 4,

> Which alters when it alteration finds,
> Or bends with the remover to remove.

Each of these items, 'alteration' and bending, introduces the two interpretations of mutability, in the second and third quatrains respectively. 'Alteration' lurks under lines 5 to 8, which are concerned with flux in nature (tempests and seas), while in lines 9 to 12, 'bends' speaks of time as decay and death, the human situation in 'rosy lips and cheeks' and the relativism of our 'brief hours and weeks'.

The world of mutability therefore points up by contrast the constancy of love. Love transcends time in the way that essential beauty ('distilled' in sonnet 5) and art transcend its ruinous effects, unlike breeding (sonnet 12), which merely gives the illusion of cheating time. Breeding an heir lends the impression of evading time's effects, yet the individual person is still subject to time. Love, beauty and art in their abstract essences are not of the human sphere of time and are therefore immune to its destructive influence.

Plato proposed that goodness, truth, beauty and justice are qualities all beyond time. Conversely, Shakespeare nominates instead love and beauty, and proposes that these are essential to good art: love and beauty, as sonnet 18 tries to demonstrate, are prerequisites to the eternal life and power of art. In the opening two lines of sonnet 116 he also includes justice, in the form of moral duty (the legal and ecclesiastical imagery, plus the word 'worth' in line 8, also point in the direction of themes of ethics and justice).

Moreover, Plato believed that for these ideals to reach perfection (as 'forms') they would have to be suffused with the essence of the ultimate virtue, the 'good'. So, Platonic love exists in a non-physical realm as an ideal or perfection. For his part Shakespeare sees 'love' as performing the same function on earth (though the marriage is of 'true *minds*'). Thus love as the 'ever-fixed mark' and the fixed star, not only evades time and mutability but is central to and a standard for mortal life and all that is mutable in it.

Conclusions

In the film *Annie Hall*, Woody Allen reminds us of the old joke about two elderly women in a restaurant complaining about the food: one of them protests about the terrible quality of the food, to which her friend adds, 'Yes, I know and such small portions!' The sonnets which we analysed in Chapter 1 pointed to the anguish and contingency about love – the sonnets of Chapter 2 reveal how small our portions are, how short life is for loving.

After the profound uncertainties of love, time ironically offers the poet a deep-seated source of assurance – but it is not that life is any less tentative, only that Shakespeare is more confident about what makes it so. In this he appears to write from the very roots of his soul.

In his work as a whole, time is one of its most recurrent preoccupations, and in the Sonnets this preoccupation with the theme of time falls into two primary aspects: time as duration or history, and time as an active cause of change in nature.

These two aspects are connected for Shakespeare on the level of human perception: we try to exercise control over them both by naming periods of duration (hours, days, seasons, and so on) as a framework within which to observe time as change or mutability (the sonnet form itself enacts this framework as a correlative).

Mutability in the Sonnets often encompasses human decline against the backcloth of a universe in perpetual flux (associated with the threat of chaos). Mortal life itself is depicted as incessant mutability in which all follow a pattern of birth, ripening and decline. Shakespeare understands time in anthropomorphic and mythic terms – so it is frequently personified as a thief (in sonnet 77), a tyrant (5 and 16), an artist (16), the great devourer (19), hoarder (65), chronicler (123), but perhaps above all as a scythe-wielding harvester of lives (12). As a callous and pernicious figure, Time is the force that brings men and women to the mature pitch of their beauty and minds, but is also the force that destroys them.

In an age striving to overturn the shibboleths that had traditionally dominated and controlled mankind, time persisted for the Elizabethans as *the* tenaciously obdurate power. Time is the other great rival – we might even say that for the Elizabethan humanists it is the final frontier.

The sonnets are very much preoccupied with the sovereignty of time towering over vulnerable humanity and they offer a variety of strategies for transcending or cheating time, the 'great devourer': by begetting an heir (sonnets 5 and 12), through love (116) but above all through beauty in art (60). Because of our individual personal stake in the process of time none of these is likely to convince as a way of defeating time but only serve as consolations for the reality of 'nature's truth' (60:11) or even as metaphysical abstractions.

On the other hand, Shakespeare's is an eminently realistic approach, confronting the actuality of death. Accordingly, his more persuasive take on time can be summed up as, 'seize the day and make the most of that day, for in effect that is all there is'. Yet, amid all of Shakespeare's unstable harmonies and metaphysics there is little recognition in his dialectic for the compensations of religion.

In the discussion of the theme of time, Shakespeare demonstrates again how open and flexible the sonnet form can be and how much its internal framework is responsive to different treatments and emphases. In its tightly wrought economy of statement and rich formal dynamics the verse enacts the meaning, form and substance fused together. In correlating a framework of time each individual sonnet also signifies an expression of its author's attempt to conquer time. A sequence of sonnets (such as 1–17) amounts to a broader microcosm, with its ambiguities and ellipses, shifts in meaning and voice, and so on. As an allegory of time the sonnet also manifests the very human desire to impose the illusion of order on it. Accordingly, a great part of the appeal of the Sonnets lies in Shakespeare's ability to poeticise the intricate metaphysics of time, interrogating and humanising its complexity.

Further Research

Read or re-read sonnet 18, 'Shall I compare thee to a summer's day...'. What in this dazzlingly beautiful poem does Shakespeare say about the relationship between time and art and nature? It may help in your analysis of the poem to begin by identifying the imagery of time, all the words and images that refer to time, and then work out how the poem progresses through them. What is the structure of the poem and how does each quatrain differ from the others in terms of its theme, its attitude to theme and the author's voice? Have a look at sentence structure (for example, what is the effect of the question in the opening line?) and also at the patterning of sound.

3

Art: Clever, Very

> Scorn not the Sonnet; Critic you have frowned,
> Mindless of its just honours; with this key
> Shakespeare unlocked his heart.
>
> (William Wordsworth, *Miscellaneous Sonnets*)

Although many other arts are referred to in the Sonnets (for example, music in Sonnet 8, painting in 24, and acting in 23), what I am primarily interested in here is literature, and poetry in particular, and what Shakespeare says about his own art.

All art is concerned in one way or another with deception or attempted deception. Artists are essentially con-men, con-women. In his compelling study, *The Rhetoric of Fiction*, Wayne C. Booth advises that

> since any sense of composition or selection falsifies life, all fiction requires an elaborate rhetoric of dissimulation. (W. Booth, 1961, p. 44)

In this respect, poetry is no different from any other art form and engages with the reader in a discourse, a language of dissimulation or deviousness. This is its lifeblood.

As readers or 'consumers' we are accustomed to sleight of hand, deception, of having the rabbit pulled from a literary hat, our disbelief forcibly suspended. We are accustomed to having things palmed off on us under a welter of patter and hocus pocus. This, however, does not stop us being hoodwinked and we never seem to tire of it. It takes us out of ourselves and makes us 'patrons of the arts'. Shakespeare is no different (trust me on this).

Art in the Sonnets is manifested in many ways and with many threads. These topics are multifarious and interrelated but include the following – the imagination, art in the service of friendship and seduction, time, language, creativity and beauty. Some of these are allowed more detailed attention than others; for instance, art as seduction, literature and posterity, and Shakespeare dwells long on the nature and purpose of his own poetry. The sonnets themselves become, reflexively, a topic for themselves.

I have chosen to look in detail at sonnets 23, 55, 100 and 106.

Sonnet 23 'As an unperfect actor on the stage'

Sonnet 23 is an excellent example of deception in action. John Keats warned that we resent poetry that has a 'palpable design' on us. Yet 23 has just such a design, on someone anyway. Like many of the love sonnets, it sets out to persuade.

23

As an unperfect actor on the stage,
Who with his fear is put beside his part,
Or some fierce thing replete with too much rage,
Whose strength's abundance weakens his own heart;   4
So I, for fear of trust, forget to say
The perfect ceremony of love's rite,
And in mine own love's strength seem to decay,
O'ercharged with burthen of mine own love's might: 8
O let my books be then the eloquence
And dumb presagers of my speaking breast,
Who plead for love and look for recompense,
More than that tongue that more hath more expressed.   12
    O learn to read what silent love hath writ:
    To hear with eyes belongs to love's fine wit.

Sonnet 23 (like sonnets 118 and 60) opens with a simile that to a large extent controls the octave of the poem. Comparing himself to an actor reminds us of the author's own actual artistic background both as a dramatist and as a performer (tradition has it that Shakespeare took some minor parts such as the ghost of Hamlet's father) but modestly so, since the opening line also introduces the poem's important idea of a flaw or a deficiency. From the beginning the self-effacing poet humbly sets himself in inferior position to the reader.

The poem surprises by opening with a negative – 'unperfect' – (compare this effect in other sonnets, such as 14, 55, 107 and 130). Perhaps this is to undermine our position or expectations, and we are likely to feel there is some jockeying going on. An 'unperfect actor' is one who is unskilled, not word-perfect in his lines, and therefore tentative, lacking in confidence.

The words 'actor' and 'stage' are significant too in pointing towards an artform that is manifestly illusionist. It involves at heart a deception, and one that the audience readily adopts: it necessitates, as Coleridge tells us, the 'willing suspension of disbelief'. In line 2 the word 'part' is also an element of the poem's theatre imagery (referring of course to the actor's lines as well as his role). Stage nerves can produce the fear to make an actor forget his lines, or corpse ('put beside'), but the words are now beginning to open up more figurative possibilities too. He is not simply 'unperfect', lacking skill, but what skill he does have is undermined by some 'fear'. (Helen Vendler suggests he is more likely tongue-tied through having too much to say; Vendler, p. 138).

Line 3 adds that his performance is further diminished by his having too much passion bursting from within. He is reduced to the level of a dumb animal, 'some fierce thing', and then in line 4, the oxymoronic phrase 'strength's abundance weakens' reveals that such strength of feeling amounts in practice to a weakness as it impairs his performance. The first quatrain ends on the word 'heart', which is important since having opened with a metaphor of the theatre, the poet arrives at the figurative subject of the poem. It is expressed with something of that 'wit' which the final line of the sonnet aims for. Animal lust ('rage', 3) is contrasted with genuine love ('heart', 4) and he finds it difficult to vocalise his love openly and clearly because of all these restricting factors.

The second quatrain echoes these concerns but in a different idiom, though one which picks up some key words from the first. 'Fear' and 'strength' are reprised while the 'unperfect' of line 1 is translated to 'perfect' in line 6. Line 5 introduces the tone of nervous hesitation in the octave's argument. As if to deepen the poet's humility it is only now that he speaks as 'I', immediately qualifying any trace of assertiveness by reminding us of his imperfections, 'fear of trust' and 'forget to say'.

His 'fear of trust' reinforces the hesitation in line 2 but what was an indeterminate anxiety has become something more specific. The poet fears his own ability still but with the recent references to love it now embraces uncertainty about his lover's feelings towards him. Just as the actor's performance is diminished by stage fright, the lover is undermined by insecurity over whether his feelings are reciprocated. So it is not any lack of love that makes him neglect to declare his love in

> The perfect ceremony of love's rite,

but simply his reticence or, as line 7 suggests, the very strength of that love (compare sonnet 125 for a similar slant).

Lines 5 and 6 are important in stressing the theme of speaking: while confessing his weakness in seducing his beloved the poet admits that he has got neither the knack nor the patter and so cannot deceive her ('ceremony' and 'rite', which may also connect with sonnet 116:1–2). He is so poor a lover that he even forgets to say 'I love you', the 'perfect ceremony of love's rite'. He is poor at speech and the pun on 'rite' draws on the words 'writ' and 'wit' in the poem's couplet.

The litotes of line 7 further extends the poet's protestations of incompetence, especially in the light of his love's vigour. Line 8 parallels the confession of the first quatrain, gathering up and loading more imagery of power and weight. Yet love makes him a poor speaker, in fact it even makes his virility 'decay' or wilt away while he dithers. Passion subordinates his more courtly or gracious love, which is a purer if more vulnerable emotion.

The word 'burthen' in line 8 offers a familiar Shakespearean pun (for example, see *As You Like It*, 3.2.243); 'burthen' can be an 'oppressive load', or 'care', or a 'poetic refrain', and as such it cunningly presents a transition here between the octave and the sestet, drawing the attention away from spoken arts to written. The exclamation 'O' announces the start of the sestet, echoing the large 'O' in 'O'ercharged' (compare a similar effect in sonnets 22 and 32). The /o/ sound becomes the dominant vowel in the latter part of the sonnet (i.e. between lines 6 and 14) so that once again the piece as a whole sighs aloud, mixing love and dismay. The change of mood marks a break but also comments in frustration on those weaknesses set out earlier. The line declares that books (i.e. writing in general) now take over as his strength, or 'eloquence'.

The original 1609 Quarto of the *Sonnets* has 'books' in this line but some editors choose to emend it to read,

> O let my looks be then the eloquence.
>
> (line 9)

This has the merit of creating a more alliterative line and presents no major thematic conflict; the line would then paraphrase as something like, 'let my eyes be the true window of my feeling'. But in the sestet, writing and reading assume authority as sources of truth and expression, and the word 'looks' seems awkward as the subject of 'look' in line 11.

'Books' is an apt subject, of course, and it governs the hendiadys in 'eloquence / And dumb presagers'. This and the oxymoron in 'dumb presagers' or messengers/mouthpiece are yet another example of the exquisite 'wit' of this poem. In addition the word 'books' naturally refers reflexively to the Sonnets themselves. 'Speaking breast' (line 10) extends this theme of 'eloquence', while 'breast' harks back to 'heart' in line 4, now a metaphor for the poet's feelings. In terms of the theme of art, 'eloquence' smartly encapsulates the idea of creativity, being shrewdly supple in language.

The wealth of complex figures here invests the sestet with an easy charm, as its opening, extended, sentence urges its way smoothly forward. It flows artfully onward now with a confidence markedly in contrast with the fitful octave.

His writings 'plead', as a lawyer might speak in advocacy of his client, here speaking for himself. They 'plead for love', implying they do it for affection, to contrast with the 'rage' or passion of line 3. But they also do it without fee, while hoping for 'recompense' in requited feelings (though the word also carries a detracting sense of 'reward').

The poet's cunning reaches its climax in the crucial line 12:

> More than that tongue that more hath more expressed.

The poem seems to cascade headlong in this buoyant, artful line, swirling with an intricate interplay of 'more' and 'that'. There is a multitude of available interpretations, though the most immediate sense is that books (or even looks) are more succinct or truthful than speech in projecting the truth of a lover's devotion. Another sense is that the poet in his writing may say more, or more sincerely, than his honey-tongued and loquacious rival in love – the rival may have spoken more, yet meant or articulated less.

As so often, the couplet summarises the sense of the foregoing. His imploring 'O' again marks the structural break here with another emotional plea. The strength of the emotion once more iterates the frustration felt with language (though words are literally all he's got). The very intensity of this feeling now pulls us out of the difficult mists of line 12 with a straight-talking imperative: learn to interpret words and signs whose meanings are not immediately obvious or active. The idea of silence has been building from early on with 'dumb' and even the actor 'put beside his part'. While words are all he has, he urges his beloved to look beneath the surface of his words, especially since writing does not seize the attention (is 'silent') in the way that a speaker may.

Line 13 may also allude to the Elizabethan proverb 'Those that love most speak least', recorded by Shakespeare in *The Two Gentlemen of Verona*, when Lucetta tries to mollify her love-struck mistress:

Julia: They do not love that do not show their love.
Lucetta: O, they love least that let men know their love.

(1.2.32)

(and see Sir Philip Sidney's *Astrophel and Stella*, sonnet 54:14).

The line steers the reader–beloved back into the poem to read with new eyes and discover his unspoken love. 'Learning to read' reminds us too of what actors do, again pointing the reader back to the beginning. The final line of the poem, with yet another oxymoron in 'To hear with eyes', hints at the technique his beloved should use. Refined or courtly love (another contrast with the passion of 'rage') is concerned with more gentle, subtle seeing. The final line draws together the two sides of the written art that must be fulfilled: writing must be done with 'wit' but also requires the perceptive reader to fulfil it by providing a cogent interpretation.

Elizabethan poets were eminently concerned with 'decorum' in art: the precept that the style of a work should be appropriate to its content, art matched to matter (for more on this see Chapter 7). Sonnet 23 has two related decorums for us to consider: the aesthetic and the psychological. We can work towards a detailed analysis of the two of these by examining both the techniques of the sonnet and the poet's role in it.

As we have noted, this sonnet is organised as octave-plus-sestet. In simple terms the octave here consists of one complex sentence, outlining the poet's frustration in conveying his love; the sestet replies with a solution, that he *write* of his love since his writing is more expressive than his speech. The mood of the octave is composed and indicative, yet we may get caught up in its occasional imprecision such as '*some* fierce *thing*' and 'seem' (most of the nouns are abstract too). The sestet consists of two demonstrative entreaties ('O...').

The poem springs then from the poet's avowed deficiency: his failure to express affection is due not to a lack of devotion but to his inability to speak it. What's more, he can write his love but it still needs his beloved to interpret it correctly. The poet's character is the starting point of the poem's subject, adopting an inferior position predicated on his expressed weakness yet turning this to his advantage by contrasting it with the great power of his feelings.

> And in mine own love's strength seem to decay,
> O'ercharged with burthen of mine own love's might.
>
> (7–8)

The vigour and novelty of his position plus the deliberative energy of this seductive enterprise generate an almost palpable momentum but its primary vitality issues from the poem's many rich ironies, a point signalled in the final key word of the poem, 'wit'. At the same time the pathos of the poem turns partly on the poet's careful modesty but chiefly on the rhetorical movement that structures the spine of the poem: from statement and understatement to petition.

The poem's many contrasts and conflicts are also a valuable source of tension and interest in this marvellous lyric. These include the contrast once more of lust and courtly love, of speech and silence, speech and writing, 'tongue' and 'eyes', feeling and rationality, 'rage' and constraint (constraint implicit in 'ceremony' and 'rite'), strength and weakness, and so forth (there is the implicit counter too between the two lovers, though we do not see the other). The sonnet's system of antitheses and alternatives relates to its embedded theme of striking the balance, and yet they have another important function, defining the immediate limits of the poem's experience by tracing the limits of the speaker's anxiety and ambition.

Although we see only one of the lovers, the poem prompts the reader into constructing its narrative. It does this both by what is said ('what silent love hath writ') and what is left out ('forget to say'). At root it is a narrative regarding the poet's insecurities over his beloved and, ostensibly, the effectiveness of his artistic ability. Both ideas are figured in the references to 'fear' (2) and 'trust' (5). In the world of the poem his love is, ironically, the truly silent one. Outwardly diffident, he admits to not coming up to scratch (perhaps sexually too – see line 7) and makes this the excuse for his other failure: the failure to remind her sufficiently of his devotion. His apprehension about her and about his artistry is given an added twist of urgency by the shadowy presence of a potent rival who has already demonstrated his vocal eloquence,

> that tongue that more hath more expressed. (12)

The poet's own character is relatively clear. He has that avowed modesty over his spoken skills (comparing himself to an 'unperfect actor' and a fierce beast) and a steadfastness in love. On the other hand he does have a cocky self-belief in his writing, as we might expect, and the poem itself bears this out. He is above all a devious fellow.

He is devious because he is an artist. Art is here both Shakespeare's theme, speech versus writing, and his method, writing versus speech. It is thus a self-conscious, reflexive poem, a type of meta-art, attempting to demonstrate in action what its manifesto states. This is another of its ironies, that it writes what it would rather speak.

In sonnet 23 the theme of art manifests itself in three ways. In quite simple terms art is the relationship of style and matter in speech and writing. Then, more intricately, art here examines the creative interaction of speaking, writing, and reading (the product of what we would normally think of as an artist). And finally Shakespeare considers art as deception. We can take each of these points in turn.

In *Hamlet* Gertrude becomes impatient with Polonius's garrulousness and chides him,

> *Gertrude*:   More matter with less art.
> *Polonius*:   Madam, I swear I use no art at all.
>
> (2.2.95–6)

Brevity may be the soul of wit yet Polonius is neither brief nor witty and, to be fair, his art is tedious. But as we have noted in Chapter 7, to the Elizabethan writer and courtier, matter without art or ornament would make a very dull prince. Matter atoned with style is the very soul of speech and writing. This is the aesthetic decorum, the ideal refinement in art, referred to above. Francis Bacon urged that even philosophical writing should adorn itself in some embellishment, though ornament was more appropriate to creative writings,

> for the expressing of affections, passions, corruptions, and customs we are beholding to poets more than to philosophers' works; and for wit and eloquence, not much less than to orators' harangue.
>
> (*The Advancement of Learning*, Book II, IV:5)

In sonnet 23 Shakespeare is much concerned with the idea of performance. Not just as the 'unperfect actor' whose performance is marred by nerves but also as the speaker. He excuses his poor skill in speech and looks to books to carry his words home. Since the words would be quite similar in each, the difference is taken up by the performance.

In spite of his disclaimer in relation to speech, many of the sonnets have an oratorical feel to them. They often read like dramatic soliloquies and, as we would expect, they use similar vocal techniques of spoken rhetoric (and the word 'sonnet' comes from the Italian *sonnetto*, a small sound). It is another of sonnet 23's ironies that it too actually imitates speech, well-rehearsed speech, admittedly. This effect emerges chiefly from the vagueness injected in some of the diction, the aside in line 5, as well as the double outburst of 'O', passing off as spontaneous emotion. But it is, of course, very carefully crafted and this is the joke.

The poet is unable to speak and without a voice he is finished as an artist, which is another of the poem's many jokes. In the octave he complains that his silence is due to the fact that he has too much too say. He becomes tongue-tied and his strength as an artist is withered by his strength as a lover.

In the poem's second idea of art Shakespeare develops the theme of poetry as eloquence. Art for the prince is ornament or style and it is equally important as wit, particularly in that the poem seems to act out the show of courtly love. Courtly love involves a sequence of conventional codes and postures, important among which is understatement, especially of the man's prowess. Propriety is pre-eminent.

Othello is accused by Desdemona's father of using unnatural arts and potions to seduce his daughter. But Othello defends himself by claiming only to have spoken plainly to her. His plea has much in common with sonnet 23's.

> Rude am I in my speech
> And little blest with the set phrase of peace.
>
> (*Othello*, 1.3.81–2)

Desdemona's father is still unconvinced by his avowal and the suspicion lingers here too, but with better reason (in *Richard III*, Richard makes a similar defence at 1.3.47–50).

In sonnet 23 the litotes in line 7 extends the poet's protestations of inferiority so that he begins to acquire some adroitness in it. The whole performance betokens self-effacement through its stress on weakness though this is a rhetorical posture. Katharine M. Wilson offers the interesting insight that the 'theme of the lover so replete with passion that he is dumb is part of the ancient tradition that Petrarch built on' (Wilson, p. 179).

Part of the poem's cleverness lies in the poet's prompt distancing of himself from acting. He separates these two elements of the stage – the writing and the performing – but his real focus is to contend that he is no actor, no faker or pretender, and that what he writes is true.

His superb artistry is manifest in, on the one hand, the exquisite phrasing of the sonnet, and on the other, the staggering range of rhetorical figures that the poet musters. The phrasing and poise of the poem are delightful but it is in the poem's tropes that his brilliance emerges. Its mere fourteen lines (brevity being the soul of wit) include: simile (lines 1 and 3), oxymoron (4, 10 and 14), metaphor (4 and 10), litotes (1 and 7), antithesis (4, 9 and 10, 11), hendiadys (9 and 10), personification (11 and 13), chiasmus (11 and 12), pleonasm (12), synaesthesia (14), plus a wealth of fertile imagery; all of which establishes the poem's decorum. To this we can add the highly intricate tracery of sounds; for example, from 'unperfect' the sound separates out into the phonemes of fear, fierce, fear and forget, back to perfect and burthen, books and so on. The whole is an example of *occupatio*, the poet brilliantly protesting his incompetence.

In terms of literary technique the whole poem is itself a litotes writ large, an ironic understatement of its literary eloquence, curiously wrought. Yet, as a further witness to the poet's mastery, none of this sophistication is especially obtrusive. It leaves the clear impression that this poet rather than loading his work mechanically simply thinks readily in these terms. All of this represents the literary decorum of the poem: the irony that the poem itself demonstrates *implicitly* what the poet *explicitly* declares,

> O let my books be then the eloquence
> And dumb presagers . . .

> (lines 9–10)

Such fine erected wit is one essential element of courtly lovers' dalliance, of sharp and supple word play. The other important element is irony and the poem has a wealth of examples, especially in its oxymorons as we have noted above: dumb books speaking for the poet, hearing with eyes, and strength as a source of weakness. The chief source of the sonnet's irony is the wit of holding disparate elements in comic opposition.

Sonnet 55 'Not marble nor the gilded monuments'

Where sonnet 23 is very much focused on a theory of art in terms of creativity and the effects of verse on the reader, the emphasis of sonnet 55 is on art in the context of time and eschatology, that is, on final matters, death and judgement day. To posterity and beyond.

> Not marble nor the gilded monuments
> Of princes shall outlive this powerful rhyme,
> But you shall shine more bright in these contents
> Than unswept stone, besmeared with sluttish time.   4
> When wasteful war shall statues overturn,
> And broils root out the work of masonry,
> Nor Mars his sword, nor war's quick fire shall burn
> The living record of your memory.   8
> 'Gainst death and all oblivious enmity
> Shall you pace forth; your praise shall still find room,
> Even in the eyes of all posterity
> That wear this world out to the ending doom.   12
>   So, till the judgement that yourself arise,
>   You live in this, and dwell in lovers' eyes.

The stridently assertive, even triumphant tone which opens this sonnet is unwavering throughout. Its message is relatively clear: neither marble edifices nor the rich tombs of monarchs will outlive this poem. The memory of the beloved will not only outlive *this* stone but will outshine even newly cut stone. Equally, although the violence and fire of war destroy civilisation's works (statues and masonry), the vital record of your name will endure.

Mankind is at war not only with nature or time but also with itself. Yet, resilient of death and oblivion, 'your' name will endure even to the end of mankind itself, to the day of judgement (12). Until that day, when you yourself will be stirred awake, you will be kept alive through this poem and in the eyes of other lovers.

In the opening line, the synecdoche 'marble' stands for the opulent edifices built by princes during their lifetime, while 'gilded monuments' represent their tombs or burial chambers (probably the most famous monument in Shakespeare is the scene of the queen's suicide in Acts 4 and 5 of *Antony and Cleopatra*; also see sonnet 123:2–6). Although proverbial, substantial and long-lasting as a bulwark against time, in terms of preserving the memory of their builders, stone monuments are ironically as nothing compared with the life of this poem written on flimsy paper.

Shakespeare may have had in mind, among other tombs, that of Henry V, who was buried in Westminster Abbey in 1422. His gloriously gilded effigy had by 1600 become a much desecrated and headless torso. In his play of *Henry V*, Shakespeare expresses a great prince's anxiety over his posterity, as he prepares for wasteful war:

> Or lay these bones in an unworthy urn,
> Tombless, with no remembrance over them.
>
> (1.2.228–9)

Sonnet 55 can be seen as a modern challenge to this antique and outmoded concept of the emblazoned sepulchre of 'lovely knights'.

This 'powerful rhyme' refers to poetry in general of course and to Shakespeare's own poems in particular. The point is echoed in line 3, where the phrase 'these contents', as well as pertly implying the contents or words of sonnet 55, may refer to the contents of the *Sonnets* as a whole. Continuing the hyperbole of the opening, his beloved shall outshine even newly cut, therefore as yet 'unswept stone'. The irregular comparative form 'more bright' is phrased to match the iambic rhythm but has the added advantage of spelling out its description, taking up and extending the idea of 'gilded' from the opening line. It introduces a moral element too, that the lover's reputation will be not only longer but also clearer and happier (and we cannot help but recognise the suggestion of 'happiness' in 'these *contents*' with its stress on the final syllable). The deixis in lines 2 and 3 ('this' and 'these') is also important, as we will see later.

That the stone is 'unswept' is intended to suggest that it is brand new, but together with 'sluttish' it accuses time of being neglectful (and so anticipates 'oblivious' in line 9). The stone is gradually 'besmeared with sluttish time': it becomes eroded and discoloured. But time is personified as 'sluttish', implying a sloppy and neglectful, even promiscuous cleaning wench who ought to care for man's art work (keeping it 'bright') but fails to. The defiant, hubristic belittling of time as a slovenly servant is all one with the sonnet's up-tempo start – though ironically it is this slapdash drab that is the destroyer of mankind's creation.

In the opening quatrain the works of civilisation are attacked by nature and time. In the second they are attacked by man himself, through the folly of war. At this point line 5 opens an alliterative, rhetorical effect extending the imposing resonances of the early lines.

When wasteful war . . .

Just as time was personified in the first quatrain, now it is the turn of war. War is the agent of chaos, destruction and human catastrophe. It overturns statues while 'broils', or strife, ruin the fine work of masonry. 'Statues' is an important word here in that it includes the physical objects of stone mentioned earlier and it is metonymic as a tag for civilisation in general. Further, in that a statue often venerates the memory of some famous figure it refers to the poem's themes of time and preserving a reputation into posterity through art.

With regard to the theme of time, line 5 looks both backwards and forwards simultaneously. Januslike, it glances back to a classical scene of statues and the distant past but the use again of the word 'shall' projects the attention forward to the future (and the dismal prospect that mankind will continue to warmonger even to the crack of doom).

The structure of line 7 echoes that of the opening of the sonnet. The intensity of this line's description of war is increased by its complex alliteration of /w/ and the assonantal /ɔ/ sounds, bonding together the destructive elements,

Nor Mars his sword, nor war's quick fire shall burn.

The Elizabethan genitive form ('Mars his sword') and the 'Nor...nor' construction maintain the early grandiloquent, prophetic tone. The reference to the mythical god 'Mars' also makes the poem look back, with a Roman thought. The vivid monosyllables – sword, war, quick, fire, burn – deepen the passion of this section: 'quick' here means aggressive, fierce, while 'burn' can be translated as 'waste'.

'Burn' links this line with line 3's metaphorical 'shine more bright', light now presented as a destructive force. And yet, war and its devastating effect cannot destroy this poem, that is, literature or art in general, the 'living record of your memory'. This too recalls a previous reference: in line 2, that even undamaged stones cannot 'outlive this powerful rhyme'. Living and vitality (as in the 'quick', fiercely destructive fire) are key themes that seek to galvanise the poem and are all one with the word 'shall', which pulses through the poem to the final line's promise of 'live' and 'dwell' (note too the assertive beat of the /b/ sounds in lines 1 to 4, and /p/ in lines 10–11).

That verse or literature should be a 'living record' is clearly significant and is contrasted with the relatively chill and sterile torpor of marble and masonry. The point is, of course, that stone tributes are inert, simply fossilised memorials. The phrase 'living record' is synonymous with 'memory' at the end of the line since the latter includes not just a trace of the loved one's likeness or portrait but also his or her personality.

Verse or literature, then, is a powerful, ever-living artform capable of personifying its subject. By transcending time it stands as a buttress, defiant, 'Gainst death', not literally but in a mysterious non-material sense. Thus, in lines 9 and 10, Shakespeare can reassure his friend that he shall 'pace forth' or outlive death and 'all oblivious enmity'. The latter phrase is a crux, though its likely meanings are probably congruent. 'Enmity' revisits wasteful war, broils and 'quick fire' in men's folly. But 'all oblivious' suggests on the one hand a hostility or perhaps spiteful envy that is indifferent to and therefore cruel to everyone. Or it could be a hostility that reduces everything to oblivion, forgottenness. His lover will, against these outrages, 'pace forth', a strutting phrase that surprisingly implies both indifference and impatience in the face of time's destructive effects.

Ambiguity continues in line 10 with the objective genitive 'your praise'. The sense is 'your glory', or public worship of you, will endure always, even to the end of human generations, to the end of posterity, the end of time itself. The reference to 'eyes' in line 11 is interesting in suggesting the admiration of future generations. It also suggests 'watching', and thereby 'waiting', the slow process of elapsing time in contrast to the violence of war (compare 'Devouring time' of 19:1). Shakespeare implies that such attentiveness gradually wears out and thus outlives the mortal and material world. The lover's glory will last to the end of mortal life, to the 'ending doom', or doomsday ('even to the edge of doom', 116:12). Indeed the eyes of the world are more enduring than the marble and gilded monuments, while the word 'wear' carries an echo of war, with which its slowness is to be contrasted (note too how Shakespeare, by separating the parts of the verb phrase 'wear out', stresses its gravity).

In her edition of the *Sonnets* Katherine Duncan-Jones interprets this line as a typically Shakespearean vision of apocalypse: that in his writing as a whole Shakespeare regards the history of the world as one of continuous decline, worn out by succeeding generations (Duncan-Jones, 1997, p. 220; in support she cites *King Lear*, 4.6.136–7).

Line 12 in effect functions as the climax to the poem. There is the customary hiatus at the end of the line and this serves to deepen the anticlimax that follows. In contrast to the preceding *douzaine* (and to most other sonnets), the couplet here is disappointingly limp and lacking the incisive wit and sparkle we have come to expect.

> So, till the judgement that yourself arise,
> You live in this, and dwell in lovers' eyes.

Line 13 connects with the 'ending doom' of the previous line, with a pun on doom/judgement (and with 'eyes' in line 11, a metaphor for 'opinion'). The line looks at first like a solecism, unless we read it as meaning, 'until the day of reckoning when you awake from death, or until the judgement that you yourself bring about'. The pronoun 'yourself' calls attention to the singularity of the beloved, and like the many instances of the deictic 'this' it contrasts with the anonymous throng who simply watch as time goes by. Nevertheless, the overall effect is to weaken the already flat bathos of the couplet.

Until the day of judgement the beloved will live in 'this powerful rhyme'. Significantly, Shakespeare at this moment drops his repetition of the auxiliary 'shall' but uses the simple present to stress the ever-living memory of his lover in his ever-living art. After the familiar mid-line caesura in the concluding line, Shakespeare's final phrase seems to imply a causative connection between its two halves: in other words, because of this poem and my preserving your memory, you dwell forever in lovers' eyes. His point seems to be that future lovers will read about you and find in you a model, a perfect archetype of the lover, and a solace for their own tribulation (thus restating the theme of the strong third quatrain).

Accordingly the couplet is distinguished not by any epigrammatic crispness but by its summarising function, and leaving the end a little sweet if a little prosaic. The final word 'eyes' gazes back to those eyes of the great multitude of generations that have watched out mortal time in line 11. It also pulls together the little cluster of judgemental terms towards the end.

Compared to most of the other sonnets we have examined in detail, the structure of sonnet 55 is much looser, less intense, and is organised around its diction. The structure of the poem, like its syntax, is of the 'English' type: the *douzaine* of three more or less connected quatrains with the *volta* immediately before the couplet. The first two quatrains are closer in tone and, typically, the second quatrain restates the message of the first. The *douzaine* is held together as much by the dogged beat of the word 'shall' as by a common theme. The couplet again integrates the two chief concerns of the poem: my sonnet and your memory.

The chief technical driver of the poem lies in the structure of its sentences. Of the five sentences, only one (lines 10–12) is not a suspended sentence, and it is these plus the drama of the opening quatrains that power the forward movement. Thus the climax of the poem, in technical terms at least, becomes that extended sentence in the third quatrain. In essence the couplet rephrases the substance of the fourth sentence.

The poem's discourse is in the vocative, addressed to the poet's beloved – though there is also a strong sense in which it is addressed to time, or posterity, itself. Although the opening of the poem sounds as if it is going to be a very open public scenario the focus gradually narrows down, via lines 3 and 8, to a more private and intimate scope. The tone is earnest, urging, orotund even, but not severely so. The thumping repetition of 'shall' instils a sturdy prophetic air too. On the other hand, Shakespeare's unmistakable tone of reassurance actually suggests a mysterious narrative undertone to the poem. Some part of the whole picture is missing and we must construct the unspoken part, namely that the dispirited lover has come to utter doubts or insecurity about their relationship and mortality.

This off-stage insecurity permits the poet to adopt a slightly superior posture here. At the same time there is the undoubted self-confidence, perhaps arrogance, in Shakespeare's own art and its potential, though he broadens this to cover all of art (he is of course carving his own monument here). The unwavering confidence of 'this powerful rhyme' contrasts with that of sonnet 107's apology for 'this poor rhyme' (though the couplet of that sonnet revisits both the theme and imagery of 55). In spite of a certain overflow of hyperbole in the voice there is a strain of something punctilious here, which issues from his desire to insist on reason and to illustrate it with some objective, almost corporeal imagery.

Beginning with the particular art object (the poem before us) Shakespeare makes us see the connection between it, and what it represents, as well as the awesome prospect of eternity – even if his ultimate intention is to make us aware of the mortality of the particular observer (the reader). The monumental imagery helps here, naturally, and there is much tension in a viewpoint that repeatedly switches between the local or particular and the eternal or universal; for example, 'these contents' versus 'sluttish time'.

A vital role in this effect is played by the diction too. As we would expect, it reflects the nuances of the poem's themes (erosion and destruction, the shortness of life, the longevity of art, and so on). 'Shall' both asserts a claim on time but also looks long within time, pressing the poem forwards and outwards. The poem's deixis is significant too,

> this powerful rhyme ... these contents ... his sword ... your memory ... live in this.

This-ness is contrasted with ever-ness. The vividness of the present 'now' (the paper of this poem, for instance) is set against a mysterious and speculative 'posterity' and judgement day. The imagery of monuments and falling statues, princes, wars and fires have a sort of vague and cautionary otherness about them but the poem is always conscious that what is important for its characters is what these mean for the specific self. There are 'lovers' in general and monuments in general but we all know that the real urgency lies in the specific 'you', and this is what Shakespeare's voice and the medium of art, the poem, seek to reassure:

> The living record of your memory.

This is clearly consistent with the Renaissance humanist concern with individual and personal fame. Posterity's all very well but what's in it for me? Shakespeare's answer is that the beloved will remain individualised through the unique prestige of this poem(s), or poetry in general,

> and dwell in lovers' eyes.

Not especially modest, perhaps, but there is a good reason for that. Shakespeare does his best to reassure his lover through argument and assertiveness but he also seeks to reassure himself. Above all he hopes that it is his own name impressed on the 'living record', the title page, that will guarantee immortality for the artist, since without this, neither identity will endure. Art offers if not the possibility of avoiding the grim reaper at least that of avoiding the levelling anonymity of death.

Apart from the sonnet there are other examples of art in the poem: works of marble, gilded monuments, statues and stone masonry. Mostly architecture and sculpture, and far from offering immortal renown, these substantial works seem anonymous and constantly at war with the elements and time. They are intimately implicated in the atmosphere of perpetual turmoil that appears to characterise mankind's temporal existence: turmoil, overturning, war, wear, broils, sword, pace, quick fire. It is a brief, volatile and on the whole sluttish period. Time's destructive streak is matched by that in man.

Art is recommended here as the stillness of history, unravished and silent through slow time. Art, as shining, contrasts with besmearing time and as a living record it opposes 'wasteful war'. Death, love and art present escape from a life of turmoil and danger, as the final line points out:

> You live in this, and dwell in lovers' eyes.

The word 'live' here points to merely subsisting, while 'dwell' offers a still point and a significant, truly enduring existence.

Why should art in the form of this sonnet, literature, survive where other art works have passed away (a question also posed in the first quatrain of sonnet 65)? After all, stone is manifestly more durable than paper. Philip Martin believes that Shakespeare confers on the poem a robust structure, a solidity, in order for it to seem stronger than the monuments and statues that lie crumbling (Martin, 1972, pp. 108 and 157). This may be true, and there is certainly a strong sense of power working through nature and time's effects (for instance, in lines 2, 5 and 12). But a more convincing reason lies in some of the other sonnets. In sonnet 18 Shakespeare promises his friend that 'thy eternal summer shall not fade' (9), and then famously,

> So long as men can breathe or eyes can see,
> So long lives this, and this gives life to thee.
>
> (18:13–14)

This resembles in construction and sentiment the couplet of 55. Until mankind (and time) ceases, this will persist. But this does not explain the cause. Tastes change, paper rots and, alas, ink fades. The very materiality of monuments and statues makes their eventual destruction inevitable. Yet line 8 of sonnet 55 declares itself to be a 'living record'. The couplet of sonnet 65 answers that art has a mysterious power (a 'miracle'; 65:13) but a more rational solution lies again in the metaphysics of sonnet 5 (and see 54:14).

> But flowers distilled, though they with winter meet,
> Leese but their show; their substance still lives sweet.
>
> (5:13–14)

Sonnet 100 'Where art thou Muse that thou forget'st so long'

In which the classical theme continues and the interrogation of the poet's Muse is used as the starting point for a discussion about the role and place of the artist in his/her society. Time too is an important figure in this.

> Where art thou Muse that thou forget'st so long,
> To speak of that which gives thee all thy might?
> Spend'st thou thy fury on some worthless song,
> Darkening thy power to lend base subjects light?   4
> Return, forgetful Muse, and straight redeem
> In gentle numbers time so idly spent;
> Sing to the ear that doth thy lays esteem,
> And gives thy pen both skill and argument.   8
> Rise, resty Muse, my love's sweet face survey,
> If Time have any wrinkle graven there;
> If any, be a satire to decay,
> And make Time's spoils despised everywhere.   12
> > Give my love fame faster than Time wastes life,
> > So thou prevent'st his scythe and crooked knife.

In the ancient Greek religion there were eventually nine muses, each venerated for a particular genre or art of poetry and song. Here Shakespeare probably has in mind either Calliope (muse of poetic inspiration), Urania (of lofty, refined verse) or Polyhymnia (of lyric poetry). Significantly they were all daughters of Mnemosyne, goddess of memory. In ancient days the invocation was probably taken as a serious affair (as Dylan Thomas might have said, they'd have been damn fools if it wasn't). Shakespeare is in more playful form though his theme is nonetheless heartfelt.

The opening question accuses his muse of forgetfulness, with no little irony, her mother being the apotheosis of memory. But if it is not amnesia then perhaps it is neglect. She has failed to visit and inspire his work.

Then Shakespeare takes a surprising turn in the second line: her neglect is not of himself, not initially at least, but of his beloved or of love itself. If he refers to his beloved here then the phrase 'that which' seems once more deliberately equivocal, avoiding personal pronouns. As the poet is inspired by his muse so her power depends on and is inspired by love or a lover, who 'gives thee all thy might'. If it is love that the poet refers to here then perhaps his love has neglected the muse, implying that, after all, he himself is really to blame in a vicious circle.

The question is, of course, a confrontational device. It challenges the reader or listener too, at first anyway. The poet's frustration is not exhausted and the next pair of lines contains another expression of his irritation with her. Receiving no response, he expands his interrogation with a gentle taunt. He queries whether she has been expending her 'fury' or passion on some other poet's trivial efforts.

> Spend'st thou thy fury on some worthless song,
> Darkening thy power to lend base subjects light?

Perhaps 'song' implies something less profound than the poet's own higher work, his 'gentle numbers' (line 6). Has she been slumming it by visiting unworthy rhymsters? 'Darkening' implies dulling her power and degrading it, but 'darken' can also mean, metaphorically, to reduce her fame, which is the antithesis of the idea in line 13. He practically accuses her of diminishing herself in order to enhance the efforts of other writers. That he somewhat peevishly considers them demeaning leaks through the pointed diction here: worthless, darkening, base, idly.

'Lend' (4) may also imply that her arrangements are transient or perfunctory but it calls to mind a similar characteristic ascribed to nature in sonnet 4,

> Unthrifty loveliness why dost thou spend,
> Upon thy self thy beauty's legacy?
> Nature's bequest gives nothing but doth lend . . .
>
> (lines 1–3)

The notion of transience accords well of course with the sober reminder of mortality at the end, that 'Time wastes life'. The Muse spends and lends, yet can regenerate her power in art while Time *wastes* us with an awful finality.

In line 5, 'Return' and 'redeem' hint at this idea of the regenerative power of art, a power that he hopes at the end will thwart the work of time. After the opening two interrogatives, the second quatrain begins with two positive-sounding imperatives. As well as being ironic again, 'forgetful' looks tactful or circumspect but is followed by a more snappy 'straight'. She can immediately redeem the profligate energies in lines 3 and 4, the 'time so idly spent', as Shakespeare reminds both us and her. Instead of dallying on the vulgar work of other men, she may assist on his more 'gentle numbers', namely a more refined, noble and therefore virtuous verse (which implies that Urania is the Muse in mind here). Once again the poet displays no self-doubts whatsoever about his own worth as a writer.

Another imperative in line 7 ('Sing') anticipates the idea of the reader too. He bids his Muse sing to or inspire his own ear initially, one which can appreciate and glorify ('esteem') her verse, or 'lays'. As the first reader of the Muse's material, the poet can use this to apply both art and wisdom, 'skill and argument', in the process of composition.

But lines 7 and 8 are complex. The 'ear' is a metonymy for both the poet and the poet's beloved – remember that line 2 suggested how the Muse herself was inspired by the beloved. The poet hears the Muse and what he composes will be read by his lover. 'Thy pen' is another metonym, for the Muse's contribution as well as for the poet's (though Shakespeare is vague about the real nature of this). Accordingly the Muse receives 'skill and argument' from the lover and in turn the poet applies his own 'skill and argument' as a craftsman.

Yet, we should ask, what does the Muse actually bestow on the poet? Much depends on how we interpret the word 'argument' and there is more on this below.

The third quatrain continues the run of imperatives or petitions,

> Rise, resty Muse...

Are these imperatives, tetchy demands, impatient rebukes, claims, or are they more like prayers or wishes? Or perhaps they simply represent and instil an awareness of that sense of urgency made more explicit in the poem's couplet. It is not easy to decide, and yet this is important for understanding the relationship between the poet and the muse (though in reality they are directed at himself).

The poet's tone grows in confidence and there is more than a hint of hubris in his voice. The mood is pacey now but controlled, both aspects generated by the brisk series of imperatives, heightening the tempo with each pair of lines, which comes to resemble a ladder.

The poet prolongs the momentum, with the challenges on his Muse. Where the octave looks to the past and how the Muse can redeem time wasted, the sestet now directs the Muse to particular actions aimed at achieving success through the intended work.

'Rise', in line 9, marks a break between the two sections of this sonnet. It arrests the attention of the reader and, hopefully, the Muse too. It sounds like a necromancer summoning his familiar spirit. As far as he is concerned she has been 'resty' or indolent (compare *Cymbeline*, 3.7.7), and now she is to examine the 'sweet face' of the poet's lover for wrinkles to see if she presents any signs yet of ageing ('wrinkle graven'), recalling sonnet 60's warning that

> Time doth transfix the flourish set on youth,
> And delves the parallels in beauty's brow.

> (60:9–10)

Engraved wrinkles also anticipate the work of the 'scythe and crooked knife' in the final line of sonnet 100.

At this point the Muse becomes more explicitly understood as a metaphor for the proposed poem. Both lines 10 and 11 begin with 'If', although it is used differently. Their effect is to soften the poet's tone, making his commands briefly more conditional as well as existential.

He implores the Muse to 'be a satire to decay'. This of course quibbles on 'satyr' and 'satire' though the ultimate effect is pretty much the same. As the satyr was a composite beast of classical mythology (half man, half goat; note *Hamlet*, 1.2.140), the poet asks her to be a brute towards Time and halt its destructive advances. Alternatively, the Muse may act as a satirist and scorn the process of decay. Either way the Muse should make Time's desecrations universally despised (though this seems to me an unnecessary enjoinder).

Typically, lines 11 and 12 embody a complexity of possibilities. However, the main thrust seems to be that the Muse's poem should act as a counter to the corrosive ravages of Time, replacing the lines or wrinkles on the beloved's face with lines of poetry. The Muse, art in general, can produce a flattering or deceiving image by concealing, seemingly to defeat time, with which mankind is in conflict.

The couplet offers a further cheat on time. Not only can art mask or deceive but, as we saw in sonnet 55, it can outlive time 'Even in the eyes of all posterity'. Here, in line 13, Shakespeare offers a variation on this idea:

Give my love fame faster than Time wastes life.

The poem closes with an epideictic plea: that the Muse through his poem should present the beloved with a perfect image ('fame') one that is 'faster' (i.e. 'more fixed'), fastened more permanently than the long duration of mankind as a whole. Faster in the sense of 'quicker' too carries great purpose since time to the Elizabethans must have been the touchstone of speed. Thus, once more, she will cheat Father Time and death, emblematised conventionally in the blades of the scythe and sickle.

The beloved will become preserved in art, poetry here, and preserved from oblivion. This theme contrasts ironically with the forgetful Muse of the early lines. Although lines 11 to 14 hold out the promise of a kindly outcome, the final word of the poem, 'knife', hovers like the Damocletian hazard and as a reminder too.

Acutely apprehensive about writer's block, the poet conjures his powerful Muse to employ her 'fury' and 'light' to inspire him. He invokes her not for himself initially but in the interests of his beloved: to make her immortal through poetry. A series of imperatives emphasises the deep intensity of the poet's anxiety for his craft and for his love. And what does the Muse get out of this? Nothing apparently. It's her job: this is what Muses do.

Written in pairs of lines, each sentence occupying a pair, this sonnet is loosely organised into octave and sestet. As we have noted, the octave embodies a general appeal to the Muse while the sestet directs her to more specific tasks concerning the effects of time (this specificity is reflected in the large number of concrete nouns in the sestet). The two sections are linked by the overarching voice of the poet and the common themes of poetics, the Muse, and time. The sonnet opens with some uncertainty, registered in the questions there, but closes on an up-beat exclamation of fervent and scornful defiance.

Once more the bare fourteen lines of a sonnet are supercharged through rich thematic complexities, focused on the subject of art. Let us take a deeper look at these themes, beginning with the Muse herself, the poet's inspiration.

We can begin by asking what sort of a creature this Muse is. In sonnet 79 she is 'my sick Muse', in 101 a 'truant Muse', while in 103 she is impoverished. Here she is a forgetful Muse and a 'resty Muse'. But there is more.

We have already noted her classical pedigree. Traditionally, poets called on the assistance of the Muse at the outset of a poem (though, as here, the poem was already written, of course). It was a sort of prudence, an insurance, a feeling that the work was under the guidance and protective aegis or patronage of the appropriate goddess. Thus Homer sets out in *The Odyssey* and *The Iliad* with just such a a dutiful invocation. By the Elizabethan period this was little more than a poetic piety. Yet the characters of Homer and those of Herodotus, Virgil and Ovid had achieved immortality, in literature at least. Shakespeare impresses upon us the idea that he is writing within a tradition, a continuity among the poets, stretching back to Homer.

For Shakespeare the Muse is in effect a handy poetic device by which to address the poem. She is his narrative object, his audience, by which to reveal that for some time he has not been able to write. She is a personification and a metaphor for a range of ideas and theoretical poetics and the poem is marshalled around some of her abilities: she can speak, inspire, sing, survey, satirise and bestow fame. But in the end she is intended to remain elusive, an enigma.

His Muse is identified with light, and the commonplace metaphor of inspiration as the bringing of light.

> Darkening thy power to lend base subjects light?
>
> (line 4)

She is both ear and voice: this poem is addressed to her and the poet hopes she will convey the proposed poetry to him. She is a kind of angel, or perhaps two kinds of angel. She seems to be a type of personal guardian angel for the poet in whom he can confide his woe. On the other hand, as inspiration she is a sort of messenger. James Joyce in *A Portrait of the Artist as a Young Man* conceived of inspiration in a similar way. He compares the Muse to the archangel who visits the Virgin Mary, filling her with the word of God, and thus the artist receives a mysterious artistic spur 'in the virgin womb of the imagination' (*A Portrait*, chapter 5). She is a mysterious figure, a simulacrum of a mysterious process.

But this Muse is no schmaltzy Tinkerbell. Line 3 points to her 'fury' and 11 to her potential as a satyr (a protean character, at times the paragon of lyrical beauty, at others, a lascivious brute, half animal, half man). Nevertheless, art here can have a tempering effect, traced in the transition of the imagery from might, fury and power in the first quatrain to gentility, 'skill' and 'sweet' in the second and third.

The device of a Muse and of her representing the creative process is nothing new, of course. It is by Shakespeare's day somewhat hackneyed too. So how does he imbue this feature with new vigour? A significant aspect of Shakespeare's Muse is the mystery surrounding her. She cannot easily be formulated as representing or functioning one thing or anything. She is elusive and unpredictable, capricious too. For Shakespeare she is evasive, having forsaken or even jilted him. The sestet of the poem articulates her power to control and deceive (key elements in art of course).

She is depicted too as a capricious spirit, a shifting, shadowy presence in the consciousness of the poem (compare the woman in the 'Dark Mistress' sonnets). All the same, the poet seeks to summon her, and the association with black arts and conjuration lends to her an extra frisson of desiring. On the other hand, her capacity to control Time makes her a stern demigoddess.

She is a woman of forgetting and desire, both of which exasperate the poet. She is the elusive object of desire, elusive in the sense of being fugitive, slightly beyond his reach. But she is elusive for him, and us, in the sense of being insubstantial and indefinable. This is mirrored in the complexities of lines 2 and 7, which strive to delineate her exactly,

> To speak of that which gives thee all thy might?
>
> (line 2)

This Muse is, then, variously a protective spirit, a bringer of light, a reader, a messenger, an angel, a satyr, a sonnet and a metaphor. She is other things too which we will examine. And she is a mystery, a strong focal point of timeless fascination here but also an apt analogy for the imagination and the mysterious processes of artistic creation. Yet, what does she actually do?

From the point of view of this chapter this really translates as what she contributes to the creative process. As a poetic construct or personification, she appears to inspire the writer to compose. Which is not to say much. Does she merely generate the right conducive mood and a vague stirring, or does she stimulate the poetic imagination as a species of catalyst, or perhaps she produces the actual words of the poems themselves? She may even be the imagination itself.

Lines 4 and 8 seem significant in trying to answer these questions:

> Darkening thy power to lend base subjects light?
>
> (line 4)

> And gives thy pen both skill and argument.
>
> > (line 8)

'Light' is certainly a metaphor in line 4 but this can mean that she supplies information about a subject or, more likely, insight (including understanding, new perceptions, awareness, innovation). Metaphors can be slippery customers. Line 8 is even more equivocal. Her 'pen' can mean almost anything here. As a metonym it is surprising that the Muse has the 'pen' while he brings art and wisdom, order or even the matter of the poem itself.

Line 8 modestly admits that metaphorically the Muse rather than the poet is the source of the verse. And this offers an answer to some of the questions above. In reality the Muse and the poet are the same thing: she is just a useful externalisation of a process. None the less, the problems raised are interesting since they reveal the poet's view about his nature and his role in society.

The poet sees himself as a conduit or vehicle for the Muse, implying that poetry comes from some external mystical source. A poet is thus only a kind of medium, a passive intermediary between the mortal and the spirit worlds, a creation myth that originates among the ancients. For instance, the Romans regarded a poet in this way, as a *vates*, a prophet, high priest or bard, divinely pre-ordained to speak for the gods and for his community. With the Renaissance rediscovery of the Classical world such ideas were buzzing in the air and Shakespeare, perhaps picturesquely, adopts this view of the poet as a priest of the eternal creative imagination

> Sing to the ear that doth thy lays esteem,
> And gives thy pen both skill and argument.
>
> > (lines 7–8)

Sonnet 106 'When in the chronicle of wasted time'

Sonnet 106 is a strikingly beautiful poem whose beauty lodges no less in its themes or images than in its rich musical timbres, notably in lines 4, 6 and 9. The closing line brings together the music of these and other lines, combining in a dazzling finale of theme, tonality and poise.

> When in the chronicle of wasted time
> I see descriptions of the fairest wights,
> And beauty making beautiful old rhyme
> In praise of ladies dead and lovely knights;   4
> Then in the blazon of sweet beauty's best,
> Of hand, of foot, of lip, of eye, of brow,
> I see their antique pen would have expressed
> Even such a beauty as you master now.   8
> So all their praises are but prophecies
> Of this our time, all you prefiguring,
> And, for they looked but with divining eyes,
> They had not skill enough your worth to sing: 12
>   For we, which now behold these present days,
>   Have eyes to wonder, but lack tongues to praise.

The poem's highly resonant first line immediately seizes the reader's attention through its peremptory initial word, 'When'. Introducing the theme of time, this is immediately reinforced in the familiar ring of 'chronicle of wasted time'. 'Wasted' here simply means 'spent' (compare this word used in sonnets 12 and 100), and on a literal level the phrase might refer to documents of time: diaries, journals, public records, making the poem sound highly ironic, which it is. But Shakespeare equally intends the metaphorical idea of 'looking back', of taking stock. Some readers see a pun on wasted/waisted in the sense of weakened and gaunt and this is distinctly sympathetic with the 'time' theme in this section of sonnets (and compare 55:5).

The second line reinforces the idea of chronicling descriptions. The 'fairest wights' are elegant or courtly people, a reference echoed in line 4. The word 'wights' was already archaic by Shakespeare's day, an early indication of the irony at work in the sonnet. 'Of' in this line is ambiguous, suggesting that these descriptions may be either written by or be about the 'fairest wights'.

But why did Shakespeare write 'see' in line 2 instead of 'read', which might seem more precise? Probably because 'read' would be too precise and he really wanted to get across the visual impact of descriptions. Although the poem has little in the way of visual treats it is much to do with seeing and the effects of that seeing – as the final line strongly hints.

The chronicle, if literal, is in 'beautiful old rhyme' ('rhyme' may simply mean something like 'language'). But, again, line 3 is slippery and has lots of possible interpretations. What makes the old rhyme beautiful is the beauty of the people who are its subjects (see the following line). Or it may be that its qualities of charm and splendour are due to the artistry ('beauty' being used as synecdoche) that the ancient writer invested in his writing.

What is certain is the artistry that Shakespeare employs to furnish line 4 with such alliterative music. The line sings as well as speaks and appears at the moment that he laments deficiencies in contemporary literature. 'Ladies dead' and 'lovely knights' refer, of course, to the subjects of courtly writing, courtly love, with echoes of Petrarchism. The knights were amorous as well as handsome, while 'dead' in reference to 'ladies' implies heroic postures or perhaps simply melodrama. The reversal in 'ladies dead' has a quaintness, a ring of nostalgia for the old verse that it emulates, which 'dead ladies' comes not near.

The line is also important in terms of the object, the 'beautiful you' of the poem. Once again Shakespeare offers no clue to the gender of his beloved and by referring to both 'ladies' and 'knights' he keeps open the possibilities.

In the first quatrain, the preposition phrase at the start of line 4 is decisive because it introduces the key theme of exaltation. The theme of praise grows in importance until it reaches its climax in line 14 and it is the final, resounding, word of the whole poem. The quatrain began with negative tones in 'wasted' but seems to end on a brighter vision with 'praise'.

'Blazon' in line 5 extends this rising sentiment (as do 'sweet' and 'best' here) and the word itself has clarion effect. It looks and sounds dramatic, as well as both jubilant and radiant. 'Blazon' as we have seen before is, appropriately and ironically, an heraldic term. Originally it was a shield or coat of arms but in rhetoric it meant, for Elizabethan writers, a catalogue detailing the parts of a beloved's beloved body. A poetic convention, it was a list of a woman's virtues or beautiful physical attributes, 'of sweet beauty's best' (5). And in the next line this is exactly what the poet does itemise,

> Of hand, of foot, of lip, of eye, of brow.
>
> (6)

The first two items take in the physical extent of the beloved, from head to foot, implying posture or grace, and then the eye focuses trenchantly onto more alluring features relating to sexuality and personality. 'Brow' refers literally to her or his face, but also to charisma or demeanour. Again it is a distinctly musical line, savouring the magnetism of every part, and making a fine virtue of the sonnet's metrical constraints.

The start of line 7 ('I see') echoes that of line 2 but is an example of antanaclasis, that is a word used twice in different senses. In line 7 'see' means 'perceive' but here it has the sense of 'recognise' or 'realise'. He *sees* that their 'antique pen' would have been able to express beauty in eloquent measures. 'Antique pen' is clearly a metonymy for art or skill, but who does 'their' refer to? This pronoun is both gnomic and deictic: Shakespeare seems to assume we know who it applies to. It refers of course to the writers from the past, those behind the 'antique pen', their 'descriptions' and 'the beautiful old rhyme'.

These writers would have had the ready skill to capture the beauty possessed or mastered by his beloved. And they would have achieved it in their own prepossessing style. The octave ends with two forms of hyperbolic praise: of the ancient writers and of his lover, 'Even such a beauty'. At the same time, if we take 'beauty' to include 'art' (as in line 3), then this line could be interpreted as the beloved surpassing or eclipsing even artistic perfection itself.

The poem is structured as a rhetorical argument, with four major turning points: 'When' (line 1), 'Then' (5), 'So' (9), 'For' (13). These are the key controlling markers in the development of the argument. At the end of the octave the adverb 'now' brings that passage of the argument, the account of the former writers, to a close and aptly answers the opening adverb, 'When', and the chronicle of passed time.

The final and therefore significant word of the sonnet, 'praise', first appears in line 4, reappearing in line 9.

> So all their praises are but prophecies
> Of this our time.

Beautiful as they were, the praise of those ladies and knights was only an anticipation of his loved one's beauty. These are exquisitely poised lines, with such exuberant consonance, that Shakespeare's shrewd irony is becoming increasingly conspicuous.

Having looked at the past he now puts that past into his present. The alliteration in 'praises' and 'prophecies' draws the two themes together and then connects in line 10 with 'prefiguring' and then 'divining' in line 11. All of their achievements have foreshadowed the beauty facing Shakespeare as he now writes this.

Line 11 is not an easy line but one possible reading of it is that the only reason the antique writers did not quite match the beloved's beauty is that *they* did not have the actual person before them and so could only guess (or 'divine', foretell). They had eyes but could not sing – notice how the final line takes up these thoughts again. Although the antique writers were the most skilled, even they could not predict such 'worth', or distinction.

This slant makes an interesting contrast with sonnet 59. There the poet believes that 'divining' is not quite so tentative because the ancient writers produced an archetypal form of beauty. Since the beloved embodies the archetypal beauty they did not require him/her to be physically present. In any case, Shakespeare concludes, they tended to overpraise inferior beauty.

> O sure I am, the wits of former days
> To subjects worse have given admiring praise.

(59:13–14)

The idea of 'divining' in sonnet 106 does have, however, at least one other significant implication. A divine in the sixteenth century could be a clergyman of the Church or a soothsayer, that is a prophet. As many critics have pointed out, by suggesting that the ancient writers acted like Old Testament prophets in 'divining', Shakespeare secularises a spiritual activity, and as such lays himself open to the charge of blasphemy.

However, where in sonnet 59 Shakespeare practically accused former writers of deception, 106 has none of this and the past is used as a foil to the present in terms both of artistic skill and of the beauty of his beloved. As we would expect, the couplet foregrounds both of these issues:

> For we, which now behold these present days,
> Have eyes to wonder, but lack tongues to praise.

The opening word of the couplet, 'For', is very astute – it looks at first to mean 'because' and so connect with the rest of the poem (as the same word does in line 11), but it really means 'whereas', which thus sets up a contrast. So Shakespeare artfully seems to connect, or separate, but in practice does both.

The final line has a beautifully crafted isomorphism about its two sections, pivoting around the conjunction, 'but'. If we take the line metaphorically then it merely repeats the idea in lines 11 and 12 – we are poor artists. But if we see it in plain terms then line 14 is shrewdly ironic (as indeed is the whole sonnet) since Shakespeare does nothing but praise his love's deep and indefinable beauty and does so in such a supremely delightful phrase.

When compared with the apprehensions of sonnets 23 and 100 or the dilating consciousness of 55, the voice of sonnet 106 is much less emotionally intense. It is a bravura performance presenting a more relaxed, reasoned argument focused on the trigger words 'eyes' and 'praise'. There are no major rhetorical flourishes. A eulogy of his beloved's beauty and of past writers, the voice is on the whole conversational, unvarnished. He attempts to persuade us that he does lack 'tongues to praise' (though we do get 'beautiful' and 'lovely' plus the Platonic-sounding 'fairest' and 'best'). But the message is really in the medium.

The whole poem is usually interpreted as two long, complex utterances with their main clauses in lines 7 and 8, and then in lines 9, and 13–14 (syntactically it resembles sonnets 32 and 47). Together with its highly regular pentameter this helps impart a silky fluency to the sonnet, uncoiling and coiling smoothly and ironically through its intricately scored periods and prepositional phrases.

Sonnet 106 has a graceful decorum, matching understatement with a relatively plain style, a wry complaint about inexpressive writers. The whole piece is again a variety of litotes and any hyperbole is present in the syntax and the argument rather than the diction or sound. Yet this does not make its sincerity any the less – it enlarges it.

One of the ways that sonnet 106 differs from the other sonnets in this chapter is in making an explicit contrast between past and contemporary writers. As well as having a thematic role, this centrifugal contrast helps to suffuse the poem with its tensions: arising from the counterpoint of what was and what might or ought to be, from desire of what the past represents, as well as desire of his beloved.

To begin with the basics, the sonnet has plenty of different expressions or metaphors for art: descriptions (line 2), beauty (3), blazon (5), pen (7), sing (12), tongues (14) and praise (4, 9, 14). Art of the past is characterised as chivalric or courteous,

> In praise of ladies dead and lovely knights

while the superlatives, 'fairest' and 'best', are aimed at the antique skills. Shakespeare presents the unmistakable picture that for literature the past was best – and he himself had mined it for some of his dramas (for example, Roman Plautus for *The Comedy of Errors* and Chaucer for *The Two Noble Kinsmen*).

That said, who are the writers Shakespeare had in mind for their descriptions of 'fairest wights'? Well, apart from Chaucer the list is likely to include the courtly troubadours, plus Chrétien de Troyes, Geoffrey of Monmouth, Layamon and Brut, and the authors of *Sir Gawain and the Green Knight* and of *Roman de la Rose*. However, the poem was written at a time, in the closing decades of the sixteenth century, when English writers had at last confidently asserted a native literature, freeing themselves from Continental models. This perhaps lends another clue as to Shakespeare's irony here.

Looking closely we can see that his tone towards them is not necessarily nostalgic. He may not even have read many or any of them and he seems detached from them, naturally so. His point is that they serve his theme as a device, a gauge or standard of beauty, and the detachment created helps to mythologise their reputation so they become heroic, almost talismanic. At the same time this mythopoeic Shakespeare identifies his beloved with the distant past and its writers, for clear reasons of association.

The flip side is that his contemporaries are inadequate, having not the 'tongues to praise'. Sonnet 59 scolded 'wits of former days' for their deceptions in overpraising. But sonnet 100 represents a more penetrating literary indictment of his peers. He may perhaps have been including himself in this critique – after all, the poem finishes with 'we'. This would be consistent with a view of the movement of history as decline (some readers regard sonnet 55: 11–12 as indicative here).

There would be some modesty in Shakespeare including himself in this censure. But it seems unlikely. His judgement of the past undervalues his peers but this is not his main point, as the irony in the final lines reveals. And, incidentally, he situates us exactly in his own position then because he looks on the past writers as we are now, 400 years on, looking back at him and his own work.

It is a poem of seeing and praising, of expressing what one sees in art or 'praise'. It is a poem of viewpoints. As well as our two perspectives just mentioned, the poem itself actually embodies two viewpoints. In the first two quatrains the poet casts his judgemental eye back on antique writers but in the third they look forward from their time to his. He comments on their depiction of beauty in art and they (whose 'praises are but prophecies') look forward and comment on his beloved's beauty,

> for they looked but with divining eyes
>
> (11)

Taken with the couplet, this line divulges how the ancient writers actually comment on the skill of Shakespeare and his contemporaries.

This interlacing of viewpoints intensifies the theme of seeing and helps to structure and bind the poem (the book of these sonnets is also a book of myriad perspectives).

The point is that the poem is not primarily centred on antique writers. Its purpose is in fact a species of hyperbole, to state that even if we had the skill of the past we would not be able to capture the beauty of this stunningly attractive woman or man. No artist could. Surprisingly, beauty sets its own limits on art.

The whole poem is drafted as a paean to him or her, trying different approaches, of which the 'antique pen' is but one. The blazon of his/her beautiful parts marching along line 6 is another:

> Of hand, of foot, of lip, of eye, of brow.

This also suggests the totality of her beauty as well as the 'wonder' gaze of the artist counting the parts. Linking her with these ancient fellows imbues her with a timelessness that art itself might try to instil in her image (and the past becomes an allegory of the present).

All of this points of course to another great irony informing the poem: Shakespeare's use of the rhetorical device of *occupatio*, in which a writer modestly repudiates his skill. In a final turn of the screw he produces a brilliant poem in which to say that we can no longer produce brilliant poems. He outpens the antique pens. Employing intricate webs of phrasing, sound and diction, and an impressive, if understated, palette of rhetorical tropes, he demonstrates his own poor 'skill' (combining synecdoche, metonymy, antanaclasis, chiasmus, isomorphism, as well as blazon).

In a poem of many ironies the final twist is that even this virtuoso achievement cannot come close to reproducing the natural beauty of the lover, matchless and therefore timeless.

Conclusions

Although in the *Sonnets* Shakespeare presents us with nothing that can be regarded as an artistic manifesto, a theory of poetics, we inevitably observe him considering important conceptual issues implicit in the practice of his art. At times this reflection is as a subtext to other important themes and at others it foregrounds art as a crux in itself. Indeed, this readiness to reflect meaningfully on theoretical aspects of art is one of the key features that mark Shakespeare out from most of his literary contemporaries .

In this chapter we have explored some of these musings: his views on creativity, the manners of art, and the relationship of poetry and the poet to the wider world of readers and people in general. As a creative project, art is depicted in contrast with the destructiveness of nature, time and mankind. Shakespeare affirms the regenerative powers of art in the sense that art may be seen to transcend the corrosive effects of time, and is aligned with love, life and the eternal in nature.

In his reflections on art and time, two key views stand out. The first is that literature in particular embodies the platonic essence and this essence is what guarantees the 'best' literature its perfection and therefore immortality, a bulwark against the deterioration that metal and stone are vulnerable to. The second is Shakespeare's important view on the nature and position of the artist himself. He looks on the writer as a man in direct contact with the world of immortal ideas, whose influence speaks directly to him through inspiration and its workings on the powerful receptive imagination. It is a mysterious, quasi-religious interaction and the artist is a man set slightly apart from other men by the gift of talent or temperament. A bard, he is a special man but speaking to other men. Ironically, Shakespeare himself, as if uncomfortable from this responsibility, speaks to us in an undertone, tentatively, unsure of the Muse's delphic signification. He is thus too the archetypal reader.

Prophetically, however, the man from Stratford also demonstrates how literature is an ever-living sphere of human activity, through the interaction of texts and the continuity of the artistic sensitivity. In this way Shakespeare makes his own claim on the future. Perhaps above all and implicitly he presents the convincing case (as some of his contemporaries like Sidney and Puttenham were also beginning to) for the central role of vernacular poetry in the life of English civilised society.

Further Research

Carefully read sonnet 76 and try to explain what it is the poet complains of, about his verse. What is the cause of his complaint in terms of the poet's intended subject matter and how does he regard the style of his own writing? Lines 11–12 of the sonnet seem to contrast with the general view of past literature as presented in sonnet 106; in what ways do the two views differ? Does he believe true originality in art is possible? You may also wish to compare the themes and attitudes of both of these sonnets with those offered in sonnet 38.

4

The Rival Poet(s): a Lesson in Tightropes?

Apemantus: Art not a poet?
Poet: Yes.
Apemantus: Then thou liest. Look in thy last work, where thou
   hast feign'd him a worthy fellow.
Poet: That's not feign'd, he is so.
Apemantus: Yes, he is worthy of thee, and to pay thee for thy
   labour. He that loves to be flattered is worthy of the flatterer.
                              (*Timon of Athens*, 1.1.219–26)

Most critics believe that in their present arrangement, the *Sonnets*
contain two sequences of sonnets that focus on the mysterious characters of a Rival Poet (numbers 78–86, excluding 81 and 84) and a Dark
Mistress (127–52). While there is no external (and not much internal)
evidence to support the view that these sonnets refer to a single man
or woman it has been attractive to discuss them as if they did.

Indeed this mystery has spawned a speculative and mostly harm-
less industry bent on establishing the actual identities of these two
individuals. From time to time there emerge stories in the popular
media claiming to have discovered conclusive proof of who the rival
and the mysterious woman were, and yet, to date, all of these have
proved inconclusive. So, reader beware and have your smidgen of salt

111

at the ready. From the point of view of this literary discussion their identities matter hardly at all.

In the previous chapter we considered the subject of art very much in terms of theoretical aspects. For Shakespeare, however, as for other writers, art was first and foremost the tough means of making a livelihood. In this chapter we will examine art chiefly on this basis and the sonnets we will be analysing focus very closely on the precarious relationship between the poet and his patron in terms of economics, art and friendship. In this chapter our discussion will centre on the mini-sequence of sonnets from 78 to 86, discussing in particular poems 78, 79, 82 and 86.

To understand something of the highly competitive conditions in which Elizabethan poets toiled for their modest rewards it will be useful to include a brief sketch of the rivalry that existed between some authors. In Shakespeare's day a poet was commonly regarded as either a liar (because he distorted nature), a beggar (his trade was so poorly rewarded) or a lunatic (because of his 'wild' imagination). Writing for the print media was so poorly remunerated that almost all writers were forced to top up their meagre payment by seeking supplementary employment or by securing the financial backing of a wealthy patron.

Those poets fortunate enough to secure patronage were usually treated, at best, on a par with servants, and at worst as suspicious misfits. The poet had certainly to sing for his uncertain supper. As a result he was constrained to work within an autonomy that was qualified by loyalty to the patron. In addition he frequently had to vie with rival poets for the generous indulgence of his benefactor by dedicating works to him/her, by ghost-writing pieces, and by recourse to obsequious flattery. This rivalry could sometimes reach resentful proportions, as suggested in Robert Greene's famous deathbed dig at Shakespeare as

> an upstart crowe, beautified with our feathers... [who] is in his owne conceit the only Shake-scene in a countrey. (*Groats-worth of witte*, 1592)

Shakespeare himself almost certainly enjoyed the valuable patronage of Henry Wriothesley, third Earl of Southampton.

The hugely popular *Venus and Adonis* (1593) together with *The Rape of Lucrece* (1594) was dutifully dedicated to his lordship and Shakespeare may have received board and lodgings on the Southampton estates in Hampshire, as well as in the capital. This close connection has accordingly led many to identify Southampton with the enigmatic 'Mr. W. H.' of the *Sonnets*.

On the other hand, other writers including Thomas Nashe and John Florio also dedicated works to Southampton and so Shakespeare probably did not have exclusive or long-term affiliation with his patron.

In her enlightening study *The Literary Profession in the Elizabethan Age*, Phoebe Sheavyn presents a coldly realistic portrait of the poet in the early modern period,

> [constantly] striving to snatch for himself a share of the bounty which not all could possibly obtain. He had to live in the midst of perpetual rivalry; he must forever be striving to bid higher than his fellows. (Sheavyn, p. 21)

The image of Shakespeare in the 'Rival Poet' sequence is one very different from the commonly held idea of Shakespeare the dramatist, assured, financially independent and sustained by the admiration of the theatre community. Here we have a much starker picture of a servant necessarily dependent on the whim and largesse of a tentative patron, shuffling along an uncertain tightrope.

Sonnet 78 vividly presents an insight onto the commercial and artistic rivalry among Renaissance authors but chiefly the anxiety that was generated by it.

Sonnet 78   'So oft have I invoked thee for my muse'

> So oft have I invoked thee for my muse
> And found such fair assistance in my verse
> As every alien pen hath got my use
> And under thee their poesy disperse.   4
> Thine eyes, that taught the dumb on high to sing,

And heavy ignorance aloft to fly,
Have added feathers to the learned's wing,
And given grace a double majesty.   8
Yet be most proud of that which I compile,
Whose influence is thine, and born of thee;
In others' works thou dost but mend the style,
And arts with thy sweet graces graced be.   12
    But thou art all my art and dost advance,
    As high as learning, my rude ignorance.

This sonnet begins with an address so direct and personal that it resembles a confession. The poet submits to his patron with a hint of discomfort, self-reproach even, that he has had to turn 'so oft' to his benefactor. 'So oft' implies not only the extent of his indebtedness but also the long period of his relationship with him and, together with 'invoked', immediately introduces a vein of anxiousness into the poem.

'Invoked' reminds us at first of sonnet 100 and its 'Muse'. But here the word 'muse' indicates 'source of financial help' as well as suggesting the more flattering idea that the patron has inspired his poetry (as an 'onelie begetter' perhaps). Some editors assign a capital 'M' to the word but at this moment the sense is not quite the same as in sonnet 100. Here, the accent is on the patron as a practical provider of his living – though this alters as the poem moves on.

It is important to note the repetition of 'my' in these three opening lines. As the whole poem is much to do with retaining his benefaction Shakespeare is not reticent to sound proprietorial, claiming the patron as exclusively his own. He has turned often to and depended on this man to provide 'fair assistance' in the production of his verse.

'Fair' here means excellent but, as regards 'assistance', Shakespeare is keen to keep his meanings ambiguous. The word elaborates on what sort of 'muse' the patron represents, so it includes a range of possibilities that patrons provided for their protégés at this time: the patron's inspiration, his suggestions about composition, a stable creative atmosphere in his home, use of his library, literary contacts, as well as the necessary material subsistence. Shakespeare is not averse to giving the impression that the poetry has in fact been a collaborative effort. Thus the half-rhyme at the ends of lines 1 and 2 (used in sonnet 21 too) helps to fix the association between the poet's output and the benefactor.

The first quatrain tries to achieve a wide variety of practical object-ives. These include acknowledging indebtedness, pledging loyalty, and in lines 3 and 4 spoiling his rivals. Having in the first two lines set up his modesty and deference, the tone modulates in line 3 to a more wounding aside against his rivals, the poets seeking the patron's beneficence for themselves.

'Alien pen' is a composite entity, referring generally to the 'others', them, the producers of inferior verse who imitate Shakespeare's own poetic style ('hath got my use') and publish or 'disperse' it under the name of this patron. In other words, rival poets who formally dedicate their mediocre stuff to him. (Shakespeare writes 'verse' but they concoct mere 'poesy'.) 'Under' in line 4 reinforces the inferiority of their writing but also reminds the patron of Shakespeare's own acquiescent posture.

While the logic of the quatrain's construction (So oft... As ...) is dubious the gist of it is clear. 'Alien' is clearly a significant and powerful epithet, and because it implies that these other authors are hostile and malicious, it strengthens Shakespeare's position as the bruised victim of plagiarism, at the same time post-modifying the word 'assistance' to include connotations of 'shelter' and 'security'.

In the second quatrain the focus shifts onto the more specific effects of the patron's influence. In line 5 the 'eyes, that taught' can be unpacked in all sorts of ways: care, vision, generosity, beauty, and so on. As a symbol they are among Shakespeare's great favourites in the Sonnets. Here the suppleness of this symbol is perfectly consistent with the speaker's hyperbole: the patron does practically everything for the arts and does it stupendously well.

Accordingly, 'taught' can mean moved or showed or directed or perhaps initiated. The patron does this to, or for, the most humdrum of poets, making them 'sing' or write lofty poetry at the highest level. The paradox of eyes causing song seems again to express the excep-tional powers of this patron. Furthermore, he has fostered scholarship as well as poetry, teaching 'heavy ignorance' to reach lofty heights of culture. This metonymy ('heavy ignorance'), like the metaphor 'dumb' in the previous line, is intended, I think, to refer to those alien pens, Shakespeare's rivals, but in the light of the final line of the sonnet he ultimately includes himself (secretly he recognises the adversary's story as a mirror of his own).

However, the phrasing is ambiguous and not all critics agree with this reading. Some, such as Helen Vendler, interpret the poem as dramatising a debate 'between *ignorant* Shakespeare and the *learned* rival poets' (Vendler, p. 351). On the other hand, the context appears to represent Shakespeare as superior in potential at least and thus more deserving of his support. In this sense he figures himself as a type of Cinderella figure. At any rate, in his submissiveness Shakespeare is, by the end, happy to acknowledge that he too was ignorant and dumb before coming within the prestigious aegis of the patron.

The flying metaphor is extended vividly into line 7 where even the already-learned have benefited. The image of adding feathers derives from falconry, the process of 'imping out' or repairing a bird's wing by grafting extra feathers (see *Richard II*, 2.1.292; and Sidney's *Astrophel and Stella*, 75:4). 'Feathers' recalls too the 'alien pen' or goose quill, to create a complex conceit of rousing writers to soar to great heights of literary achievement. Tangentially, perhaps, the reference to feathers similarly brings to mind that famous and bitter remark of Greene's, a real rival poet, quoted above: pinioning the young Shakespeare as 'upstart crowe'. Feathers are thus emblems of artistic prowess, to be sported in the cap when the cap is not in the hand.

Lines 7 and 8 focus, not unfittingly, on donation: adding and giving. Not only has the patron brought on the weak and ignorant but he has improved even those who were accomplished,

And given grace a double majesty.

'Grace' contains overtones of generosity as well as refinement, excellence or nobility. He has endowed those who were already graceful, cultured, with a double majesty (or the patron himself has enlarged his own grace by acts of generous munificence).

The second quatrain deals with the ameliorative influence of the patron – two negative ideas become positive and two positives are enhanced – as part of the poem's imagery of refining (note also 'mend' in line 11 and 'advance' in line 13). In the next part of the poem, the sestet, Shakespeare continues this idea but concentrates it more specifically (and for obvious reasons) on its effects on himself.

As we have come to expect, Shakespeare marks a fulcrum between the octave and sestet with a pause and, here, also with the sentence adverb 'Yet'. However, in this sonnet the second quatrain does not repeat the substance of the first, the typical pattern of a Shakespearean sonnet. Instead, here it is the third quatrain that returns to the subject set out at the start: what you, my patron, have done for me in particular.

The eulogy continues but, cunningly so, Shakespeare now including himself in the panegyric,

> Yet be most proud of that which I compile.

Although he may sound like a pet puppy grovelling for attention the stress returns again to the writer of the poem, the 'I'. Where the rival poets 'their poesy disperse' Shakespeare does the opposite and compiles, or composes it. It isn't much but it sounds effective in this unabashed self-advertisement.

Shakespeare is pitching for his livelihood, of course, but what would the patron hope to get out of the arrangement? The word 'proud', part of the imagery of height and aspiration, offers a clue. A patron might hope to be immortalised in the poetry of his protégé by having his virtues extolled, by being identified as an outstanding patron. So the subtext of line 9 craftily says, 'I am your man because I can create great poetry about you,' poetry that will live after you.' Sonnet 60 says it more clearly while trashing the competition,

> And yet to times in hope my verse shall stand
> Praising thy worth, despite his cruel hand.
>
> (lines 13–14)

'Praising thy worth': as long as this poem lives, this gives life to you.

The economic reality was that, in perpetual competition, Shakespeare had to flatter his patron extravagantly. He claims that his poetry is to be proud of but lays the whole credit for this on the patron's 'influence' (10). By this he means the cause or inspiration (compare 'assistance' again in line 2) in both financial and spiritual backing.

Alternatively Shakespeare may be arguing that his poetry's influence on others, its good effect or reputation, is wholly down to the benefactor. 'Born of thee' points to the idea that without the patron it would never have seen daylight but, since in the 1609 Q this was printed as 'borne', he may even be claiming that his output is sustained by him too (cleverly hinting that he still depends on his bounty to continue).

Where the second quatrain duly acknowledged the good influence on his rivals too, here Shakespeare is anxious to qualify any whiff of altruistic fellowship. The patron has been instrumental in the verse of his rivals but only to 'mend [or, improve] the style' (11). This has faint echoes of a similar sentiment in sonnet 100,

> Spend'st thou thy fury on some worthless song,
> Darkening thy power to lend base subjects light?
>
> (3–4)

Not quite as blunt but the same idea, that the patron really ought not to waste his time on his rivals' worthless songs and sordid subjects.

In sonnet 78, line 12 reiterates an idea from line 8 through the repetition of 'grace'. The thrust seems to be that the patron improves only the ornamental skills of the others, their 'arts'. The poem tries to charm the listener's ear with its play on 'graces graced' and in the couplet does the same with 'art', and quibbles on its various meanings (skill, wit, the copula, my literary career).

The couplet draws into itself words and ideas from the rest of the sonnet (art, high, learn, ignorance) to prepare for what is a relatively modest climax. This is in keeping with the ostensible humility of the speaker, of course. The patron enlightens him, provides insight into high culture and so promotes one who would otherwise be a crude lout. 'High', 'learning' and 'rude ignorance' tie the ending of the poem to its second quatrain. Having seen off the rival opposition Shakespeare now feels confident to confess that patronage has cultivated what was once 'rude ignorance'.

The mainspring of the poem is the anxiety of the poet to impress on the patron his indebtedness as well the desperate need to extend his backing. It shares with the 'begetting' poems (1–17) both a persuasive intent and a deference towards its listener, though now chiefly for economic ends. This anxiety is manifested in the profusely hyperbolic tone, which borders on self-parody. Except on purely artistic terms it would surely drive any but the most dull-witted egoist to wince with mortification.

As we have noted, however, it does have a recognisable narrative form in which its strategy is moulded. The form mirrors the themes of the poem: the octave a testimonial of what the patron has done, and the sestet the poet's petition, soliciting the patron's particular attention for himself. The two parts are connected by, among other things, the poet's unctuous note of duty and indebtedness. It is framed by the I/my at beginning and end, which together embrace the poem and the patron in a possessive hug. Line 13, with its play on 'art', underlines the idea that the style and form of a sonnet are actually its subject;

> But thou art all my art and dost advance...

Because all his verse derives from the patron so the patron fills all his verse as its subject matter.

Shakespeare's enterprise is two-pronged: to boost his own verse and to scorn that of his rival poets. This is indicative of what Phoebe Sheavyn calls the 'sordid rivalry' among authors of the early modern period (Sheavyn, p. 32). Artfully, although this sonnet is ostensibly about his immense debt, Shakespeare converts it into an advertisement of his own worth. In simplistic terms: you inspire my verse, which is so great that my obtuse rivals imitate it. As a variation on Greene's bird image, what we have is a form of cuckoo syndrome in which Shakespeare strives to wrench his rivals from that feathery nest that had been exclusively his own.

One strategy here is in the deployment of sound: for example, the enchanting effect of the interplay of 'I', 'thee', 'thine', plus repeated reminders of grace and art. Flattery works through the rhetoric of key sounds (and by Shakespeare's time rhetoric had declined to a technique of right-sounding spin). Equally, a patron was unlikely to make a close textual analysis, so sonnet 78 desires that the interplay of its melodies and the sound of key words (such as 'muse', 'assistance', 'disperse', 'grace', 'art') do the job. The patron would expect to *hear* praise and he gets it laid on with a trowel.

Another approach involves the poet adopting a supine position, to heighten the patron's superior status:

> Thine eyes, that taught the dumb on high to sing,
> And heavy ignorance aloft to fly.

This has the double value of making the patron feel better while emphasising the poet's great need.

The poem's eternal triangle of patron–poet–rivals is in constant tension and Shakespeare's own nervousness at the centre of this is evident. In fact his very nervousness threatens to undermine the poem for the sake of the petition.

Yet, there is manifestly not one particular rival but a shadowy archetypal 'others' (3), coalescing into a general consciousness of a grey, minatory presence: those other 'alien' pens. Where in the sonnets of previous chapters the 'other' has represented objects of desire, such as lovers and muses, here it is divided between the targeted financial help of the patron and the threat of competitors for the pot. Since the rivals are a constant presence these tensions are doomed to be unresolved and so do not find closure by the end of the poem.

This tension is dramatised in the poem through its many antitheses: compile/disperse, I/thee/others, dumb/sing, heavy/high. Perhaps more specifically there is an antagonism of positive and negative poles: fair/alien, learned/ignorance, grace/rude. Shakespeare tries to marshal these along lines of allegiance, and to define and magnify the difference between himself and them.

If Shakespeare resembles a complaisant puppy before his master then this simply reflects the commercial reality of the literary marketplace. It also conveys how brilliantly he can make art out of prostration. Pride struggles from this uncomfortable posture by the speaker's reminding himself of his real worth,

> Yet be most proud of that which I compile,
> Whose influence is thine, and born of thee.
>
> (9–10)

Shakespeare's importuning must tread a narrow tightrope between pride and humility. The game plan of the sestet as a whole is to praise the patron's good influence. This is not primarily to aggrandise Shakespeare but to persuade the patron that his largesse has been most effectively (and gratefully) deployed here. In fact, as in sonnets 100 and 106 too, for instance, the poet must somehow disingenuously diminish himself as among the rudely ignorant (line 14) while bragging of his outstanding poetic prowess. He attempts to resolve this by locating the patron at the centre of them both (and in the couplet the patron unites both form and content).

Above all his many devices here, Shakespeare sets out to be clear in his message to the patron. Sonnet 78 is a relatively plain, modest production. It is 'compiled' in perfectly regular iambic pentameter throughout, with little music and very few figures. But one of the outstanding characteristics of the sonnet is its clarity and the impression projected is that the poet is careful to avoid any verbal or aural tricks, any equivocation or dubiety coming in the way of the business message (for instance, note the looseness of the clause structures, relying overmuch on the repetition of 'And').

Although the dumb have been taught to sing and the heavily ignorant have had flying lessons this is a declaration of art rather than a performance of it. The self-confidence and assertiveness are still evident as they were in the earlier sonnets. But we get the feeling that this poem has distracted the speaker from more important artistic business, a necessary bugbear of the patronage system.

Thus an unintended irony of the poem is that for all its claims it is certainly not one 'to be most proud of'. There is no grace, no memorable images nor artful word play as in, say, sonnets 5, 12, 55 or 116. It cannot match 100, which brazenly sought to convince us that the Muse had actually deserted him.

Unfortunately the success of the poem is made to be the practical success of its petition and this is ultimately its weakness. It turns the attention away from the internal workings and tensions towards the external, towards an artistic void.

Sonnet 79   'Whilst I alone did call upon thy aid'

After sonnet 78's relatively cautious position, and the threat of loss, Shakespeare in sonnet 79 now begins to shimmer again with accustomed vigour.

> Whilst I alone did call upon thy aid,
> My verse alone had all thy gentle grace;
> But now my gracious numbers are decayed,
> And my sick muse doth give another place.   4
> I grant, sweet love, thy lovely argument
> Deserves the travail of a worthier pen,
> Yet what of thee thy poet doth invent,
> He robs thee of, and pays it thee again;   8
> He lends thee virtue, and he stole that word
> From thy behaviour; beauty doth he give
> And found it in thy cheek; he can afford
> No praise to thee but what in thee doth live.   12
> Then thank him not for that which he doth say,
> Since what he owes thee, thou thy self dost pay.

What is likely to strike us first about sonnet 79 is how it begins in similar vein to sonnet 78 with the same slightly compliant vocative tones. The two begin with synonymous phrases: where 78 has 'So oft', 'invoked', 'fair assistance', 79 begins with 'Whilst', 'did call upon', and 'thy aid'. There are many such similarities in diction between these two and the others in the. 'Rival Poet' sequence, and they represent one of the major binding or concatenating elements of this series.

Differences are thus made all the more conspicuous and the single item that stands out in the start of sonnet 79 is the word 'alone', sombrely underlining the point that the poet has been spurned by his patron. The conjunction 'Whilst' and the use of the past tense make the once-happy association even more distant: past perfects 'did' and 'had' despondently emphasise both the pastness and its irrevocability. The repetition of 'alone' in line 2 insists on his new solitude while the echo of 'call' and 'all' sets up a slightly murmuring lamentation like a sigh in these opening lines (the dominant sound of the first seven lines is /ai/ ('I', 'my', etc). However, these belie the spark and brilliance to come.

'There was a time when, dependent on your financial support, my verse had exclusive call on your largesse or "gentle grace".' Simultaneously, it suggests too that his poetry alone enjoyed that same noble refinement as the patron himself displays. The first two lines clearly look back with poignancy to a time even before sonnet 78; and then the third line with its ironic opening of 'But now' thrusts us into a complex web of irony and delicately cunning virtuosity. His marvellous verse before us is both a repudiation of the rival and a sly if tactful riposte to his former patron.

'But now' in line 3 turns our attention with a cadence to the present and does so with an unmistakable tone of self-pity. Yet, in the light of the poem as a whole, line 3 is very much ironic (the start of the poem's many ironies). Now, this verse (or 'numbers'; see sonnet 100:6) which once was permeated by that 'gentle grace' has declined, cut off from your assistance and inspiration, since my waning, ailing poetic prowess must yield place to another poet. As Colin Burrow points out, lines 3 and 4 combine the 'poet's fear that his art has been superseded with his anxieties about his own decrepitude' (Burrow, p. 538). Sonnet 79 intensely sublimates so many emotions, anxieties and ironies within such a finely succinct narrative poem.

In what senses then can his muse be described as 'sick'? First, the word 'muse' may refer to Shakespeare's own poetic power, and 'sick', taking up 'decayed' in the previous line, makes explicit the fears of an older, possibly outmoded poet challenged by a new generation of virile writers after his 'place'.

On the other hand, if 'muse' in 78 is interpreted to include the patron himself then we find a different slant on the line: the 'sick muse' could mean that the patron himself was misguided in giving a rival precedence or inspiration. A third possibility for this richly suggestive section is that Shakespeare himself is the active (or reactive) agent and must seek another patron, 'give another [your] place'.

In line 5 Shakespeare makes another slight but significant change in direction and tenor. He concedes that a subject as beautiful as the patron ('thy lovely argument') merits the pains or efforts of a more skilful writer than himself. Addressing him as 'sweet love' aims to assure his ex-benefactor that there is no bitterness, no hard feelings, about this loss (though other elements in the sonnet suggest otherwise).

The word 'grant' in line 5 offers punning contrast with the 'donation' imagery of sonnet 78 (a patron being the one normally doing the 'granting'!) and anticipates the figures of traffic and finance to come below. Here (at this crucial turning point in the sonnet), where the poem turns from 'poor me' to 'bad he', the poet's deference is a sign of his cunning reversal of their relationship. This deference plus his renewed blandishments may lead us to expect utter submission again, but no – he adamantly refuses to grant that the rival poet *is* the 'worthier pen'. Shakespeare uses these as the platform to introduce the third element in the poem's triangular set-up.

'Yet' in the next line is a pivotal word and it turns us in the new direction towards the rival poet.

> Yet what of thee thy poet doth invent.
>
> (line 7)

With 'thy poet' Shakespeare seems here to scorn his rival as a mean, lowly servant. The 'what' that this poet seems to invent is made clearer in lines 9 to 12 but the speaker prefaces this with a charge against the man's honesty, as a robber.

The word 'invent' has a sharp mocking edge to it because while it contains the surface meaning of 'to originate' or 'to discover', for Elizabethans it might also mean 'to relate what is already known' (see sonnet 59 for Shakespeare's view on 'invention'). In other words, the charge is that this contemptuous fellow purports to dream up virtuous and beautiful praises but in reality he is a deceiving charlatan.

In reality he derives or robs his flattering homage from the patron. He does not invent anything at all. Any fine qualities in his verse are really the fine qualities of his subject, the patron. In this sense he returns, 'pays it thee again', what he takes from the living man to begin with. The point is repeated at the end of the poem, except that here the impostor pays whereas at the end the patron pays. In fact, Shakespeare's argument that the patron pays twice.

The language becomes markedly incisive now, querulous, with 'robs' heading Shakespeare's astringent accusation. Its true significance is that it reveals Shakespeare's own emotional distress at his loss. There follows a catalogue of the impostor's offences drenched in the contemptuous language of traffic and finance, thereby reducing the rival to the status of a pilfering trader and prostitute of his art. At first, anyway. The three charges are presented as a formula:

he *lends* thee virtue and he *stole* it from you (lines 9–10)

he *gives* thee beauty and he *found* it in thy face (lines 10–11)

he *affords* (yields) thee praise and he *took* this from thee
(lines 11–12)

The rival's actions are at each point first portrayed in terms of donating (ironically reversing the normal direction of patronage). Then Shakespeare attempts to further outrage the patron by claiming that the swindling ingrate had in any case pilfered all these from him in the first place.

All three charges are adamant that he has no originality and that he is an impostor–thief. They are presented in a succession of enjambements in lines 9 to 12, thereby making Shakespeare's straddling charges appear quite extensive.

At the start of the couplet the adverb 'Then' signals another change in tone and direction. Occurring at the end of five isomorphic structures the couplet acts as a release, an epigrammatic conclusion turning towards the reader. Turning directly towards the patron with an imperative, Shakespeare entreats the man not to thank his new poet for *what* he writes (its subject matter) because he simply trots out what is there before him. He sells to you what you already own. Essentially the final line of the sonnet reworks the substance of line 8, 'He robs thee of, and pays it thee again', two lines being tallied through the word 'pay' .

With its slew of sibilants the couplet whispers provocatively, conspiratorially, directly into the patron's ear. It insists obsequiously, maintaining the pressure, and memorises it. The bald final statement 'thou thyself dost pay', with its repeated pronoun, is obviously intended to reverberate beyond the poem's end, in the porches of the patron's ears.

The final line is important in a variety of ways. In artistic terms it reminds the reader that the surrogate poet invents nothing. In patronage terms, it reminds the patron that he foots the bill for the deception: the patron owes his man nothing but he does the paying. It reminds the patron too that he also pays by suffering the loss of Shakespeare as his main man. Judiciously the speaker does everything but call the patron a fool, yet he firmly plants the idea.

Not surprisingly, much of the attraction of sonnet 79 derives in part from within itself but also, and in greater part, from its being a component in a close-knit sequence. The 'Rival Poet' sequence is closely integrated by theme, tone, attitude, diction, and so forth, as well as by its shared characters. Examining this 'Rival Poet' series points up the true nature of a sonnet sequence, albeit a very brief one: a dynamic of graduated modifications in tone and feeling, inflected in the fine nuancing of voice.

Sonnet 78 understands and sharply articulates the fear of loss of love and livelihood to rival poets from without. 79 goes on to present a sudden shift in perspective, to that of the outsider, ejected from the comfortable bourn of patronage. It is in the differences as much as in the similarities between sonnets 78 and 79 that the possibility of a sequence narrative is set up. This, as I have tried to demonstrate, is not solely in the shared diction (of which there is a great deal) but in the subtle alterations in verb (most notably from mending to decline and from giving to robbing).

The devil is in the diction. For instance, three key words adverbially refer to the new order of figures in the drama of sonnet 79. In line 4 'sick' refers to *me*, the poet and my poetry, decayed; in line 2 'grace' refers to *you*, the patron's elegance and beauty; and in line 8 'robs' refers to him, the rival poet who robs both you and me. The incidence of pronouns in the poem reveals its form. Lines 1 to 6 are predominantly concerned with first person, 'I' and 'me', while lines 7 to 14 switch to 'he', identifying and accusing the rival poet (the poem, however, has an amorphous thematic structure, its particular form depending on how exactly you read its themes).

Although sonnet 79 deals at length with an external circumstance – basically, the loss of patronage – it has a surprising amount of interiority. There is a profound crisis and consequently we share more closely and intimately the pain of Shakespeare the man as well as, necessarily, the poet. Because of this crucial circumstance, the 'Rival Poet' sequence, moved by urgency, anguish and disaffection, allows us to think of this series of poems as bringing us closer than anything else to the intimate core of Shakespeare himself.

Moreover, we glimpse for the first time Shakespeare's own *lit. crit.*, and something of a theory of literature. Poetry, he charges the rival, is not about the slavish production of naive realism, producing the facsimile of a subject,

> he can afford
> No praise to thee but what in thee doth live.

Artistry is what poetry is to be about, '*gracious* numbers', the beauty in the subject and the beauty in the ornamented style.

Loss of patronage is, of course, only part of the story. The rejection by the patron represents not simply a financial but also a deep emotional loss. As well as the voice of the redundant professional we hear the voice of the forlorn spurned lover. He has lost the love and protection of the patron (and with it something of a paternal figure too, perhaps).

Shakespeare is a jilted friend. He dwells in that strange and uncertain no-man's-land, following the loss of an intense partnership. Stripped of the commercial flattery of 78, we now hear a man less solicitous, more sensible, but trailing the vestiges of a deep loyalty. And this, as we would expect, deepens the anguish of the voice in the wilderness here. Equally natural, is the concomitant tone of rancour that emerges in the latter part of the sonnet (many of the poems in the group 27–51 share a similar grief and confusion at loss).

At heart there is an ambivalence in the voice which betrays the deeper confusion about where he is now in a limbo relationship. The patron is linked with 'gentle grace' but (if we take a broad reading of 'muse') he is in some way 'sick', implying a poisonous influence from the deceiving rival. Yet, strictly speaking, his desperate spleen is not aimed directly at the former benefactor nor should we forget that the poet continues to write exquisite poetry in his patron's honour.

And then the rival; what can we say about the rival poet himself? Here we meet the 'alien pen' referred to in sonnet 78. He is in essence accused of being a swindling charlatan. By contrast with the stolid (outwardly at least) Shakespeare the other man is untiringly active: he robs, pays, lends, stole, gives, found, and owes. He is referred to throughout in the active subject form 'he'. Someone as active as this fellow must be up to no good.

Shakespeare's thrust is twofold: the rival deceives you, being in truth a common criminal, and he is artistically incompetent into the bargain. The conspicuous imagery of traffic and commerce work subliminally against the rival, cleverly colouring him as a menial pecuniary, a prostitute even (contrast Shakespeare's 'sweet love' in line 5), and the charges are intended to play on a patron's worst fears about a domestic servant, that he filches from the household on his own account.

> He robs thee of, and pays it thee again;
> He lends thee virtue, and he stole that word.
>
> (lines 8–9)

By contrast Shakespeare claims his love was based on frankness and honest loyalty.

The poem originates in a crisis of confidence in connection with the loss of patronage. It is a crisis seeming to stem from Shakespeare's profoundly radical appraisal of his powers as an artist in the wake of the anxieties of sonnet 78. His strategy is to belittle the downgraded rival but also to belittle him through a brilliant display of mastery which is aimed less at the rival than at the bereft patron, and a boost to his own self-respect. To demonstrate his greater prowess he must and does outshine his rival – and if, as many believe, that rival is George Chapman then he is indeed a formidable opponent.

In the 'Rival Poet' sequence, unlike any other sequence or series in the Sonnets, each successive poem elucidates more clearly some of the decisive feelings underlying its predecessor. One result of this is that in this sequence we witness Shakespeare the poet come closest to

Shakespeare the dramatist. It is in this group that he sets up a system of concerns and tensions that pulsate between figures dramatised within the poet's consciousness and engage with the reader in a manner akin to the stage scenarios. We are likely to feel that these are first enacted as external dramas and then internalised as the poet's personal demons. Sonnet 82 exemplifies this feature of the 'Rival Poet' suite.

Sonnet 82   'I grant thou wert not married to my Muse'

At this stage in the sequence, Shakespeare is fully aware that the sundering of the relationship between himself and his patron is complete. He still addresses these sonnets to him but the feeling is only one way. Yet the poet refuses to accept that the situation is irrevocable.

At the start of sonnet 82 we get a hint that Shakespeare is still on speaking terms with his former benefactor and perhaps it is this that sustains hope. It reads like a reply to the patron's rebuff.

> I grant thou wert not married to my Muse,
> And therefore mayst without attaint o'erlook
> The dedicated words which writers use
> Of their fair subject, blessing every book.   4
> Thou art as fair in knowledge as in hue,
> Finding thy worth a limit past my praise,
> And therefore art enforced to seek anew,
> Some fresher stamp of the time-bettering days.   8
> And do so love; yet when they have devised,
> What strained touches rhetoric can lend,
> Thou, truly fair, wert truly sympathized,
> In true plain words, by thy true-telling friend;   12
>   And their gross painting might be better used,
>   Where cheeks need blood; in thee it is abused.

This is clearly a reply to something said by the patron. But what? Now with his new poet, the patron has protested that Shakespeare is behaving as if they had actually been married.

The sonnet begins in conciliatory mood, a reply that tries to abate a misunderstanding. Conversely, the words 'grant' and 'married' in the opening line are so strong that the opening resembles a challenge, making a pass, to the sometime benefactor. The word 'marriage' introduces a sexual element to the poem and at the same time calls to mind sonnet 116's celebrated opener, 'Let me not to the marriage of true minds / Admit impediment.' Both are to do with admitting something, but here Shakespeare is less stoical and love is less an 'ever-fixed mark', at least from the patron's point of view.

On the other hand, sonnet 78's patron was identified as 'my Muse' and that fact makes this break seem all the more agonised. Not being committed to Shakespeare (or any one poet for that matter) the patron may without discredit or moral taint support any other devoted writers. 'O'erlook' in line 2 is ambiguous. In a neutral sense it means to study work which has been dedicated to the patron, based on words specially selected to praise him. But crucially and in a more pointed sense, it means 'to ignore' – the patron can blithely disregard whatever he chooses.

'O'erlook', then, is attached to the theme of loyalty and commitment (via the words 'married', 'dedicated', 'enforced' and 'strained'), and to learning (via 'knowledge', 'truly', and 'fair'). But the purport of Shakespeare's message is that the patron is not so much wilful as simply led astray: again he accuses the patron of a blunder in forsaking his former protégé.

But lines 3 and 4 concede he may patronise whom he will, 'blessing every book' that is dedicated to him ('blessing', though, is modified here either by the patron, 'thou', or by 'dedicated words', the writers of them).

'Blessing' is an important metaphor in that one mark of Shakespeare's brilliance in these 'Rival Poet' sonnets is his knack of combining flattery and detail through some very sardonic diction. 'Blessing', too, works in this way. On one level, the patron simply endorses the works dedicated to him, but, on another, in 'blessing' them he seems to have holy powers of making these works successful (as a king was once believed to have healing powers; see *Macbeth*, 4.3.141–7).

The patron is also declared 'fair' and Shakespeare continues to make these fertile words work fulltime. He is 'fair' in that he is just, open-minded, without any moral tinge (see line 2 again) yet graced too with beauty and refinement (as he is delineated in sonnets 78 and 79).

The second quatrain, as we have come to expect, mirrors the theme and even something of the structure of the first. The word 'fair' (5) expands on the same word in the previous line by explaining that the patron is both well educated ('in knowledge') and beautiful ('in hue'; compare sonnet 20:7, 'A man in hue...'). The reference to 'knowledge' links this poem with sonnets 78 and 79 (the patron had taught 'heavy ignorance' to fly; 78:6). 'Fair' can also include 'just', of course, and eventually this will take in truth too, in line 11's 'truly fair'. But for now, being fair he will not need the 'gross painting' that his toadies indulge in, as the couplet relates.

Shakespeare's conciliation continues and deepens as, in line 6, he once more combines flattery and detail. He concedes too that the patron realises his poetic skill is not up to the difficult job of praising 'his worth' though this is, with profound wit, another example of rhetorical *occupatio* (paradoxically, he apologises for his weak effort but excels in doing so). 'Worth' connects with sonnets 79 (line 6) and 80 (line 5) and the same notion of 'quality' or 'rank' appears again in 83 (line 8).

The patron is therefore 'enforced', compelled to 'seek anew', or afresh. The use of 'enforced' (line 7) makes the patron sound compelled by his own decision and carries a similar sense of duress, as 'married' and 'dedicated' do in the first quatrain. The repetition of 'therefore' makes him sound as if he is compelled by logic too. However, by an ironic contrast his former poet is now a free agent, however unwillingly.

'Anew' puns on 'a new poet' and in the context of line 8 incorporates a slightly pejorative smack about it. He charges his former patron with merely following fashion,

Some fresher stamp of the time-bettering days.

(8)

He seeks the latest model in poet, not necessarily the best. 'Stamp' opens up an interesting metaphor since it can mean the mark or colophon of the printer (and so glances back to line 4). The indefinite pronoun 'Some' is of course contemptuous.

'Fresher stamp' is hence an important oxymoron combining the idea of 'newness' with that of 'something fixed' or 'of long-standing'. A 'stamp' on a coin refers to its impressed pattern, implying an ingrained character and therefore something established or time-honoured, and thus contrasts with the fresher ornaments, the new-fangled style of the tyros.

'Time-bettering days' challenges the patron (and the period itself) as merely fashion-conscious, whimsically pursuing the latest craze. It is an intricate paradox and at the heart of this is the writer's acerbic metaphor that these days (i.e. poets) think they can improve on the past, on those reliable antique 'pens'. The young generation of rivals, with their ornate and 'strained touches', nevertheless 'lack tongues to praise' (106:14) when compared with the old hands, and Shakespeare strategically aligns himself with the past.

The third quatrain begins on a palpable note of truculence.

> And do so love; yet when they have devised,
> What strained touches rhetoric can lend . . .
>
> (lines 9–10)

What a brilliant phrase is 'strained touches rhetoric can lend', exquis-itely compressing within itself all manner of ideas and tensions. 'Strained' implies that their work is not a natural reflection of their benefactor. It also implies they are overextending their ability, toiling to wrench distorted images from callow pens (cf. the 'stretched metre' of 17:12). At the same time, 'touches' supports these ideas by suggesting that their rhetoric produces mere impressions, purely superficial effects, consonant with the idea that their faddish produc-tions are just that, transient, ephemeral.

'Lend' is borrowed from sonnet 79 and its context there (and in 84:6) amplifies this theme of shallow effects. Every word is carefully selected for its trenchant as well as its musical effect in a perfect decorum. We hear a great unstrained economy of eloquence, tightly organised against the form, and this is of course the nub of his *occupatio* here: you dump me for him and yet, look at my work – can he get even close to this?

'Sympathized' is yet another element of this richly potent decorum. I have, he says, expressed you with sympathy: that is, matched your character faithfully, conscientiously and lovingly. For emphasis Shakespeare adds extra value, dazzles his ungrateful reader with an imposing word play, expertly setting down a barrage of cognate lexis for instant effect: truly fair, truly, true plain, true. The message is hit home even to a dull reader only half listening. As a 'true-telling friend' his 'plain words' are frank and simple, but clear – no straining or distorting (he protests). But the epithet 'true' also hammers home Shakespeare's own deep sense of loss, and his incomprehension at this loss. Through the repetition of this tag, 'true', he exposes the terrible irony that he has been scorned as a friend, even as a lover, as much as a mere employee.

The couplet of sonnet 82 begins in the same way as lines 2, 7, and 9 began, with the continuer 'And'. Shakespeare seeks to give the poem a sense of loose organisation, to suggest that these claims came to his mind spontaneously. However, to create this effect actually requires him to be very highly structured in his approach.

In the phrase 'their gross painting', the word 'their' lends weight to the view that Shakespeare has more than one rival here. The phrase and the hyperbole in 'gross' testify again to the deep strength of his feeling about the 'strained touches' of these new-generation writers. 'Gross' similarly links with 'strained' as an expression of distortion or crudeness (compare *Hamlet* 4.7.170) while the metaphor 'painting' in the Sonnets as a whole is nearly always linked with counterfeiting and deception (see 16:8, and *Hamlet*, 3.1.143). It connects back to 'hue', 'fair' and 'stamp'.

Once again the efforts of these new poets are merely cosmetic. That such painting *'might* be better used' casts some scorn on these flatterers but the poem finishes with its own dedication: Shakespeare flatters the patron that he does not need flattery. 'Cheeks' is once again synecdochic (as in 79:11), signifying natural beauty or complexion; thus these rivals lay on the 'painting' where it is most redundant and so, misused. This misuse contrasts with a 'truly fair' patron and a 'true-telling friend', drawing together the preceding themes of honesty, knowledge and loyalty. By ending sonnet 82 on the word 'abused' Shakespeare once more leaves reverberating in the air the idea that the patron is being ruthlessly swindled.

Shakespeare reminds his ex-patron that he is still here, attentive, still his true-telling friend. He is still available and this sonnet again flaunts his high-octane skills, notwithstanding the *occupatio* in line 6. Desire continues to drive *him* too – he reaches out and refuses to release the patron. As a 'true-telling friend' his central aim is to advertise the fact that by trusting some 'fresher stamp' of a rival(s) the man has made an honest ('fair') mistake, and that he fails to recognise the further deception by the other man that this has led to.

Shakespeare maintains his emotions under firm control so that he can present a soft-sell case founded on argument instead of sentiment. Instead of saying 'take me back' he advises the patron on the problems each of them faces, the result of the patron's regrettable lapse. What he lays before him is a kind of incomplete dialectic, or syllogism, addressed to his former benefactor that leads him so far, with the hope that he will complete it. The syllogism, a figure from classical logic, is worked out through the word 'fair' in its sense of 'being reasonable' or 'just'.

First, Shakespeare affirms his true dedication to a 'fair subject' (4), then the patron is identified as that fair subject, being described as a 'fair' friend (11). The third, unstated conclusion of the argument is that the patron as a fair man ought to reinstate him. This unspoken imperative hangs like a shadow or an injury over the final part of the poem.

As we would expect, the poem's diction supports this rationalistic approach. Each section uses 'therefore' or 'so' (lines 2, 7 and 9) to emphasise the consequences of the patron's earlier decision to dismiss Shakespeare. The diction also encapsulates the outline of the sonnet's larger argument: in the first quatrain the man is free, 'not married' and 'therefore mayst'; but in the second he is 'enforced' by his mistake; then in the sestet Shakespeare offers release by first inviting him to 'do so love' (9) then shrewdly reiterates the consequences of so doing. Key words are accordingly marshalled at decisive moments, so we hear the bare bones of a narrative: I, thou, days, yet, friend, abused. This skeleton is fleshed out in 'plain words': married, attaint, dedicated, blessing, worth, anew, love, strained, fair, true.

It is a brilliant piece of calculated, reasoned discourse. There is nothing strained about any of *its* neat touches, though he pushes the diction hard: compounds 'time-bettering' (8) and 'true-telling' (12); the coinage in 'sympathized' (11); the paradox in 'time-bettering days' (8); and the pleonasm in line 12. These are so brazenly foregrounded (they are hardly 'plain words') that the words begin talking about words (note too the diction about diction: words, book, rhetoric, words). Above all, these exude an acute sense of self-esteem regarding his ability as a poet. Only the dullest of patrons could fail to realise his mistake in releasing this poet.

In talking about words Shakespeare necessarily talks once more about literature. Again the style of the sonnet is its subject:

> The dedicated words which writers use
> Of their fair subject . . .
>
> (3–4)

Similarly, the poem reveals again Shakespeare's anxiety about his place in the coming new order of poets. Where in sonnet 79 he bitterly criticised these *upstart crowes* for their lack of ornament, here he tries a slightly different tack with his own ironic affirmation of 'true plain words'. A poet ought to be honest, both in his dealings with a patron and in a realistic depiction of him. Shakespeare hints strongly that the new man is neither. His replacement is a cheat, a 'deviser', who has conned the patron into believing that what he needs is artifice and flattery

> And their gross painting might be better used,
> Where cheeks need blood; in thee it is abused.

These new poets, the fresher stamps, are not only conmen but they are clumsy with it. Yes, by all means use rhetoric, argues 79, but 82 argues these new mannerists offend nature by overdoing it with blatant exaggeration, abusing nature (which Shakespeare's treatment had 'truly sympathized').

The phrases 'fresher stamp' and 'time-bettering days' also offer two important shades of time: one is Shakespeare's awareness of his own ageing and the other is the lure of the new ('enforced to seek anew'; 7). He strives to link the idea of personal ageing with the continuity of traditional poetic values, and with ethics of truth and loyalty. The antithesis of this foundation myth is the shallow modishness of a new generation of poets whose art is essentially deception, an abuse lending colour to a cheek that needs no extra blood. These new hubristic lads try to better time itself, and Shakespeare the steady old hand is a bastion of time,

> No! Time, thou shalt not boast that I do change.
>
> (123:1)

It is a tight tightrope and there is room for only one showman on this poetic highwire.

At this point in our analysis of the 'Rival Poet' sequence we need to pause briefly in order to consider the image of the patron built up within it. The *Sonnets* appeared during the English Renaissance, a period characterised by among other things a shift in artistic attention towards the individual, leading to, in painting especially, the sudden rise of the personal portrait (and painting is a recurrent motif in this sequence). In the 'Rival Poet' sequence Shakespeare presents us with a series of powerful psychological insights building towards a self-portrait, a highly personal, individualistic response to the loss of patronage but also, and more profoundly, the loss of the love of someone he had come to regard as more than a friend. In the process of doing this he inevitably constructs an impressionistic study of his former patron.

Starting with the more obvious, the patron must be wealthy and leisured, of course. He appears to be (or Shakespeare makes him so) aloof and impersonal, capricious, insouciant, sovereign of his minor demesne, perhaps even a tyrant. We have only Shakespeare's partial portrait but he comes over as vain, even foppish, readily flattered, unpredictable, and moody. Sonnets 79 and 82 are impressed by his erudition and there is an assumption in the sequence that he fancies himself as a connoisseur of arts, most likely painting in addition to literature. Shakespeare thinks he is easily swindled but is probably wealthy enough to fund this with indifference.

The relationship between himself and his patron in this sequence gradually shades away from that of the explicitly feudal, in which the poet-servant would entirely submit himself to be silent and undemonstrative (as happens in sonnet 78, for example, and compare sonnet 26). 'Explicitly' is apt here because Shakespeare is readily aware of the economic and social realities governing his own position. Yet the relationship is more complex than that of a servant to a patron. He is not a figure entirely subordinate to the master's will, in service, and there are strong vestiges of love involved not wholly accountable in terms of power and desire.

A key element in the great appeal of these sonnets lies in Shakespeare's refusal to act within the framework of a fixed or conventional patron–artist relationship. His strategy is to question in minute detail the nature and dynamic of the failure of that relationship, to envisage its problem in terms of loyalty and language.

So, what the 'Rival Poet' sequence does, specifically with regard to Shakespeare and his patron, is to deconstruct, on the one hand, the conventional notion of the servant, and on the other, the conventional belief in the stability of language. He shows us that the insecurity of the relationship is essentially linked to the instability of language, leaving a strong suspicion that at the heart of the failed relationship lies an unspeakable secret or sin which the evasive and gracious language and its silences conceal yet dramatise.

Sonnet 86　'Was it the proud full sail of his great verse'

In the final sonnet of the 'Rival Poet' sequence we witness an important change in Shakespeare's frame of mind, a change that holds out the possibility of an aesthetic if not an ethical closure to the sequence. It is a change that is intimated from the very first word, its past tense setting that tone of despondency and of irrevocable finality that ensues.

Was it the proud full sail of his great verse,
Bound for the prize of all-too-precious you,
That did my ripe thoughts in my brain inhearse,
Making their tomb the womb wherein they grew?   4
Was it his spirit, by spirits taught to write
Above a mortal pitch, that struck me dead?
No, neither he, nor his compeers by night
Giving him aid, my verse astonished.   8
He, nor that affable familiar ghost
Which nightly gulls him with intelligence,
As victors, of my silence cannot boast;
I was not sick of any fear from thence.   12
     But when your countenance filled up his line,
     Then lacked I matter, that enfeebled mine.

What was it that transfixed my writing into silence: the strutting rhetoric of my rival's great verse? Or its exceptional vigour? No, I had nothing to fear from the rival's work or even from the sinister methods he resorted to. The thing that devastated me was the discovery that you had finally championed him in my stead.

The word 'full' in line 1 hints at these conclusive currents and it is repeated in the past tense in line 13 where it is the patron doing the filling. Here in the complex opening line, 'full' seems to complement the word 'proud' but also to overlap it, as many other pairs of words do in this poem. 'Full', though, implies finished, complete. The rival's metaphorical 'sail' is resplendent and ascendent, borne before him like a ship's. The 'sail' is a conspicuous echo of the 'proudest sail' and the marine imagery of sonnet 80. The 'if' conditionals of that sonnet and the fears of becoming 'wracked' and 'cast away' here become menacingly true.

The opening line bombards the reader with a turbulence of the other man's mighty verse. The sounds too have a daringly dramatic beefiness, with plosive /b/ and /p/ booming proud, bound, prize, precious, ripe and brain. His sails almost explode with noisy grandeur.

'Proud' hints at the virility of the eminent conqueror ('victors', 11) and thus contrasts with Shakespeare's own infirm situation of the 'sick' (12) and 'enfeebled' (14). But, as we have come to expect, his words have an antinomy about them – in a different mood we may interpret the first line in a pejorative light, so that 'proud' may be understood as 'overblown', that is puffed to excess (compare *A Midsummer Night's Dream*, 2.1.91).

In this regard and in the context of the preceding sonnets, 'his great verse' looks ambiguous in terms of Shakespeare's tone. Perhaps it is bitterly sarcastic, though line 12 seems to challenge this idea. 'Great' can be weighty, eminent, or again, full. It could mean overdone, windy in the sense that the rival's rhetoric is too much, with 'gross painting' once more (see 82:13). Equally it may refer to Marlowe's 'mighty line', in Ben Jonson's words, hinting at the identity of one of the rivals. Or it may again point to another candidate, George Chapman, whose seminal translation of Homer's *Iliad* was done in a 'great' fourteen-syllable line.

'Bound' in line 2 poses a multiplicity of suggestions. Repeating the vowels of 'proud' it is integral to the dramatic plosive alliteration that opens the poem, the phonetic equivalent of the 'proud full sail'. It recalls the sense of 'bonds' in 87:4 and even 'tongue-tied' in sonnets 80 and 85. Books too are 'bound', but the word also suggests the inevitability of the course of their relationship together with its irrevocable pain, contrasting with flight in sonnet 78. So, continuing the nautical metaphor, the rival can now be understood as headed for the cherished love of the patron.

In 'Bound for the prize', 'prize' is significant in implying a 'prize ship', rich plunder for a daring buccaneer. The word has resonances too of 'praise' from earlier sonnets ('riches' too in 87) and 'precious phrase' in 85. Now it is the patron who is the one 'all-too-precious'. This is a curious phrase in itself. It can sound on our ears as bitterly sarcastic but it may equally mean 'beyond my reach', especially as 'precious' can again mean its opposite, 'worthless' (see 85:4 and compare *Cymbeline*, 4.2.83).

Was it this that transfixed my writing, brought about the death of my thoughts before they could even be brought forth? For once the readiness was all, because although the speaker's poetry was ripe, ready and refined, his words are dead in the womb before they can be expressed as verse. 'Thoughts' were 'good thoughts' in sonnet 85 while 'tomb', anticipated in 83:12, may bring to mind the repeated idea of 'dumb' (85:10) and so back once more to 'tongue-tied'. The words, their sounds and associations, are as we expected very tightly marshalled, again indicating how all these dread anxieties were bound in mind all along and, now ripe, are at last realised.

The opening question remains for now unanswered, naggingly suspended over the second question, beginning in line 5,

> Was it his spirit, by spirits taught to write
> Above a mortal pitch, that struck me dead?

In sonnet 80 the phrase a 'better spirit' referred to both a writer, his vigorous power, and a spiritual being, probably the Muse. Here, in 86, the first mention of 'spirit' is directed at the rival poet, his Muse or perhaps, more generally, his genius since one reading of this sentence is that the rival has created not only 'great verse', but immortal verse, perhaps dealing with lofty metaphysical themes, where Shakespeare's work has been rooted in the ground.

Conversely, a more striking interpretation is that he has been 'taught to write' by demons or fiends, having conversed with the supernatural, 'Above a mortal pitch', beyond the human reach. This contrasts sharply with Shakespeare's praise to his patron in 78:5, who had taught mortal writers to reach towards heaven in their artistic work. The rival here has communed with supernatural forces and 'pitch' implies the associated darkness and moral defilement. In this case 'his spirit' refers to his own local protective demon (as it does in Marlowe's *Doctor Faustus*) and thus anticipates 'affable familiar ghost' in line 9.

He merely speculates and by this, of course, disconcerts himself as much as his reader. Ironically, although his rival is accused of intimacy with the supernatural it is Shakespeare himself who has been 'struck dead'. This metaphor rehearses the allusions to funerals and silence in the opening quatrain.

Then lines 7 and 8 burst out in splintering rage (most of the caesurae occur in this part of the poem). We might have expected a decisive, substantial reply to the earlier, grievous, interrogations but the answer is only partial and the full revelation suspended until the final line. The cause of his humiliation was not the rival spirit nor his demonic collaborators, 'compeers', of the night (contrast the 'time-bettering days' of 82:8). It was not they who supplied 'aid' – though the bitter irony remains that this is what Shakespeare begged of the patron in sonnets 78, 79 and 80. The success and popularity of the rival serve to deepen his sense of solitude and failure, his verse becomes 'astonished', struck dumb or confounded (as *Hamlet*, 3.2.319).

No, not my rival, nor his familiar. In line 9 a 'familiar' is again an attendant demon or, here, a ghost, to resume the play on spirit(s) in line 5 and taking up the deathly figures. In Elizabethan English the words 'affable' and 'familiar' could be synonymous. This is curious since the line has, exceptionally for this sonnet, a quite irregular rhythm, suggesting that Shakespeare went out of his way for a tautology by insisting on 'affable' perhaps for some private ironic reason (just as conversely he contorts line 11 to achieve a regular scansion there).

> He, nor that affable familiar ghost
> Which nightly gulls him with intelligence,
> As victors, of my silence cannot boast.
>
> (9–11)

For a second time the rival is linked with the night. The reference to 'intelligence' contrasts significantly with ideas of knowledge in 78 and 82 because where earlier the patron's knowledge is suggested as something full such as insight and wisdom, here the rival's demon supplies mere *intelligence*. This word in an age preoccupied with espionage and suspicion implies a questionable piece of information, mere hearsay, dubiously attained or bought from a stooge.

As an insult, line 10 is particularly incisive. After being accused of deception in earlier sonnets the rival himself is now presented as the victim of flattery – his spritely nightly friend dupes him (or even 'torments' him) into believing that he has high intellect.

But neither of them are the cause of the speaker's own dejected silence. He had nothing to fear from that quarter. The assertion of the first-person subject 'I' in line 12 injects a brief sense of conviction. Its bold, direct statement draws the speculation to a short but forceful standstill, blocking off that line of rumour. There is still a strong sense of pride here too, even in admitting the sickness that had moved the poem (the word 'sick' contrasts with the theme of mending in sonnets 78 and 82).

Line 12 also raises the emotional bar just sufficiently to magnify the surprise of the blow in the couplet. The poem's dramatic arc of suspense sweeps down to line 12 to be halted by the ominous cadence in 'But' at the start of the couplet. The adverb heralds the descent again into a complex of meaning and feeling, driving the attention from 'I' to an accusative, confrontational 'your'.

The formidable energy of the couplet is actuated by the shrewd pun on 'countenance'. On the one hand, the rival's 'great verse' (or 'line') is filled with the face, the presence, of his patron – and we infer this is the source of its greatness. But, on the other, 'countenance' functions as a synecdoche, the face standing for the whole man, the rival is the complete victor; at the same time it functions as a metonymy for his beauty, replacing the word 'cheek' used as such in sonnet, 79 and 82. But worse still lies in his 'countenance'.

Anyone who wishes may write about the patron, so the final bitter blow arrives in the word 'countenance', meaning the patron's 'favour' or 'approval'. The couplet invites a number of possible interpretations, one of which being that it is Shakespeare, exasperated by the patron's gullible ignorance, who actually rejects his employer.

Alternatively, the couplet may be Shakespeare's declaration that with a breach of faith by the patron their relationship has finally reached an aesthetic (and a personal) impasse. The patron, by countenancing or approving the rival's verse, confirms the new man's appointment in the household as well as in the patron's affections, in place of Shakespeare (for this sense of 'countenance' see *Hamlet*, 4.2.16). This is the final straw. The patron's tacit rejection of him meant that he no longer had a subject matter to write about (sonnet 38 is crucial here because it expresses how much the verse relies on his actual subject matter).

The diverse meanings of this sonnet develop once more as a dialectic triggered off by the two opening periodic questions, filling out into its unusual 6 + 6 + 2 form. The first part of the poem is composed as two direct 'syntax' questions, embedded and extended, musing on why the poet's creative vitality has been wrecked. Answering these, in lines 7–12, the poet's voice paradoxically repudiates the hypotheses of lines 1–6, spattering it with seven negative words. This all builds forward to the dramatic revelation in the couplet.

The poem's strong impetus is worked through its key lexical pointers: 'Was it ...?' (lines 1 and 5), 'No ...' (7), 'But ...' (13), 'Then ...' (14) – with two *voltas*, at lines 7 and 12. The long twelve-line suspense brings to the couplet great moment and acuteness.

The mainspring of the poem is only partly accounted for by its mystery and by the suspension of the speaker's revelation. It is driven too by the equivocal discourse once again, and by Shakespeare's own vexed sense of disorientation (expressed in the questions of the first section). Still in part impelled as before by desire ('all-too-precious you'), its tensions are now energised more internally by dejection and frustration.

From the beginning of the 'Rival Poet' sequence the consciousness of the sonnets has been stalked by a strange phantom and in the final poem it reaches its actualisation. As it does so we can recognise it as a variation on the Othello syndrome: a predisposition to doubting and distrusting the object of desire. This begins in desire and anxiety but breaks out eventually as jealousy and suspicion. It becomes so strong that it constructs the object of its own dread, brings about the dreaded object as if to prove its existence to itself. Thus in the final line of sonnet 86 it is possible to detect a sense of relief in verifying this self-constructed phantom.

It attests to the underlying angst inherent from the outset in Shakespeare's relationship with his patron, part-servant part-lover, predicated on social inequality and imbalance. This is all one with his construction of the fantasy that the rival has colluded in the dark spirit-world, part of the strategic narrative that he weaves for himself and for us.

In sonnet 80 an idea is mooted that the rival was intent not merely on securing the cherished patronage but also on silencing Shakespeare completely:

> spends all his might,
> To make me tongue-tied ...

> (lines 83–4)

Shakespeare had ruffled a few feathers on the Elizabethan literary scene, as Robert Greene's 'upstart crowe' attests, and he must have been alert to any ill-will against him. The theatre business too had become a cut-throat enterprise where success was measured in poaching audiences and trouncing rival companies.

From a group of rivals at the start of the sequence ('every alien pen'), a generation of new upstarts, the competition is narrowed here to one writer, focusing and intensifying the speaker's scorn. Narrowing the range of contestants to one, further helps to create an atmosphere of a *psychomachy*, a battle for the soul (see sonnet 144, and Chapter 5 for a discussion of this). On the face of it, the battle would be for the soul of the patron but in effect it is for the soul of Shakespeare. The struggle is between himself and the rival for his own soul, and it is at this point that we might begin to recognise that there are not three but four characters in play. Shakespeare loses his soul, his importance, disastrously,

> Then lacked I matter.

But Shakespeare only *loses* his soul: the rival sells his, or at least that is the charge. It is not the first indictment against the rival(s); he is arraigned for plagiarism (sonnet 78), fraud (79), gross flattery (82 and 83), and deception (85). Some of these have looked like the desperate measures of a despondent loser. As Helen Vendler points out, the world is out of joint: 'tombs are wombs, mortals write above a mortal pitch, ghosts gull human beings' (Vendler, p. 378).

Sonnet 86 begins in apparent if reluctant admiration for the rival's astonishing 'great verse', written 'Above a mortal pitch', but this modulates into scorn for a writer using low and devious means. Even if we do not accept the charge of necrolatry (unnatural dealings with the dead) Shakespeare still accuses his rival of cronyism, that he prevailed only through the help of some influential associates,

> his compeers by night
> Giving him aid
>   (lines 7–8)

Shakespeare labours hard to attain the ethical high ground over his rival and even suggests that his rival was motivated by base materialism in striking out like a grasping pirate for a 'prize' ship (2). This reproach plays on snobbery and the contemporary distinction between the gentleman-writer composing poetry solely for the sake of art and the grovelling hack scribbling for material remuneration.

The imagery of tombs, ghosts and night helps lend the impression that the other poet is not as genuine or as salubrious as the 'proud full sail' at first implies. Instead it creates an image of him as a resurrection man, picking among the dry bones of dead poets, manipulated by occult influences for which he slavishly ventriloquises. His image jars against the Elizabethan perception of a poet as gifted, a natural genius, not a mere man.

Conclusions

The 'Rival Poet' sequence of sonnets is among the most richly fascinating of the whole collection. It certainly presents the best example of a formal sequence, closely organised around common themes, predicament, tone, attitude, imagery and characters, all finely nuanced across an unfolding narrative. It also focuses closely together themes of love, time, and art, enabling us to see the interaction of these issues within a subtly changing dynamic.

On the historical level this sequence is a direct impression of the commercial realities facing the Elizabethan writer in terms of the competition among authors and also of the pressing need for financial patronage. On a specifically private level these sonnets brilliantly explore the unfolding crisis that the poet undergoes in his relationship with his patron as well as his attitude to his own writing. In these poems we witness Shakespeare tread a very narrow psychological as well as financial tightrope, revealing how each depends on the other.

A deeply intimate study, this sequence exposes the private trauma that develops from the loss of love and patronage to a challenger. Art and love are shown to cohere in a profoundly interdependent connection, with Shakespeare the man and Shakespeare the artist as an indivisible identity, 'all my art'. Failure of one becomes failure of both, with the consequence that in despair he almost loses his identity in the shock of losing his appointment. For this reason, and for the intense pain and anxiety expressed here, we come closer than anywhere else in his writing to hearing the intimate voice and personality of Shakespeare.

Because of the unified aspect of the man and the art, these poems also reveal something of Shakespeare's (or the period's) poetics, his ideas about what literature should do. Crucial to his position in the triangle here is his need to adopt a posture of respect and humility towards his patron while strongly asserting the high worth of his own work, as a moat defensive against the 'alien pen' of his foe. His dazzling solution lies in the use of *occupatio*, the brilliant verse that repudiates his own brilliance, at the same time shrewdly arguing that what creative skills he does possess spring from his patron's affection and munificence.

Through his denunciation of the 'heavy ignorance' of his rival, Shakespeare also offers something of a note towards a definition of poetry. He reveals the degree to which certain literary features are valorised. Above all, poetry is not about the unmediated reproduction of reality, naive realism, but about 'gracious numbers', that is, cultivating an ornamented style directed at creating artistic beauty in a text. '*Elocutio*' or graceful adornment is the keystone of the new style of rhetoric.

But this affirmation pitches an uncertain Shakespeare towards another artistic and personal crisis. Sonnet 82 most clearly witnesses his anxiety about time, specifically that at the heart of his dilemma is simply the process of ageing, that he has become outmoded. He fears that his emphasis on a literary style that is genuine and well-crafted has been ousted by the glossy, fine-sounding but essentially shallow rhetoric of the new generation of poets. His patron is taken in by this and, since patrons sought to project themselves as connoisseurs of avant garde-literary fashion, Shakespeare finds himself thrust aside.

Further Research

I have suggested that part of Shakespeare's crisis comes about because of his need to promote his own verse without seeming conceited about it. Take a detailed look at sonnet 85 and try to describe how Shakespeare envisages this problem there, particularly in his relationship with his patron. In what ways is silence a crucial element in this poem?

5

Fair's Fair: the Dark Mistresses

Fair is foul, and foul is fair.

(*Macbeth*, 1.1.11)

In the 1609 Q order of the Sonnets there are twenty-six so-called 'Dark Mistress' sonnets, numbered 127 to 152 (some critics also include 153 and 154 while others have included numbers 35, 40, 41 and 42). Although some people refer to these sonnets as the 'Dark Lady' sequence there is no reference in them at all to 'lady' and the word 'dark' occurs only once, at the end of sonnet 147. The allusion to her colouring as 'black' appears in only five of the sonnets, while only three make any praise of her colouring. 'Dark' or 'black' may refer to her personality or manner, to her eyes, her hair or her complexion, or indeed to all of these.

As we would expect there have been numerous and continuing attempts to equate the Dark Mistress with an actual contemporary woman. Some readers have identified her as a woman from the West Indian colonies or a Creole. Some have gone further and recognised her as Lucy Morgan or 'Black Luce', infamous madam of a Clerkenwell brothel. Other favourite Dark Mistresses have included Rosa the Italian wife of John Florio, Amelia Lanyer another Italian (née Bassano), Penelope Rich (the dark mistress of Sidney's *Astrophel and Stella*) as well as Anne Hathaway, Pembroke's mistress Mary Fitton, and even the Queen.

George Bernard Shaw also championed Fitton in spite of the fact that portraits of her show her to be fair, not black-complexioned (32:13–14), having brown hair not 'black wires' (130:4), and with grey eyes not 'raven black' (127:9). On the other hand, as Jonathan Bate observes, in Elizabethan love poetry 'fairness and darkness have a great deal more to do with social status than with actual hair and eye colour' (Bate, 1997, p. 58). So she may be more legible as a symbolic or archetypal figure than as a real woman.

To try to get a clear picture of what the dark mistress (or mistresses) means literally and figuratively to Shakespeare I will take four sonnets from this sequence for close analysis: 127, 130, 144 and 152 (see also Chapter 1 where another of the 'Dark Mistress' sonnets, sonnet 129, is discussed).

Sonnet 127   'In the old age black was not counted fair'

127

> In the old age black was not counted fair
> Or if it were it bore not beauty's name;
> But now is black beauty's successive heir,
> And beauty slandered with a bastard shame;   4
> For since each hand hath put on nature's power,
> Fairing the foul with art's false borrowed face,
> Sweet beauty hath no name, no holy bower,
> But is profaned, if not lives in disgrace.   8
> Therefore my mistress' eyes are raven black,
> Her eyes so suited, and they mourners seem
> At such who not born fair no beauty lack,
> Slandering creation with a false esteem;   12
>   Yet so they mourn, becoming of their woe,
>   That every tongue says beauty should look so.

The sonnet begins with a conventional story form akin to 'Once upon a time', an archetypal starting out, and this theme of origins is repeated later in the words 'creation' (line 12) and even 'nature' (5).

The 'old age' refers to the myth of the Golden Age, the past when things were done differently, better. The poem then outlines a sort of fall.

In Classical mythology black or dark is associated with chaos, the state out of which light and order will emerge (the 'fair'). The opening line of the sonnet enacts the archetypal beginning. From Genesis:

> And the earth was without form, and void; and darkness was upon the face of the deep...and God divided the light from the darkness.   (*Genesis* 1:2–4)

For an Elizabethan reader this was a commonplace and he or she would immediately recognise that the Fall in mind here is that of Adam and Eve. Shakespeare identifies his dark mistress with the Eve of the Creation and Fall, order and chaos, and these, plus reason and confusion, are key topics to which we will return below.

In the poem as a whole, blackness is linked by Shakespeare with chaos. It is further defined by lines 4, 6 and 12, as well as by its antithesis, 'fair'. In these lines blackness is linked with 'bastard shame', foulness, and twice with slander and shame. There could not be a much more damning notice for this shade. With the statement that, in the past, black or dark features were not esteemed as 'fair', the words begin to wobble and slip, especially when we actually reach the word 'fair'. 'Fair' could mean 'light-haired' or 'pale-skinned' and it could generate a pun on 'reasonable' or 'beautiful'. Of course, all of these are intrinsic to the word. However, and crucially, 'counted fair' introduces the keynote idea of moral evaluation. Thus, from the first line Shakespeare sets out the collision of the two modes of aesthetics and ethics, two ideas that reverberate throughout this sonnet and through the sequence overall.

In the past, black or dark women were not considered beautiful. Or if they were, then they were not described as such – no one used the *words* 'fair' or 'beauty' about them even if they found their darkness attractive. The phrase 'Or if it were' seems to be saying that many have been reluctant to admit an attraction for the foreign, the 'other' sort.

But the crucial point here is the word 'name' because in it
Shakespeare sets up the linguistic topic of his essay. As we have seen
in previous chapters he has the knack of simultaneously making a
point and commenting on the making of that point in a metalan-
guage. The word 'beauty' also makes clearer what he means by 'fair'
in the previous line.

The third line begins with a fine ironic, colloquial touch. Sounding
like a chatty bit of tabloid gossip, the speaker announces 'But now'
(and with some irony) the whole order is overturned, so much so
that black *can* now bear beauty's name. Modern readers have to try
hard not to hear a horse in this line, but they may rightly hear a pun
on 'heir' at the end of it and think of sonnet 130 (relating 'hair' to
all the other body imagery here). Dark, or black-haired women may
now be regarded as beautiful.

Black is beauty's successive heir. 'Successive' in the sense of 'next'
implies with some sarcasm that where once beauty was defined in
absolute terms, now as fashion changes anything can become counted
in (this line has illuminating parallels with sonnet 131:12 and the
quasi-sonnets of *Love's Labour's Lost* – see 4.3.249). Beauty has
become subject to fashion and therefore to change, and change is
one of Shakespeare's problem concepts. He is much happier with a
Golden Age of absolutes and definites.

'Successive' in the Elizabethan period also bore a legal connotation
of being legitimate, by right of birth. The idea thus brings out the
irony and bitter spleen of line 4 with its 'bastard shame' (and with
the idea in lines 7 and 8 that, being illegitimate, having no 'name' or
reputation, darkness hides in disgrace). Line 4, and the first quatrain
as a whole, carries the full force of a racial onslaught and its strutting
plosives (black, bore, beauty, black, beauty, beauty, bastard) hammer
out his annoyance. Beauty is slandered ('profaned', line 8) by this
change. 'Beauty', personified as a goddess and pure, is mocked and
besmirched by this surprise reversal.

At the end of line 4 there comes another example of linguistic
slippage while 'shame' keeps up the ethical tone of the poem. On
the face of it, 'bastard shame' seems to mean 'the dishonour of
being illicit or false'. On the other hand it could equally mean 'a
false shame', that dark beauty as the successor to fair beauty need

not feel ashamed now. If we accept this possibility then, ironically, Shakespeare himself is also turning.

But then the next quatrain shifts back to the idea of countering nature,

> For since each hand hath put on nature's power,
> Fairing the foul with art's false borrowed face,
> Sweet beauty hath no name, no holy bower,
> But is profaned, if not lives in disgrace.

(lines 5–8)

Where in the opening quatrain the offence against nature was that dark women could now be esteemed as beautiful, the offence in the second quatrain is that conventionally, dark women have tried to deceive by concealing their darkness through cosmetics. 'Each hand' is a metonymy for 'artificial action': every dark woman could or has, usurped the role of nature, deceitfully making fair what was 'foul'. 'False' and 'borrowed' as well as 'put on' signify a sense of something unwarranted and shallow, we might even say 'unfair'.

Such artifice is to be regarded as an offence against the divinity of Nature. These hubristic women try to play at Nature in their manipulations of it and this resurrects the theme of the Fall here because, having committed this 'sin', beauty is left with 'no holy bower' (line 7), no garden of Eden. Dark women who artificially affected blondeness committed an offence against nature, but further, according to line 7 they have also sinned against language and thereby against the social order it contains. 'Sweet beauty' having 'no name' indicates that by their use of cosmetics, confusing fair and dark, wresting 'beauty' away from its fixed roots, the word 'beauty' has become meaningless. Thus the concept of beauty is 'profaned', reduced to chaos.

After two relatively simple statements in the opening quatrain, the second quatrain presents the most complex sentence in the poem. A convoluted period, its function is, as Stephen Booth points out, to present the grounds on which the opening contentions are made (S. Booth, 1969, pp. 41–2). The two quatrains are joined by the word 'For' which, as well as acting as a connective, strikes a fairly off-hand even simplistic note, as if the facts were almost self-evident, an irony fundamental to the poem's satire.

Dark beauty is the inferior, illegitimate offspring of fair beauty, who is now out of favour and metaphorically disgraced, her virtue and fairness disunited and estranged. Beauty, whether fair or dark, now has no identity.

In line 9 the word 'Therefore' seems at first to introduce a non-sequitur, prompting us to stop reading and turn back. The word carries the same ironic, off-hand tone as 'For' (5), which it echoes. Using a trochaic foot here draws attention to this and to the *volta* here.

The speaker's casual tone advertises the poet's sense of helpless infatuation for his mistress and her modish darkness. 'Eyes' is a metonymy for 'beauty'. Witch-like, her beauty has turned him round, turned him into a hypocrite and he must eat his own words with all the salty irony that this entails.

'Therefore' is therefore pivotal. The sonnet's satire revolves on it:

> Therefore my mistress' eyes are raven black.
>
> (line 9)

The line looks forward, appearing to say 'and so my mistress has made her eyes black', but its main thrust is again ironic, 'and so I have chosen a dark mistress – in spite of my earlier denunciation'.

In line 10, some editors are unhappy with the word 'eyes' and often amend it to 'brows'. Yet the original word makes sense here. As Katherine Duncan-Jones argues in her edition of the Sonnets, the woman's dark eyes are well matched to the current fashion (and they are well suited to her character: see 131:13). 'Suited' thus implies 'appropriate' or 'becoming' as her dark eyes are in line 13 (Duncan-Jones, 1997, p. 368).

His mistress is naturally dark-featured and her eyes seem to 'mourn' or pity those women who 'not born fair no beauty lack'. This enigmatic phrase quibbles on the multiple meanings of 'fair' set up in the first line. One solution is to see it thus: his mistress pitied those dark women (not born light) who have tried to make themselves attractive ('fair') by artificially painting themselves white.

But a converse reading is also possible. His mistress mourns for those women who are naturally light-toned but as this is no longer fashionably beautiful (or 'fair') they still make themselves artificially appealing by use of dark cosmetics – 'each hand hath put on nature's power' (line 5). The poem has made a *volte face*: where in the second quatrain dark women made themselves light-coloured, now blonde women can 'foul the fair' to make themselves dark. The concept of natural beauty is utterly overturned, leaving the poet entirely baffled. The sonnet achieves the same magical confusion as does a Shakespeare comedy of mistaken identity (but a romantic rather than a satirical comedy).

Sonnet 127 centres its discussion on ideas of language, race, and the metaphysics of beauty. The poem must also be seen as writing counter to the spectre of Petrarchism, the old literary convention of courtly love, with its strict ideals and manners (for a Shakespearean variation on Petrarchan manners see *Love's Labour's Lost* with its courtly protocols, in which masks and sonnet-writing figure strongly; see Chapter 6 below, too).

As we have noted above, the 'old age' in line 1 can be thought of as referring to a 'Golden Age', a mythical time conveniently distant enough to represent the lost ideals that an author desires to resurrect or use as a foil to more modern ethics. In this way Shakespeare historicises both the topics of beauty and language. While selfishly clinging to antique modes of ethics, he is still happy in the 'Dark Mistress' sonnets to deconstruct/abandon/criticise the notion of courtly love in favour of a more earthy, erotic desire (flagged up by the adjective 'dark' in 127 and the ensuing sonnets).

In these sonnets, there are still vestiges of Petrarchism, for instance in the accusations of her insouciance and cruelty to the man, and in the moralistic diction (examples in sonnet 127 include 'counted', 'esteem', 'suited', 'shame' and 'disgrace'). He is frequently abusive to her ('bastard' and 'foul'), indicts her for sleeping around, and dwells on her unconventional physical charms. The sensuality of this love is also reinforced in sonnet 127 by the almost haptic alliteration and the geometry of bodily imagery: hand, face, eyes, tongue.

Shakespeare's anti-Petrarchism in the poem is manifested in two interrelated directions, the themes of beauty and of language. His objections are that women can and do artificially distort nature, and that language is being misused to accommodate the shift in taste that now judges black as beautiful. Each constitutes a form of deception.

The poet reluctantly praises black while reproaching the decline in aesthetic standards. This sonnet also revisits some of the well-trodden themes from the plays: notably nature versus nurture (e.g. *The Tempest*, 4.1.188–90) and substance versus appearance (e.g. *Hamlet*, 1.2.85; and see sonnet 83). As Vendler points out, the tenor of this poem, like that of sonnet 20, immediately reveals 'there is something amiss that needs to be explained' (Vendler, 1997, p. 540). The common view is that black is in vogue ('every tongue says so'), and at heart Shakespeare finds himself in an ambivalent position: ineluctably attracted to this woman, he cannot square this with his rigid views on language and aesthetics.

In the past beauty was defined and fixed in essence, or at least he believed it to be. This is the neo-platonic or Classical view of beauty, that what counts as beauty is absolute and fixed by definition based on the properties of a classical ideal of the Golden Age. This ideal is, ultimately indefinable, but may be known intuitively by a certain seer-elite, or so the theory goes. Thus, in this context, Shakespeare claims one of the key attributes of beauty is predefined as 'being fair'. It is, he believes, an a *priori* truth, a point manifested essentially in the pun on 'fair' (fair is fair; compare *Astrophel and Stella*, 5:9–10).

By this definition then, a dark woman cannot possibly be fair, or beautiful. Regretting the new relativism that has crept in, the speaker believes that the current fashion for dark beauty is a contradiction that renders the language of aesthetics meaningless. His anxiety is that if this continues then eventually language itself becomes relativistic, contingent upon taste.

> Sweet beauty hath no name, no holy bower,
> But is profaned, if not lives in disgrace.
>
> (lines 7–8)

This a threshold moment and the implications of it go much further. Shakespeare's neo-platonic view of beauty is further revealed in line 6, 'Fairing the foul with art's false borrowed face'. Plato claimed that all art was imitation of nature and that art thus distorted the truth. Any imitation of nature is therefore a diminution of nature and so a distortion. Shakespeare is ultimately accusing fashionable society, the court (but also women who change their appearance, dark or white), of deception and of sinning against nature.

Yet he cannot escape the fact that he still desires this raven-dark woman. This rankles. Shakespeare does not object to dark *per se* (the joke is, after all, that he is actually attracted to her), only to the relativism behind the change in public opinion. So much so that we may begin to wonder if his protestations are little more than a strategy in his sexual politics. He seems to be saying, 'Yes you're sexually attractive alright but not what anyone would actually call "beautiful".' The imagery of physical parts seems to confirm this, translating a fluffy metaphysical idea into corporeal reality.

Once again Shakespeare situates his theme inside history. Something has gone amiss but his answer is that he is the only one in step: fashionable taste is hypocritical since it did not formerly accept black beauty and women themselves are ever deceivers in covering their pale substance with dark show.

But what precisely was 'dark'? What was Shakespeare referring to in the 'black' of the old age? Perhaps there is a racial dimension in the answer to both questions. The Dark Mistress, counterpart to the Petrarchan ideal and to the fair youth of the earlier sonnets, may be a composite portrait of mistresses, or she may have an exact biographical counterpart, or she may simply be the poet's erotic fantasy (compare *Astrophel and Stella*, sonnet 7, especially lines 1–2).

This is all very well but what did a Renaissance cover-girl look like? Ideally she would have blonde hair and dark eyebrows, while dark eyes were preferred over blue, which were scorned as chilly (green was linked with evil). A chalk complexion flushed with red marked the paragon of beauty. Red hair was a turn-off, frequently associated with evil, and freckles were equally reviled (Caliban is a 'freckled whelp'). The Sonnets' 'dark deceiver' by contrast is likely to be the Shakespearean model behind Cleopatra, Beatrice, Kate, and Romeo's 'hard hearted' Rosaline.

So, in what sense is black or dark significant to the poem or to the woman? The strong phonemes of 'black' allow the speaker to snarl or spit out the word either in jest or denigration. But Shakespeare is not disparaging of her in particular. In fact he is sneakingly attracted to her darkness.

In early modern sonnet sequences it was common for the woman addressed to be exalted through a classical or romanticised name: Laura, Celia, Delia, Diana and so on. Set against this practice it is easy to see how Shakespeare tries to define his anonymous mistress by deconstructing the convention. She is characterised, in part, on the basis of a contrast between the present and the past. Where the young man of the 'begetting sonnets' (1–17) is identified by continuity with the past, here the dark woman is identified by a break with it.

Her unconventional beauty confronts the Petrarchan model of literary beauty. This model crucially entails a courtly or platonic love, whereas Shakespeare draws attention to the exoticism of his woman, a point that ought to eroticise her, but this aspect is diminished by his holding her, up as the incarnation of his essay on ethics and aesthetics.

Instead what comes through is a sort of uneasy admiration. He might have preferred to have framed her within the Petrarchan fable but she repudiates this formulation and he would like to love her for it. She stubbornly refuses to conform to the fashion for painting over darkness, the false beauty. The speaker champions the scorn she addresses to her timorous sisters,

> Slandering creation with a false esteem.
>
> (line 12)

This forthright refusal (he calls her 'tyrannous' in 131:1) as much as her dark elusiveness may be a source of her irksome power over him (A. D. Cousins believes we should even see her as a demonised version of Laura; see Cousins, p. 192).

Shakespeare is 'mad in pursuit' and she has reduced him to confusion and awe. But she is ahead of him. By redefining language she has defined herself and thereby put a stamp on her existence. Shakespeare by contrast comes across here as fossilised and frustrated, or at least one whose protests are an expression of his anxieties with this woman, disguising his real objections (beauty, her looks, and language) in order to vent the pent. Here (and in, say, sonnets 86 and 131) he appears as a weak, helpless middle-aged sourpuss at odds with and a little confused by his sexual world.

For this reason the style of the poem is once again its subject. I argued above that the poem enacts a myth of origins, light emerging from the darkness of confusion, into creation, and it also reveals how quick bright things like the reader can come to confusion.

> And beauty dead, black chaos comes again.   (*Venus and Adonis*, 1020)

Sonnet 127 has so many puzzling plays, ironies, and quibbles – beginning as we have noted with 'black' and especially 'fair' – that the speaker takes the language close to the abyss of meaninglessness. The poem buzzes with pairs of echoing items and homonyms: including shame/disgrace, slandered/profaned, suited/becoming and so on. Our discussion has already noted some of the sonnet's puns, while the antistasis in 'so' (lines 10, 13, 14) and 'mourn' (10 and 13) has the same effect, of exposing the duplicity implicit in the language.

These parallel the perplexity that the poet himself has experienced in trying to understand changes in language and concepts, plus the deceptions inflicted on nature by fashions and art. The poem itself is, of course, an example of 'art's false borrowed face'. And this finally is the root of its decorum of confusion.

Sonnet 127 is powered by a neo-platonic theory of beauty in which Shakespeare's assessment of his mistress is grounded in an antique concept of ideal beauty which is actually impossible to discover on earth. However, in sonnet 130 he presents a ruthlessly empirical viewpoint, owing more to Aristotle than to Plato.

Sonnet 127 witnesses its speaker reduced to confusion and anxiety by its boundaries of history and fables of beauty. Both of these complexities are hinted at in the opening lines of the poem with references to time and to narrative but also to traditional prototypes of beauty. One unmistakable repercussion of this is to question concepts of beauty and to see the notion of beauty itself as problematic, a conclusion inevitably exacerbated by instabilities in the language. Ultimately 127 deconstructs the concept of beauty, an outcome that attracts extreme but curious expression in sonnet 130.

Sonnet 130   'My mistress' eyes are nothing like the sun'

My mistress' eyes are nothing like the sun
Coral is far more red than her lips' red;
If snow be white, why then her breasts are dun;
If hairs be wires, black wires grow on her head. 4
I have seen roses damasked, red and white,
But no such roses see I in her cheeks;
And in some perfumes is there more delight
Than in the breath that from my mistress reeks. 8
I love to hear her speak, yet well I know
That music hath a far more pleasing sound.
I grant I never saw a goddess go:
My mistress when she walks treads on the ground. 12
    And yet, by heaven, I think my love as rare
    As any she belied with false compare.

Sonnet 130 begins by wrong-footing our expectations not once but twice. Clearly it challenges our expectation of the sonnet's conventional exaltation of a woman. Like 127 it contradicts an accepted norm of love poetry. This is a shock and it is swiftly followed by another: the opening line with its sweeping and imperious-sounding rejection, 'nothing like', prompts us to expect the rest to be something of a vindictive swipe from a jilted lover.

But, although we must wait until the couplet for any corroboration ('And yet') this turns out to be the opening of a prolix and back-handed tribute to her beauty. The shock effect is brilliantly and famously unforgettable in its satirical wit.

The sonnet begins, ironically, with a simile – 'ironically' because one of the objects of the poem is to lay open the speciousness of figures of speech when it comes to making comparisons (but compare 49:6). Her eyes are nothing at all like the sun because, for one thing, as sonnet 127 told us, they are dark. If anything they are an eclipse of the sun. The stress is on the deictic 'My' because one of Shakespeare's goals in this poem is to stress the individuality of this woman, her uniqueness, at the same time as he showcases his own ingenious approach here. It also stresses the individuality of the poet

('I' or 'my' appears eleven times). The cadence set up in this opening is important too in introducing one of the key structuring principles of the whole sonnet (the other is difference). The shock here and in almost all of the first twelve lines repeatedly subverts any notions of idealism.

The word 'nothing' reverberates through the first line, painfully perhaps, and then beyond, through the rest of the poem. If we set a caesura after the word 'nothing', the line changes slightly in its purport. Her eyes are like two nothings, two noughts, which is in fact a bit like *two* suns.

What something will come of this nothing? The opening line initiates a catalogue of inverted comparisons detailing her body parts. Next, in line 2, her lips, which when it comes to redness are actually paler than coral, a pallid orangey-pink. Paleness here seems less modishness than a mode of sickness. Coral lips are associated with passion: lusty Venus has coral lips in *Venus and Adonis* (line 542). Note that line 2 opens with a trochee, the brief change of rhythm serving to draw attention to the list and the discreteness of each item.

Line 3 reverses the previous disapproval of white. Disdained in lips, paleness is devoutly to be approved in a woman's breasts. But his love's breasts are by comparison a dingy brown. The banality in the opening to line 3,

> If snow be white . . .

naturally serves to strengthen the assertiveness of the rest of the line (whose conclusion is strictly speaking a non-sequitur). Perhaps there is a pun on 'dun' too, done, finished, drooping. She is beginning to sound like a peaky hag.

Line 4 parallels the syntax of line 3, and the isomorphism here again underlines the naming of parts. It starts to sound tired, banal, merely trotting out an inventory of items. The down-beat tone deepens the manner in which Shakespeare describes her hair, creating an even more prosaic effect. He does not simply say 'she has black hair', but 'black wires grow on her head'. The anatomical detail of 'wires' and growing now makes her appearance resemble that of a madwoman or a freak.

Shakespeare's rhetorical technique here is that of the antiblazon. In our earlier discussions of sonnets 20 and 106 we have referred to the literary device of the blazon, popularised by followers of Petrarch, cataloguing and eulogising the physical attributes of a woman.

More popular in the early Elizabethan period, examples of blazons include Sir Philip Sidney's sonnet 91 in *Astrophel and Stella*, and Shakespeare's own sonnet 99, which uses some of the comparisons satirised in sonnet 130 (see Chapter 6 for more on blazons). Spenser's *Epithalamion* (1595) details the sort of stock similes that Shakespeare parodies,

> Her cheeks like apples which the sun hath rudded,
> Her lips like cherries charming men to bite,
> Her breast like to a bowl of cream uncruddled,
> Her paps like lilies budded...

(lines 172–6)

In part then, Shakespeare deconstructs what had by the late 1590s become a hackneyed contrivance. Sonnet 130 represents an attack on tired literary hyperbole as much as on this woman's darkness. The second quatrain tests this almost to destruction: 'Roses' takes up again the cliché of redness and is in itself a romanticised image of unattainable loves, virginity, concealment and so on. The speaker has seen them both red and white and damasked, that is, dappled with pink as in the damask variety of rose.

As a verb, 'damasked' also contains within it a hint of 'demasked', which may be a faint clue to Shakespeare's verbal trickery at work here (echoed in 'belied' in line 14). More on this later. 'Damasked' can be read as 'woven' and he sees 'no such roses' woven in her cheeks: her cheeks are not imitations in art but real. The cadences continue, introduced in line 6 with the phrase 'But no'. Her cheeks are as pale as her lips.

By this point in the poem it comes as little surprise that the woman's breath is less fragrant than 'some perfumes' ('some' injects a note of wry irony). For the Elizabethans 'reeks' did not

necessarily imply 'stinks' or 'stench'. It could mean more neutrally, 'emanates' (for this neutral sense see *Love's Labour's Lost*,
4.3.136–7). But it helps if we take 'reeks' literally. However, the
contrast here is not as strong as in the earlier lines – breath rarely
smells as sweet as perfume, except perhaps in the sinuses of the
infatuated.

This easing of tone is even more noticeable in the third quatrain
as the mistress takes on an even more commonplace character.

> I love to hear her speak, yet well I know
> That music hath a far more pleasing sound.
>
> (9–10)

Line 9 begins like so many of the preceding lines with an eminently
simple statement of fact, perhaps underlining the speaker's plain
talking or coolly rational presence of mind. It begins too with a
positive, both about her and about himself: 'I love to hear her speak.'
It is as though after all the persistent cadences he is trying to reassure
us of his connection with her. And then, perhaps inevitably, the tone
turns downward after the word 'yet'.

Once again, as in lines 7 and 8, the comparison is not unreasonable.
Very few of us have the speech of music. Line 9 and the third quatrain
as a whole tells us more about the speaker than about his mistress.
He *knows* 'well' (9), *concedes* that he 'never saw a goddess go' (11)
and is *aware* that his mistress is a walker on the earth not an airy
fairy ideal. Importantly it is not just the woman but the observer
himself who has his feet planted firmly 'on the ground'. The crucial
point is that unlike the over-romanticised Petrarchan poets he has
no illusions about this woman or about love itself. He sees the skull
beneath the skin.

When in line 11 the speaker admits that he 'never saw a goddess'
he expresses his own as well as the woman's ordinariness. It is another
of the poem's deconstructive cadences and another expression of
difference.

Line 12 starts by recapping the opening words of the sonnet with
a clearer stress on possessive 'My'. The anacoluthon (inverted syntax)
of the line ensures that the final word of the *douzaine* is the solid
'ground'. The third quatrain is more concerned with what the mistress

does rather than how she looks or smells. The syntax turns the sense of these lines towards a high expectation that he does after all see her as a goddess and the slight caesurae after 'mistress' and 'walks' lift that expectation – only to see it dashed into the bathos of 'treads on the ground'. Rather than glide, or however else goddesses move (I too never having seen one), she plods conventionally, commonly.

'And yet'. The whole poem is made to wheel completely round with the appearance of these words, the fulcrum at the start of the couplet. They suggest, among other things, a sudden rise in tone, a change of view perhaps,

> And yet, by heaven, I think my love as rare
> As any she belied with false compare.

(13–14)

'By heaven' jokingly connects briefly with the recent allusion to a goddess, and forces another caesura. The immediate effect is to lighten the tone in readiness for the even greater admission that his love is as rare as any other over-praised woman she has unmasked by comparison.

Additionally, 'by heaven', as an oath, seeks to convey a sense of honesty and commitment. It adds weight to the *volta* in the preceding words of the line, like a great intake of breath before the tremendous assertions in the couplet. And yet ironically 'heaven' momentarily connects her with the sun he had dismissed in line 1. He acclaims her as 'rare', marvellous, or exceptionally precious, uncommonly exquisite. Adopting the 'I' again reminds us of the subjective here; this is what she is uniquely to him.

This subjective, deictic point is also underlined in the final line. He implies that the use of literary figures, especially conventional similes, is specious, impotent in trying to encapsulate the vital essence of the woman. Her reality, or essence, transcends or evades mere literary devices, which have tended to deceive by misrepresenting the real woman through distorting conventions (the 'strained touches rhetoric can lend'; 82:10).

She might be ordinary in physical terms, she is certainly real, but she exposes the crass idealisation of woman and the deception that have ornamented love lyrics. 'By heaven' and 'rare' indicate that having dismissed all the comparisons in terms of physical beauties he treasures above all that essential anima in which she surpasses all others (in the final line 'she' is stressed just as 'My' is in the first line). With the final line the poem spirals away from a description of the mistress, transposing her into a discourse on language, literary tropes and the poet himself.

In general the two ruling strategies of sonnet 130 and the 'Dark Mistress' sequence as a whole are difference and cadence, each of which is predicated on the other. Difference attempts to flatter her as unique and special to the speaker, while cadence (and bathos) attempts to degrade her as common. Together, the rhythm of these two sets out to possess and control her. We can see how they operate in 130.

Sonnet 130 presents a series of discrete utterances connected through the subjective 'I' and the object, the mistress. The architecture of the poem shows vestiges of the Petrarchan 'octave + sestet' structure but in effect it is organised more as 6 + 6 + 2, the first six lines focusing on the woman's physical appearance and the second six on what she does, the expectations of pleasure.

The main tensions of the poem arise from the comic gap between our expectations of the standard rhetoric of love lyrics and their deconstructions in the withering reality of the woman. It also generates important comic energies through other shocking contrasts, such as the different perspectives on the mistress herself and the contrast between the speaker's assertions and his own underlying uncertainty, which in effect subverts them.

The poem consists of nine sentences, mostly direct statements. The two simple assertions that open it are mirrored symmetrically in those two in lines 11 and 12 that close the *douzaine*. The baldness and frankness of these catalogue statements are accentuated by the large number of end-stopped lines, closing off each statement as if refusing to flow. This projects an image of a composed and imposing speaker (contrast the speaker in sonnet 129).

To avoid the risk of the list becoming monotonous Shakespeare includes a couple of anaphoric, conditional constructions in lines 3 and 4. These slight hesitations combine with one or two uncertainties in the poem; for example, 'some perfumes' in line 7 and 'I grant' in line 11 illustrate the subjectivity of the poem in ironic contrast to its overall tone of assertiveness. All of these factors build up a feeling of uncertainty that becomes more apparent in the couplet.

Accordingly, one of the poem's key words is 'false' in line 14 since it points to themes of deception, honesty and substance apparent in the Sonnets as a whole but especially in the politics of love in the 'Dark Mistress' lyrics. Another interesting lexical item here is the adjective 'pleasing' (line 10, which echoes 'delight' in line 7)' since it refers to the bodily pleasures, the poem's starting point, and relates to the poet's sensual expectations.

As an antiblazon, sonnet 130 dramatically explicates the idea that the sonnets to his mistress(es) are not to be taken in any conventional sense as complimentary. Beginning with and repeating the possessive pronoun 'My' demonstrates that he thinks of her protectively, perhaps selfishly but above all manipulatively. The speaker may even adopt this strategy as a means of fantasising her commitment to him (though in act she has her 'bed vow broke'; 152:3). As a whole the poem stresses the subjective nature of his perception of her ('I think', 'I grant' and so forth).

An antithesis to this subjectivism is the poem's strong sense of material or external reality. There is a substantial preponderance of concrete nouns – no less than twenty – against only three abstract nouns. By the same token the verbs are predominantly active and indicative (nineteen altogether, against two subjunctives). Both of these elements work to secure a sense of material realism. On the other hand the paucity of tropes has the effect both of keeping the poem bare and simple-sounding while imposing its decorum. The final thrust of the couplet is to undermine the efficacy of conventional literary tropes in favour of something more scientific–empirical.

Shakespeare situates his mistress solidly on this sub-lunar, sub-solar earth.

> My mistress when she walks treads on the ground.

(12)

Most of the concrete nouns emerge from the catalogue of mock comparisons, conventional points of symbolic beauty: eyes, lips, breasts, hair and so on. The poem moves from her eyes and colours, the scent of perfume and breath, plus sounds, to the idea of the deportment of goddesses and women. The two dominant vowel sounds of the piece are /aɪ/ and diverse 'o' sounds (more, snow, some …) so as she 'moves' past us through the poem we again repeatedly hear the speaker sigh.

Sonnet 144　'Two loves I have of comfort and despair'

In 1598/9 two of Shakespeare's sonnets – 138 and 144 – were printed in a small anthology of poems called *The Passionate Pilgrim*, ten years before they were published in the1609 Quarto. Both exhibit some variations between the two printings, and modern scholarship tends to regard the 1609 version as a conscious attempt at artistic revision rather than as a printer's emendation (though whether the hand behind such revision was Shakespeare's it is not possible to say). Unlike the case of sonnet 138, sonnet 144 displays fewer substantive variants between the 1599 and 1609 printings and perhaps the most thematically significant is the change in line 13 of 'not' to 'ne'er'. The implications of this possibly authorial revision are discussed below.

> Two loves I have of comfort and despair,
> Which like two spirits do suggest me still:
> The better angel is a man right fair,
> The worser spirit a woman coloured ill.　　　　4
> To win me soon to hell my female evil
> Tempteth my better angel from my side,
> And would corrupt my saint to be a devil,
> Wooing his purity with her foul pride.　　　　8
> And whether that my angel be turned fiend
> Suspect I may, yet not directly tell;
> But being both from me both to each friend,
> I guess one angel in another's hell.　　　　12
> 　Yet this shall I ne'er know, but live in doubt,
> 　Till my bad angel fire my good one out.

The sonnet begins in a beguiling simplicity. A rather prosaic statement in line 1 outlines an antithesis of two lovers, one giving him
comfort and the other despair. It hardly hints at the intense and
complex drama to come. However, the cadence at the end of the first
line does parallel the forthcoming descent into hell-like torment.

The syntax of the first line is carefully arranged to enact this
ominous cadence. The subject 'I' is dislodged to take refuge between
the two off-rhymes 'loves' and 'have', foregrounding from the start
the key phrase 'Two loves', with all its varied internal and external
possibilities. The 'Two loves' may refer to two actual lovers, of course,
a man and a woman. Metaphorically, they may be forms of love
(for instance, *agape* and *eros*, platonic love and lust) or the speaker's
bisexual inclination. Equally the 'Two loves' could be allegories of
virtue and sin, or metaphorical projections of his own complex
divided psychology. And so on.

The terms 'comfort' and 'despair' have strong theological associations. 'Comfort' refers to the idea of salvation of the soul (as well as
to everyday ideas of respite and repose) while 'despair' in Christian
orthodoxy is the unforgivable sin that would preclude salvation (with
its connotations of hopelessness and anguish).

Comfort from what? Although the two words may look like opposites they point fundamentally in the same direction, towards that
deep anguish and its causes adduced in the rest of the poem. Together
they function as a sort of hendiadys on the speaker's discordant and
overwrought psyche.

After the mystery invoked by the enigmatic opening, the second
line begins to narrow down its scope. Following the metaphorical
possibilities in the 'Two loves', the simile in line 2 directs the reader
towards the drama presented in the main part of the poem, centring
on the rivalry of two spirits. The word 'suggest' can mean 'persuade'
or possibly 'provoke' and thus the line introduces the important
seduction theme as well as suggesting through the word 'still' that the
oppression by these spirits is unrelenting (and the idea is reiterated
in the word 'Yet' in line 13).

On the one hand, and with deep irony, the spirits urge him to
be still, taking up the 'comfort' idea. Yet he hardly needs this sort
of advice, his mind churning over. Conversely, we can read 'still' as

an adverb, the two warring spirits relentlessly provoking, harassing him. A further reading of 'still', and one that fits aptly with this sonnet as a whole, is 'inscrutable'. In other words the speaker becomes increasingly uncertain about his relationship with these two spirits, unable to fix precisely where he is with either of them. So, by the third quatrain, the beleaguered and frustrated poet can only 'Suspect' and 'guess', 'live in doubt' (line 13).

The two loves may thus be physically real, two rival lovers, as well as opposing metaphorical stances. Both literal and metaphorical positions dovetail eloquently within the poem. Line 3 takes us further towards the impression (if not the reality) of coherence:

> The better angel is a man right fair.

'Better angel' looks to be a bundle of tautologies, at first anyway, but a glance at line 14 reveals that the poet is using 'angel' in the sense of 'spirit' in a range of meanings, while 'right fair' suggests 'truly just or excellent' as well as literally blonde.

Line 4 extends the original simplistic antithesis by contrasting the good man with a 'woman coloured ill'. No extra marks for spotting the misogyny here, another expression of this simplism and of the poet's bitter jealousy. 'Coloured ill' refers to the mistress's familiar dark features but its moral pitch is equally unmistakable. It alludes to her fondness for painting and deception, warping and tainting the truth that the poet is so desperate to reach. But 'ill'? The poet vents his scathing resentment and frustration by reviling her as dark, ugly, wicked (carried into the next line with the metonymy of 'female evil').

As line 5 makes clearer, the poet locates himself at the centre of a psychomachy. This medieval device derives from early modern theatre and morality plays in which the hero's dilemma, a choice between good and evil, is dramatised formally into the two figures of a good and a bad angel, each of which argues the case for their favoured course of action. Good examples of this can be found in the anonymous allegory *Everyman* (*c.*1500) as well as in Marlowe's *Doctor Faustus* (*c.*1588).

In the conventional psychomachy the two spirits battle for the soul of the hero, and here, in the second quatrain, the poet/speaker depicts himself in the centre of such a deadly struggle, 'To win me soon … Tempteth … would corrupt … Wooing'. This sense of a lethal battle helps give the poem its danger, urgency and dynamic, of course, but it is not strictly as the speaker represents it or himself – more on this below.

> To win me soon to hell my female evil
> Tempteth my better angel from my side.
>
> (lines 5–6)

Line 5 firmly makes explicit the allegorical strain of the poem. This develops from the word 'hell' since the hell he refers to is less the literal medieval hell of fire and brimstone than the mental, the anguish and despair, that has driven the poem, and these become more expressive in the couplet (and see line 12). The form of hell envisaged and experienced here is again reminiscent of Marlowe's *Doctor Faustus*, in which Mephistophiles, when asked by Faustus about the whereabouts of hell, famously explains that hell is less a place than a state of mind, a torment,

> *Mephistophiles*: Why this is hell, nor am I out of it.
>
> (*Doctor Faustus*, 1.3.78, A-text)

The idea of winning intensifies the rivalry within the triangle and, with it, the speaker's view of the antagonists becomes more intelligible. His bitterness becomes more definite as he spits out his loathing at the 'worser spirit' in infuriated words, 'evil', 'corrupt', 'devil' and 'foul', while the repetition here of 'my' reveals how deeply personalised the rivalry has been made: 'my female evil', 'my better angel', 'my side' and 'my saint'. All of the situation seems to have been channelled pathologically through his personality.

'Side' in line 6 refers to allegiance, of course, and thus to the sonnet's theme of loyalty. It can also mean 'circle of influence' and even 'heart'. The 'female evil' threatens to rip him from his side, from his heart, even to using unfair diabolic means of seduction. In effect the poet accuses her of being a succubus and one so powerful that she could corrupt even a saint 'to be [or become] a devil' (7). The idea reveals the full gravity of the terror and jealous detestation in which he holds his ex-mistress – but also of his helplessness.

It is no surprise that the second quatrain is where the poem's rhythm becomes disrupted, through a most complex periodic sentence. Lines 5 and 7 are both hypermetric lines ending on feminine, unstressed syllables, and lines 6 and 8 begin with trochees, expressing his anger through discordant metre. This antagonism is also expressed visually in line 8 where 'purity' and 'pride' are held in tension, contrasted symmetrically, wrapped in the terminal antonyms of 'wooing' and 'pride'. 'Foul pride' sourly acknowledges that it was actually the woman's show that first drew the speaker to her. Note too how the alliteration on 'purity' and 'pride' draws together the two ideas for a formulaic contrast: the saintly man's simple, passive innocence; the witch's deviously ensnaring vanity.

The word 'And' at the start of line 9 signals the (weak) *volta*, a bridge from his fears in the octave to a state of knowledge in the sestet. The conjunction 'whether' introduces the incertitude to follow: whether my angel has been turned into a fiend, I can only suspect. He has no confidence of certitude if his earlier suspicions have in fact been realised, that his 'angel' has been 'turned', translated into a fiend. To the torment of losing one or both 'loves' is added the limbo of not knowing where he is with either of them or where they are with each other.

The octave was very much fuelled by strong emotional dynamics: the speaker's desire for his angel, his aversion to his 'devil', and her lustful craving. The sestet now switches attention towards the theme of knowledge and incertitude, flagged up by the word 'Suspect' in line 10 (which also draws out the idea of jealousy). The sestet has much to do with the speaker's strong subjectivism, of attitudes, suspicion, fear, uncertainty. He cannot 'directly tell' (decipher or recognise what they are up to; line 10) but he plants the idea firmly in our minds at least, so that we share the suspicions of the fallible narrator, who keeps us at arm's length, controlling our knowledge too.

In the lead-up to the couplet, the jouncing alliteration and slightly irregular rhythm of line 11 begins to mince the sense, deepening the ambiguity.

But being both from me both to each friend.

Alternative punctuations or stresses in this line can produce a range of radically different interpretations. I go for the reading that since both of these two lovers are now separated from the poet/speaker each has befriended the other. In the realm of love and lovers this is one of the most desperate of discoveries or admissions. He has lost both. Worse, since they have now apparently become lovers they have devastated his comfort. The fact that 'friend' is made to rhyme with 'fiend' serves to deepen his outraged sense of theft.

He surmises that his better angel, his male love and former comfort, is now in hell, the realm of that other, the female devil. 'Hell' is a pivotal word here and the spectre of Marlowe hovers over this line too. Hell may refer to the medieval 'hell's mouth', the physical cave-like apparatus to which the sinners in a morality play would be consigned as punishment for sins on earth. The male angel may already be in that hell. They are each a punishment of the other. Or rather he may share the speaker's mental torment, the anguish produced by the sort of unsatisfactory affair the speaker himself had suffered with this woman.

The fate of this former angel would thus parallel that of the speaker himself, finding himself the next victim to this *belle dame*, next in a series of hapless males lured to their doom (see line 5). In 129:14 hell is linked with lust, and the gaping hell's mouth here may refer to the woman's vagina, an idea which finds some support in the final line. He torments himself with the suspicion that they are already locked in intercourse. But it is only his guess. His torment, begun by the dark corrupting mistress, is flexed by his own suspicion and jealousy.

In line 13, 'Yet' makes the end of the poem remember its beginning in 'still', the ongoing, unfinished agony, and one which is reactivated in the word 'ne'er',

> Yet this shall I ne'er know, but live in doubt,
> Till my bad angel fire my good one out.

(13–14)

The poem has centred on three strong and interrelated strands and these converge in a headlong collision in the couplet. These can be logged as: the speaker's psychological degeneration; the flux and complexity of the relationships involving the three loves; the drive to resolve these strands by certainty of knowledge, a drive constantly frustrated.

'Ne'er' also captures a sense of the speaker's being adrift, which is strengthened by the idea of living in doubt (significantly, the 1598/9 *Passionate Pilgrim* version prints 'not' instead, which carries none of this psychological energy). He is forced into a predicament of perpetual open-endedness, of being undefined by love, disengaged. This is the madness in the brain that leads him to the curse that he utters in the final line.

'Till', in the final line, is a half-echo of 'tell' and 'hell' resonating back through 'devil', 'ill', and to the start with the ironic adverb 'still' in line 2. It is the antithesis of those other temporal adverbs 'Yet' and 'ne'er'. By imposing a sort of terminus on his misery, the word 'Till' holds out the uncertain forlorn prospect of closure at last. Lodged at the core of his perverse hope is 'fire', recalling the earlier references to hell. The line is not easy, not because of any indeterminacy so much as the dazzling multiplicity of meanings there. To come at it from a slightly different angle, his urgent desire seems to be that the mistress will grow tired of the friend, 'fire' or exhaust him, and then expel him. Clearly he hopes the bad angel will purge the good, making clear to him the error of coupling with a woman so 'coloured ill'.

His allusion to 'ill' also offers an elucidation of this purging since it suggests the bitter expectation that the once-good angel will inevitably contract venereal disease (corrupting the 'purity' of 'my saint'). The final line plays on a popular Elizabethan proverb, that 'one fire drives out another', and thus through the burning irritation of the hellish disease (or its mercurial remedy) he will be repulsed from her vagina. From *Coriolanus*,

> *Aufidius*: One fire drives out one fire; one nail, one nail.
>
> (4.7.54)

And Lear uses the same expression for the expulsion of foxes from their earths (5.3.23). As we noted in sonnet 20 the *'one* thing' represented the penis and this offers another possible reading here: that the speaker hopes the arrival of another penis will drive away the first.

Thus sonnet 144 ends with a faint squeak of optimism, of 'comfort', perhaps unintended. In spite of the speaker's anguished confusion he still acknowledges some affiliation with her in describing his mistress–whore as '*my* bad angel', in spite of her betrayal. But, and maybe more significantly, despite the wily cunning and pollution from this female evil and the duplicity of the 'man right fair', he still thinks of his male lover as 'my good one', holding out the possibility of redemption and reinstatement, the triangle come full circle.

Among the most striking features of this tormented, inchoate and highly charged sonnet are its intense drama and the deft way in which Shakespeare causes its focus to shuttle freely between its internal and external dramas. At the same time this dynamic keeps us firmly aware of the poem's important theme of division, which is also a recurrent concern in the plays.

It is a brilliantly provocative, challenging and elusive poem. Shakespeare's most overtly dramatic sonnet, it is a theatre of unfulfilled desire located on the theme of possession and the unresolved stresses between the 'fair youth' and the dark mistress. The poem brings out the full moral weight of the epithet 'dark' that has hovered indistinctly in previous sonnets. The grit in the oyster is that he thinks of her as a lust-driven, scheming temptress, preying on an unassuming, innocent male (she is thus in many ways a projection of himself).

The sonnet originates in a love triangle that becomes subsumed into a richly multilayered discourse and its mysteries are nuanced through an increasingly complex and sceptical epiphany. But all we ever get is a part of the story. It remains an elliptical fragment, a gnomon, while its full drama seems to be permanently turning away from the reader.

In spite of this ellipsis the poem also gives the impression of being a brilliantly full production both of intense interiority and of expanding interpersonal horizons. On the one hand it casts new light on the paradoxical phrase 'master mistress' in sonnet 20, and that sonnet's reference to 'controlling' contrasts significantly with the great sense of impotence in sonnet 144.

On the other, sonnet 144 is situated within a sequence of sonnets charting a dynamic of relationships. It is an integral part of the cycle of madness alluded to in sonnet 129, the fever of desire, lust, gratification, shame and back to desire. It extends 143's account of an irresponsible mistress abandoning him for his rival, and he achieves a momentary reconciliation in sonnet 145 when the woman's cruelty abates in 'saved [his] life', though it falls short of actually affirming love for him.

The most obvious tensions in the poem arise from the speaker's awareness of the other lover, another of the shadowy presences that so often haunt the consciousness of the Sonnets. Sonnet 144 is one of the frankest in terms of love and sexuality. As Edmundson and Wells remind us, 'Although the poetic voice of Shakespeare's Sonnet 144 is caught up in a love triangle, at least the underpinning dynamic is one of potential physical sex . . . ' (Edmundson and Wells, p. 151).

The wits of the speaker are feverishly unstable, constantly mutable inside an intricate crucible of sensitivities and possibilities that impinge upon him. We see the indirect consequences of 'lust in action' and along with it the stings of jealousy within its shifting reference points. The speaker constantly agonises about what the two lovers are up to while out of his sight, and torments himself with the worst possibilities of his imagination. The woman has repudiated him and his desire mutates painfully into anxiety.

The jealous insecurity of Othello is evoked here again but there are other plays ghosting the lines of sonnet 144. For example, we can see Shakespeare repeat the pattern of close male friendship disrupted by rivalry over a woman in *The Two Gentlemen of Verona*, *The Two Noble Kinsmen* and *The Winter's Tale*. However, in the Sonnets he presents a detailed examination of male/female sexuality stripped mercilessly bare of any theatrical fluff. In sonnet 144 the sexuality is self-wounding as well as misogynistic as he scrapes out the minutiae of despair and insanity.

The common critical view of the mistress(es) in these later sonnets is that she is a whore. Sonnet 144 does nothing to disabuse this view since the speaker treats her as a sexual thing and yet one whose promiscuity he is unable to come to terms with.

However, as we noted above, the poem's 'two loves' may be interpreted in a variety of ways, literal as well as figurative. The 'female evil' can be treated as referring to the speaker's own feminine side, and that therefore the two loves refer to sexual tendencies and to complex types of internal responses to these. If we see the poem on these metaphorical terms then we are likely to see it in reactionary terms, as a struggle to subdue feminine cunning in favour of reasserting more hard-line masculine aggression. Whether we read them literally or figuratively the poem's wretched, brooding jealousy certainly speaks of bitter misogyny.

Conventionally, the essence of the psychomachy is choice. Yet as we have seen, the speaker has no true choice for he has no effective will or power. The poem is a cruel parody. The conflict, so brilliantly sketched here, is left unresolved and the speaker himself remains stranded in a state of paralysis, impotent and uncertain. Bereft of his lover, his friend, certitude and security, the final torment is to be afflicted by the ambiguous possibility of hope,

> Yet this shall I ne'er know, but live in doubt,
> Till my bad angel fire my good one out.

>   (13–14)

Sonnet 152   'In loving thee thou knowst I am forsworn'

With sonnet 152 – and what Helen Vendler describes as 'this enormously comprehensive poem' – the collection comes to an unsettling finish, combining self-laceration, confusion, opprobrium and something approximating self-knowledge in which the three major themes of the sonnets as a whole – love, time and art – come together in a foment of self-knowledge.

> In loving thee thou knowst I am forsworn,
> But thou art twice forsworn, to me love swearing;
> In act thy bed-vow broke, and new faith torn
> In vowing new hate after new love bearing.   4
> But why of two oaths' breach do I accuse thee,
> When I break twenty? I am perjured most,
> For all my vows are oaths but to misuse thee,
> And all my honest faith in thee is lost;   8
> For I have sworn deep oaths of thy deep kindness,

Oaths of thy love, thy truth, thy constancy,
And to enlighten thee gave eyes to blindness,
Or made them swear against the thing they see;   12
   For I have sworn thee fair – more perjured eye,
   To swear against the truth so foul a lie.

The two opening lines introduce two of the poem's major preoccupations: the complex interplay of verb forms and the compulsive
returning to the word 'swear' and its derivatives, forsworn, swearing,
swear, sworn, together with its important cognate, 'oaths'. The
speaker's obsession with these words runs parallel to his infatuation with the inconstant woman at the centre of his tormented
love.

They are important words because behind their descriptive function, telling us that the two of them have lied, hovers their perform-
ative role: that is, if someone swears or promises to do something
then the act of swearing, vowing, or making an oath ought to commit
them to doing it. For the Elizabethan, too, swearing an oath carries
with it the force of a solemn religious duty, a sacred commitment.
The speaker's charge is that his mistress's promises are worthless.
Most hurtful of all, she has broken her 'bed-vow'.

That said however, their exact current relationship is ambiguous.
When he declares 'In loving thee', it is not clear what 'loving' means.
Does he mean it in sonnet 151's sense of making physical love and
therefore having the possibility of a reciprocal 'loving'. Or is this
'loving' a one-way matter, in the sense of desiring, of his being smitten
with her, and the love is now unrequited? If we see sonnet 144 as
the end of the same affair then we are more likely to see this 'loving'
as a desiring. The poem begins in something of the uncertainty that
has afflicted the speaker himself.

The first line at least sets the poem and this 'loving', whatever
it is, in the present. From this present moment the poem zigzags
unsettlingly back and forth through time and the nervy interplay of
verb tenses and temporal imagery, to the distant past and the more
recent past (but not, significantly, to the future). Their loving seems
to entail their dishonesty too since both have become forsworn or
perjured. We are likely to feel that their love has been made possible

through this portal of cheating and, as sonnet 151's bawdy makes clear, it is eroticised by it too.

In loving his dark mistress (though he has 'sworn thee fair'; line 13) he has become dishonest, he lies and probably cheats on another (many readers see this as a reference to Anne Hathaway, seemingly abandoned in Stratford; see 145:13 again). Strangely he speaks with indignation of a deflowered virgin lately jilted. He has lied but she has lied twice and out-cheated him in the very act of affirming her love to him (2). In the chiastic structure of the opening two lines the speaker tries to establish this partial alliance as a pair of liars. Line 1 begins with a present participle ('loving') and ends with a past participle ('forsworn') while line 2 reverses this syntax as a striving to establish a mutuality between them (this strategy forms one of the strong undercurrents of the sonnet). Note too the supple flexing of tenses in these opening lines as a sort of web in which to enmesh her and the reader.

However, the word 'But' in line 2 signals an important difference and hence the speaker's claim to the moral high ground. She is 'twice forsworn', having cheated or lied. Lines 3 and 4 purport to explain what these broken vows are but the details are private and obscure. To whom was the 'bed-vow' made? Some commentators see this mistress as having cheated on her husband in adultery, breaking a marital 'bed-vow' (recalling sonnet 116's 'marriage of true minds'). But she may not be married and the bed-vow simply a promise of fidelity made to the poet/speaker.

This promise is now broken ('new faith torn': line 3) in the act of discarding the speaker – 'vowing new hate'. In the 'act' of intercourse with a new lover she has broken faith with the previous one. The thick repetition of 'new' in lines 3 and 4 satirises the woman's inconstancy in her search for novelty (the anaphora here is replicated in the repetition of 'For' in lines 7, 9 and 13, and 'thy' in line 10). The speaker accuses his mistress of breaking her loyalty to himself, breaking faith with him and thus implying dislike of him after 'new love bearing'. The 'new love' refers either to what was newly created ('bearing') with the speaker at that time or to the new love she has now found, repudiating the speaker.

After a confusing maze of vows and breaches the mist begins to clear a little from line 5 as his anger abates. However, the cadence created by the word 'But' in line 5 also signals a change to a more sardonic tone (amplified by the use of a rhetorical question here). Stephen Booth points out the pulsing alliteration of the /b/ words in this section of the poem – and this seems to stress the force of the speaker's betrayed feelings (S. Booth, 1969, p. 72).

He pretends bafflement rather than shame at the idea of her breaking only a couple of vows to his twenty. Yet even this admission is tempered when in the next seven lines he puts the blame for his falsehoods at her door. It is because of her that he is the worst offender.

> When I break twenty? I am perjured most,
> For all my vows are oaths but to misuse thee.
>
> (lines 6–7)

The essence of line 7 is not easy to unearth since its crux is 'misuse', a slippery verb. One likely meaning of the line is that 'all my promises were made from selfish motives: to exploit you'. Another is that all of his testimonies had been intended only to 'misuse' her in the sense of to disgrace her or perhaps to misrepresent her to others and so deceive them about her true nature. Lust, which was the root of perjury in sonnet 129, is the prime mover here too.

The second quatrain ends with a dramatic charge: all of his proper trust in her has been utterly lost (alternatively, all of his basic or sincere trust in anything has been exhausted or wasted through her selfishness). The word 'lost' reverberates beyond the line, thus connecting with the sestet and the details of this 'misuse'. First, he claims to have affirmed her profound kindness (though significantly 'deep' can also mean 'cunning'). He has further incriminated himself (he argues) by swearing her love, loyalty or honesty and constancy (even though we might reasonably assume that 'constancy' would entail love, loyalty and honesty).

In line 11 he claims to have further embellished her image ('enlighten thee') by making eyes blind to the reality of what she is. Not only has he made others turn a blind eye to her true nature, he has lied to persuade people of the opposite of her nature, presumably by advertising the qualities set out in lines 10 and 11: deep kindness, love, and so on. In the next line he dismisses her sneeringly as 'the *thing* they see'.

A. D. Cousins makes the interesting point here that in playing on blindness the speaker aligns himself with Cupid, love's agency (Cousins, p. 206). In this context, sonnet 152 thus echoes the idea at the end of 148, that love is both blind and blinding,

> O cunning love, with tears thou keep'st me blind,
> Lest eyes, well seeing, thy foul faults should find.
>
> (148: 13–14)

The speaker has used language, or art in general, to deceive others and perhaps to deceive himself,

> For I have sworn thee fair . . .   (line 13; see 147:13)

Out of his own sense of loyalty (or lust most likely) he has represented her as a fine, honest, trustworthy, virtuous woman. The notion of foul parading as fair is one of the major preoccupying acrimonies of the 'Dark Mistress' sequence. He may even somehow have passed her off as blonde ('fair') in the face of the startling fact that she is dark, once more 'Fairing the foul with art's false borrowed face'.

Such is the power of art, and such is the power of what he now presents as a witch-like woman. She has not only sworn false oaths of love to him, then cheated on him, but she has induced him to prostitute or adulterate his art in her false service. This is the fault that has perjured him most in his own eyes, that is, his 'more perjured eye' (with that blatant pun on 'eye'). 'So foul a lie' refers both to the woman herself (yet again) and to his sin of lying vainly on her behalf.

The poem as a whole is a sort of anagnorisis, or epiphany, and with lacerating self-knowledge his newly enlightened eyes make him see once more how he has been taken for a fool, perjured as much by lust as by the duplicity of this shrewdly riggish woman. She has run him ragged. Cupid may be blind but he also has the effect of making lovers blind too, blind to the faults of the beloved. This poem marks the point of the end of that delusion, though not perhaps the end of the infatuation.

Sonnet 152 has a strong narrative thread hinting at a history of the lovers' relationship. The narrative though is much disrupted of course and scattered throughout its various verb tenses and forms along with its temporal imagery. It speaks of a past of vows and oaths, of swearing, bed-vows and infidelity. The speaker covers up what he sees as her lapses and inconstancy, including a more recent love-making that may actually only be desire. He loves someone who dislikes and has betrayed him and yet he has lied for her. In her deviance and unpredictability she represents another reworking of the problem of mutability.

As well as the play of time and tenses, their changeable relationship is also traced in the wry dialectic of prepositions: 'to' (lines 2, 7, 11, 14), 'for' (lines 7, 9, 13) and 'against' (12 and 14). At the same time the highly important anaphora of lines 7, 9 and 13 gives the impression of an engrossed mind seeking to find explanations, struggling to unravel the riddling course of this baffling love that has suborned him (these three lines represent the three replies to the question posed in lines 5 and 6).

As another symptom of this tormented consciousness the poem has a shifting, inchoate structure. It is disrupted in part by the almost palpable tensions in the turmoil of his manipulating this woman to conform to his ideal, in a language that equally refuses to correspond. The effect created is that of a disjunctive recollection which is trying to establish even tentative connections. The speaker accuses his mistress of breaking oaths, and then there seems to be the counterweight when he accuses himself of lying. Yet his accusations are no more than cleverly-turned indictments that originate in her own sinful actions. She has made him into a bad type, or so he claims.

A superficial reading may suggest the poem has little to do with love, just some grouchy remarks from an old 'ex'. But if 'loving' in line 1 refers to a current relationship then it also refers to a heavily one-sided love. It is the 'despair'-love again spoken of by sonnet 144, despair because it is rooted hopelessly in hope – and desire, of course. These are the forces pulling and building the poem's tensions as the 'love' itself, plus hope, despair, desire and resentment, fray the speaker's thinking. As ever, Shakespeare drops in markers at key turning points in the poem, markers we feel that are only half-noticed by the speaker himself – 'lost' (8) and 'lie' (14) – while significantly lodged between the two and bridging them is his 'blindness' (11).

We may also suspect that in this jumbled history of their affair the passionate instant of her 'bed-vow' – if it were ever made to him – offered him the brief illusion of success and peace, a 'bliss in proof'. But since this is now a despised memory, a very woe, he is filled with recrimination and he turns the instant against the dark woman, so that line 3 bitterly spits out a hurtful reminder that their love was nothing more than a crude bond of physical sex, no sooner enjoyed than discarded, and 'new faith torn' (3).

This breach seems to be the signal for an open season on lying. The readiness of both sides to perjure brings to mind the candour of sonnet 138 where

> On both sides thus is simple truth suppressed
>
> (138:8)

There it is the sweet core of a very wry farce. Sonnet 152 lacks the redeeming heroism of sonnet 144, so in 152 it is the cold heart of a rancorous vexation of strategy and cunning.

The repetition of 'For' in the sense of 'because' (in lines 7, 9, and 13) points to the purposive, scheming nature of the speaker's words and his attitude towards this bed 'thing' (12). It creates the impression of a man seeking to trace and untangle his own motives out of self-deception. He now claims to have lied strategically, to make her look better, in order to 'enlighten' her in other eyes,

> Oaths of thy love, thy truth, thy constancy.
>
> (11)

By addressing his words directly to her he seems to be striving to impress her with his devotion. And as I have noted already, his admission of lying tries to draw a concord with her, the other liar, a partner in perjury.

On the other hand this actually demonstrates his desperation. The transparency of his devices makes him appear piqued and feeble and as the subordinate party his admission transforms him into a hostage to her mercy. In so doing he submits himself to the flux that is implicit both in the mistress's attitude to him as well as in his own language.

As such, this sonnet presents an interesting comparison with sonnet 116, 'Let me not to the marriage of true minds'. Sonnet 116 essentially defines love as a constant, 'an ever-fixed mark'; otherwise it is not love. Its uncompromising attitude contrasts with the mistress's view of love as adventitious and language as its flexible conspirator. Behind his words in 152 the poet/speaker does still appear to believe in concepts of fidelity and love. But where sonnet 116 is an idealistic view, 152 is scrupulously realistic, its eyes opened to the problematics and dynamics of a graphic relationship (and these problematics and dynamics are the real sources of the poem's energies).

We are probably as far from Petrarch's idealised virgin as we can get without losing sight of her completely. That said, there is still something of the cruel insouciant *donna* of the courtly tradition and the speaker betrays much of the devoted imprecating suitor (lines 9–12 try to project an image of the humble knight avowedly in selfless fealty to his lady; and compare 141:10–12). He has lied to defend her in others' eyes. On the other hand he has also lied to 'misuse' her. He is here practically swearing at this promiscuous wanton, whose denial gives him a highly erotic charge.

His anger is another source of dynamic in the poem. Once again his ire is that of the jilted lover, angered by his own folly which is in thrall to lusty desire. His rancour is apparent in his confrontational address even though the poem's rhythmic structure militates against it to some extent. Alternate lines are hypermetric, extended by an extra unstressed (or 'feminine') syllable, the effect of which is to impart a softening cadence at the end of those lines.

Sonnet 131 makes a similar charge of inconstancy against his mistress,

> Thou art as tyrannous, so as thou art.

(131:1)

She resembles all beautiful women thus, even though she is dark and does not conform to the customary model of fair beauty. Throughout the 'Dark Mistress' sequence there runs the common theme that she repudiates not only any idea of this model but even the possibility of having a definition imposed on her by a man. Like 152, most of these sonnets project the view that she is elusive and this elusiveness includes her refusal for either herself or her love to be defined in masculine terms. For example, 127 declares that 'beauty hath no name', while 147 says 'I have sworn thee fair . . . '.

In sonnet 130 the mistress tries to evade such definition, such 'false compare', but the speaker of 152 aims to reverse and inhibit this freedom. He cannot possess her on his own terms and the opening quatrain to sonnet 152 expresses his despair at her protean ineffability. This is, of course, an expression of his frustration as elsewhere he peevishly abominates her as the 'bay where all men ride' and the 'wide world's common place' (137:6 and 137:10). And the word 'foul', routinely associated with the woman, runs intermittently through the 'Dark Mistress' sonnets (for instance, 127:6, 137:12, 144:8, and 148:14).

The throng of present participles at the start of sonnet 152 collaborates with this view of her nature as evasive and actively in flux: loving, swearing, vowing, bearing. In addition, the sonnet's imagery of time supports this slant since the speaker seems sensitive to her unsettling unpredictability. He tries to envisage his love as a rock of constancy against her whirlpool of instability.

Conclusions

One of the most enduring impressions to arise from the 'Dark Mistress' sequence of sonnets is how problematic the speaker finds his relationship with the woman herself or perhaps with women in general. He spends much of his time complaining about her and about their relationship. Although this sequence does not directly present a narrative in itself, it does offer vivid glimpses of the intriguing narrative that lies somewhere behind it and which provoked the writing of the poems.

The speaker is simultaneously both deeply attracted to and repelled by his dark mistress. At the centre of both impulses is her 'darkness', which makes her for him exotic and erotic in her difference from other women. He complains of her promiscuity and her infidelity, eulogises her physical attractiveness and dwells on his addiction to her sex and to sexual pleasure in general (the poems tend to focus on her physicality, body parts, and genitalia in particular). All of these are, at different times, sources of deep pleasure and dire despair.

She is characterised for him by difference from others and distance from himself. These two elements are the source in the 'Dark Mistress' sonnets of much of their tension and movement since they supply the main rhythms of fluctuation and cadence. Fluctuation relates to the dynamically changing distance between the two figures while cadence refers to the speaker's repeated failure to find harmony in his relationship via sole possession of this elusive woman. An important theme of the sequence is instability: the speaker's desire for the woman is sharpened by the fact that as a lover she is not fixed and her love is maddeningly contingent. Once again this instability is a source to him of both magnetism and intimidation.

Changes in complexion and tastes in fashion are featured in the themes of deception and of mutability in human affairs. Shakespeare uses the dark mistress and their relationship here as the basis for an exploration of the metaphysics of beauty and of the limits of language in its capacity to express and define beauty. In striving to express the key values of love as loyalty, honesty and constancy and to define the experience of beauty, art and time, the speaker is repeatedly characterised by failure, his frustration manifested in the refusal of language to delimit and define, a sharp correlative of his inability to dominate and control 'his' mistress.

Further Research

Carefully read sonnet 145, 'Those lips that love's own hand did make', and try to describe how the relationship of the lovers differs from or resembles that in sonnet 149. What is the effect of the final line in 145? With specific reference to lines 9–12, what thematic links does it have with sonnets 144 and 146? What do you notice about the metre of sonnet 145 and how does it affect an interpretation of the poem?

PART 2

THE CONTEXT AND THE CRITICS

6

Shakespeare and the
Elizabethan Sonnet

Miracle of the world! I never will deny
That former poets praise the beauty of their days;
But all those beauties were but figures of thy praise,
And all those poets did of thee but prophesy.
Thy coming to the world hath taught us to descry
What Petrarch's Laura meant, for truth the lip bewrays.
Lo! why th'Italians, yet which never saw thy rays,
To find out Petrarch's sense such forged glosses try.

(Henry Constable, *Diana*, 1592)

The sonnet is both a poetic form and an ideology. It is as much an ideology as that of the contemporary Court whose culture, with major upheaval in the ruling elite and the rise of humanism, it reflects. This chapter and the next will look at both aspects, the literary form and the ideology behind it.

Shakespeare the poet

Although Shakespeare is now deservedly famed as a dramatist it is just as feasible to consider the ambitious young Will Shakespeare of the 1580s as bent on making his living as a poet. His narrative poems, *Venus and Adonis* (1593) and *The Rape of Lucrece* (1594), were both huge commercial successes and even if he had written nothing more than the *Sonnets* and this non-dramatic verse he would still top the list of great Elizabethan poets.

Although there remain thirteen known copies of the original 1609 Quarto edition of the *Sonnets* and several manuscripts of sonnets copied out 'by other hands', no one knows for certain when the sonnets themselves were composed. They were probably written over a period of perhaps ten or more years beginning in the early 1590s and circulated in manuscript form among a close circle of friends. The earliest mention of Shakespeare as a writer of sonnets is that by Francis Meres in his *Palladis Tamia* (1598), describing him as

> hony-tongued *Shakespeare*, witnes his *Venus* and *Adonis*, his *Lucrece*, his sugred Sonnets among his private friends, &c.

In conspicuous contrast to the success of the two narrative poems, only one edition of the *Sonnets* appeared in Shakespeare's lifetime, a point which some readers have taken as evidence that the book was unauthorised and subsequently dropped. Curiously the collection appeared long after the Elizabethan vogue for sonnets had peaked between about 1594 and 1596. This was the second great flourishing of English sonnets in the sixteenth century – the first having been in the 1550s when the sonnet form was introduced from Italy by the poets Thomas Wyatt and the Earl of Surrey.

The sonnet form presents a formidable challenge to a poet. Its deceptively slight fourteen-line structure presses poetic resourcefulness to its limits, within a traditional framework imposing very strict conventions on metre, rhyme, and structure as well as on subject matter. However, within the limits of this compact yet versatile format Shakespeare not only excels but brilliantly advances its possibilities, exploring new potentialities in verse through a fresh and complex range of experiences and intimate voicing.

Shakespeare's sonnets embody a search for the limits of what words can do and a love of the perfect imperfections of language. At the same time we see an increasing concern in their author with the intricacies of language and especially with silence and deception: in other words a movement towards circumspection, a language that does not give the game away. They show a fascination with the kind of expression that conceals expression. In essence it is the language of silence and a silence that brings language closer to thought.

The sonnets have all the verbal pageantry and eloquence of the plays and yet unlike in the plays we have a close intimacy with Shakespeare himself. In the absence of explicitly biographical material, this is probably the closest we can come to the voice and mind of the man, so close in fact that we almost hear him breathing and observe his mind at work.

The sonnet form

The sonnet has proved to be one of the most versatile and enduring forms in English poetry. Long enough to admit development of form and thought, allowing variation of tone and mood, it acutely tests a poet's virtuosity and resources in terms of rhyme and metre. It is at the same time compact enough to compel brevity, subtlety and compression of thought or theme, and to exercise intensity of feeling. The sonnet is an enticing challenge to any poet and most poets have tried their hands at it.

Introduced into English poetry during the sixteenth century the sonnet form's popularity rests on its capacity to combine formal discipline with a high degree of flexibility. However, it rigorously taxes the poet to concentrate his thought, wit and invention into a condensed framework which thereby enhances those thoughts. The versatility of the sonnet form is attested by the wide variety of subject matter, shades of thought, tones, attitudes and voices which have been borne on its slender proportions: pre-eminently love, of course, but also the metaphysics of existence and time, issues of identity and sexuality, the politics of seduction and deception, allegory, decorum, ornament, and poetics itself.

The name 'sonnet', like the form, originates in Italy: *sonetto*, a small sound or short song. So trendy was this import that at first Elizabethans began to apply the label 'sonnet' to almost any short lyric (for example, John Donne's *Songs and Sonets* does not actually contain any sonnets). Poets and publishers gradually settled to the sonnet as fourteen lines. Basically consisting of fourteen lines (even if Shakespeare's sonnet 99 has fifteen lines and 126 has only twelve), usually in iambic pentameter (though sonnet 145 is octosyllabic), the sonnet in the hands of sixteenth-century English writers soon developed a broad range of rhyme schemes. However, the three most common forms of the sonnet in sixteenth-century literature are: the Petrarchan or Italian, the Spenserian, and the Shakespearean.

The Petrarchan sonnet, named after the highly influential Italian poet Francesco Petrarcha or Petrarch (1304–74), consists of two principal parts: the first eight lines comprise the octave or octet and are rhymed *abbaabba*, followed by six lines, the sestet, usually rhymed *cdecde*. This affords a symmetry of two quatrains plus two tercets. While the rhyme scheme of the octave is usually fixed, the sestet presents some variation. In general terms the octave sets out the problem or issue and, after the *volta* or 'turn around', the sestet resolves it. The sonnet's importation to England by the poets Thomas Wyatt (*c.*1503–42) and the Earl of Surrey (*c.*1517–47) heralded the first wave of fashion for the form. The following example is by Wyatt and is a quite exact translation of Petrarch's sonnet 'Io non fu' d'amar voi lassato unqu'anco' (though in the sestet Wyatt adopts a pattern of *cddcee*).

Was I never yet of your love greved,	*a*
Nor never shall while that my life doeth last;	*b*
But of hating myself that date is past,	*b*
And tears continuell sore have me weried.	*a*
I will not yet in my grave be buried;	*a*
Nor on my tombe your name yfixed fast,	*b*
As cruell cause that did the sperit son hast	*b*
From th'unhappy bonys, by great sighes sterred.	*a*
Then, if an heart of amourous faith and will	*c*
May content you, withoute doing greefe,	*d*
Please it you so to do this to doo releefe:	*d*
I, othre wise, ye seke for to fulfill	*c*
Your disdain, ye err, and shall not as ye wene;	*e*
And ye yourself the cause therof hath bene.	*e*

English sonneteers

The first major collection of Wyatt's and Surrey's verse was the highly influential *Songs and Sonnets* of 1557 (quoted by a gravedigger in *Hamlet*, 5.1.62–95) and more commonly known as *Tottel's Miscellany*).

While Wyatt is normally credited with introducing the sonnet to the English with his translations of Petrarch (following his return to from Italy in 1527), it was Surrey who brought about two important innovations to the lyric. He adapted its rhyme scheme to produce the distinctive pattern of three quatrains and a couplet, imposing the *volta* between lines twelve and thirteen, a pattern frequent to both Spenserian and the Shakespearean sonnets. Where Edmund Spenser (1552–99) employs the rhyme scheme *abab bcbc cdcd ee*, the Shakespearean sonnet generally uses *abab cdcd efef gg* (though both varieties may impose a *volta* anywhere within the three quatrains: for example, compare the position of the *volta* in Shakespeare's sonnets 86, 117 and 121). This scheme stimulates a great variety in the development of the argument or problem, with considerable flexibility through the three quatrains, closing with a resolution or epigram in the couplet. In general terms, the rhyme scheme and the position of the *volta* usually mirror the structure of the poem's argument or theme. The English couplet, with its tightly closed rhyme, moralising or summarising, offers a strong sense of closure within the sonnet architecture.

In his Preface to the Signet edition of the *Sonnets*, W. H. Auden believed the Shakespearean sonnet to be the easiest pattern for English poets because, unlike Italian, the English language lacked the great breadth of rhymes required to fit the demanding Petrarchan pattern. But he also held that the Shakespearean ran the risk of slipping into a mere twelve-line poem with a couplet after-thought (although he scorned the couplet as a 'snare' for the weakest, lame sort of ending, he praised Shakespeare for managing to avoid this trap).

One trademark feature of the sonnet introduced by Surrey was the adoption of iambic pentameter, which developed out of his translation of part of Virgil's *Aeneid*, in which he sought a modern English counterpart for the Latin dactylic hexameter. This was taken up by all the major Elizabethan poets and became the standard English metre for the form over the next four centuries.

Another unusual feature of the Petrarchan sonnet adopted by English poets needs to be mentioned here, the device known as a 'blazon'. Deriving from a French heraldic term (a shield or coat of arms), the word describes verses that catalogue and extol parts of the woman's body, pedestalling the unattainable woman and emphasising the breadth of her beauty (while opening up interesting erotic possibilities). The opening quatrain of Petrarch's canto 292 is a fine example,

> Gli occhi di ch' iò parlai sí caldamente,
> e le braccia e le mani e i piedi e 'l viso,
> che m' avean sí da me stesso diviso
> e fatto singular da l' altra gente;

> (*The eyes of which I spoke so warmly,*
> *And the arms and the hands and the feet and the face*
> *That are separated from me,*
> *Making me a lonely soul among other people.*)

Shakespeare both makes use of the blazon in sonnet 20 (see Chapter 1) and satirises it in the antiblazon in sonnet 130 (see Chapter 5).

A sonnet then is a highly sophisticated form usually consisting of fourteen lines, whose rhyme scheme represents a deep-seated sense of structure the essence and heart of which is the *volta*. The quatrain, with its cross rhymes (*abab*), represents a double-edged experience: on one hand a solid poetic unit but, within a Shakespeare sonnet, the three quatrains tending to be thus separated from each other phonetically.

One mark of Shakespeare's gifted facility with the sonnet is the variation he brings to the positioning of the *volta* and thus to the internal structure. He does this by cutting across the formal internal structures set up by the quatrain blocks, within the conventional rhyme scheme, and he does so using a variety of rhythmical, phonetic and syntactical devices. For example, he makes flexible use of enjambement and punctuation, or extends the syntax and themes across the blocks, or simply uses carefully deployed bridging words.

Shakespeare's sonnets are distinguished by their fluctuating logical and syntactical structures, through which he achieves a fine discursive fluency. In general terms, while maintaining a robust internal structure, his sonnet will typically exhibit two vigorous movements: one lateral, a momentum forward through the 'narrative' sequence and its discursive markers (and, so, for, yet etc.), while the other is centripetal, pressing within itself by its system of internal rhyme and reference.

Petrarch's sonnets to his beloved Laura are very much bound up with their origins in twelfth-century courtly ballads of the troubadours and reach even further back to Classical models of love and love poetry, particularly Ovid (see below). At a time when English verse was emerging tentatively from the strictures of medieval poetics, Petrarch and his Italian contemporaries offered more than just a handy new love lyric: they opened up the brave new world of the Renaissance, already under way for two hundred years in Tuscan and Lombardian cities. George Puttenham, critic and theorist, humbly acknowledged the enormous cultural influence of Italian writing on Wyatt and Surrey,

> Having travailed into Italie, and there tasted the sweete and statelie measures and stile of the Italien poesie, as novices newly crept out of the schooles of Dante, Aroste, and Petrarch, they generally pollished our rude and homely maner of vulgar Poesie from that it had bene before, and for that cause may justlie be sayd the reformers of our English meetre and stile. (*The Arte of Englishe Poesie*, 1589)

While Petrarch was by no means the only Italian influence (for instance, Dante – especially his *New Life* – Burchiello, Della Casa and later Pietro Bembo and Torquato Tasso were immensely influential) he effected the greatest impact in terms of the sonnet. English verse imported not only the sonnet matrix from Italy but also a great range of feature themes inherent in it. The Elizabethans owe to Petrarch much of the now-familiar scenario of courtly love and lovers which they espoused: these include worship of the idealised unattainable woman, her fatally cruel beauty, the spurned and melancholy lover, antitheses of hope and despair, and of entreaty and reproach, the themes of human mutability, language, and poetry itself, and so on. The most intense passion of his verse lies in the not-having, and what makes Courtly Love perfect is the unattainableness of its object, making every sonnet a compressed drama of emotion.

The sonnet sequence

Later Elizabethans also fervently adopted the sonnet sequence, and the craze for sequences marks the second major wave of sonnet writing in England. Thomas Watson's *Hekatompathia*, of 1582, is a series of a hundred connected 'sonnets' emulating Petrarch's 'Laura' poems but it is not strictly a sequence (and the individual lyrics themselves are eighteen-liners). Beginning with Soowthern's *Pandora* in 1584, a sonnet sequence is an extensive series of sonnets loosely unified by common central characters, situation, or themes that develop through an unfolding if loosely structured narrative. A sequence is usually connected through the author's pervasive voice, vision and distinctive language with, for instance, recurring diction and imagery.

A sequence is thus more than simply a collection of sonnets. On a deeper level it attempts to penetrate and develop the thematic potential inherent in the shared scenario, its ideas, or its allegorical and symbolic fields. On these terms, Shakespeare's Sonnets do not as a whole constitute a sequence, though as I have pointed out in the 'Introduction' there are three micro-sequences, namely sonnets 1–17, the 'begetting' sonnets addressed to a young man; 78–86, the 'Rival Poet' group, addressed to a patron; and 127–52, the 'Dark Mistress' group, addressed to one or more women.

Thomas Wyatt was most instrumental in establishing the reputation of Petrarch through his painstaking translations from the Italian. Aware of the vibrant presence of Italian literary culture, Wyatt strove (somewhat clumsily) to produce an accurate English imitation of his models. In general he was also following the practice of Italian sonneteers, who were very much conscious of their own sophisticated work as rooted in a tradition extending back to ancient Latin precursors. They tended to regard literature as an art which aspired to a higher plane of intellectual engagement than the commonplace issues which typified English airs, ballads, rounds, catches and part-songs, the staple poetic fare of the early sixteenth century. Before Surrey and Wyatt, English poets inherited little beyond what came through from Chaucer.

English sonneteers tended at first to lack the technical panache of the Italians, and settled for translations and imitations of the Italian sonnets (between 1560 and 1600 there is an enormous volume of translation from the Italian). Another snag was the linguistic differ-ence mentioned above: the Italian sonnet with only two rhymes in the octave (*abba abba*) requires an abundance of rhyming words for its musicality. For the Italian sonnet the risk lies in over-ornamentation, while for its English devotees it lay more problematically in finding an intricate and vigorous poetic idiom. Instead they began to develop their own versions of it.

With Sir Philip Sidney and his *Astrophel and Stella*, of 1591, the major sonnet sequence of the century, the English poets determ-ined to strike out in their own vernacular style. The earlier verse of Wyatt and Surrey, however, continued to display vestiges of medieval metrical devices, with their pausing metre and ponderous measure. Sidney, on the other hand, imparted to his sequence a dazzling freshness of intensity, stamped with his own colourful genius. Although Sidney early acknowledged Petrarch as his master and often adapted translations of him, he gradually came to scorn what he described as 'filching from Petrarch's pen', encouraged by his athe-istic Italian friend Giordano Bruno, whose *Eroici Furori* is dedicated to satirising the great Florentine (Shakespeare's Sonnet 130 and John Donne's 'Eighteenth Elegy' are also examples of this reaction against Petrarchism). Sidney signals this change in the opening sonnet of *Astrophel and Stella*, after recognising that 'others' feete still seemed but strangers in my way',

'Foole,' said my Muse to me, 'looke in thy heart and write.'

(line 14)

Sidney's sequence of 1591 heralds the second flowering of the English sonnet following a gap of some twenty-five years during which the form had lapsed in popularity. *Astrophel and Stella* announces the coming of age of Elizabethan verse prosody. Like Henry Constable in *Diana* (1592) and Michael Drayton in *Idea* (1593), Sidney's sonnet sequence finds its initial inspiration in Petrarch's *Rime*, but imposes his own more urgent mode of experience and discovers a uniquely personal imagery, and rhetorical devices in which to craft it.

Succinct, assertive and energetic, Sidney adopts a scrupulously Renaissance attitude towards decorum (more on this below). He visits the familiar ingredients of the knight seized by love, rebuffed by his lady, permitted a kiss and then sorrowfully parted from her. Yet Sidney constructs out of the conventional a genuinely deep-felt emotion and, as one critic has argued, 'Throughout *Astrophel and Stella* we feel the pressure, direct or indirect, of complex actual circumstances, of a day-to-day life in which the poet and his loved are enmeshed' (Prince, p. 19). Passion directed through propriety leads ultimately to virtue.

> There shall he find all vices' overthrow,
> Not by rude force, but sweetest soveraigntie
> Of reason.
>
> (*Astrophel and Stella*, 71:5–7)

Although Sidney signals the resolute reaction away from Petrarchism his sonnet form still owes more to the Italian than to the Shakespearean, adopting the octave-plus-sestet pattern. He follows and breathes new life into Petrarch by dramatising and thereby objectifying a more personal mode of poetry.

In his own sonnet sequence, *Orchestra*, Sir John Davies (1569–1626) offered Sidney as an exemplum of a poet who begins as an imitator of models and who transforms them into his own,

> Yet Astrophel might one for all suffice,
> Whose supple Muse chameleon-like doth change
> Into all forms of excellent device.
>
> (*Orchestra*, stanza 130)

Though not published in his lifetime Sidney's great 108-sonnet sequence (composed *c.*1582) circulated widely at Court in manuscript and was enormously instrumental in inspiring younger poets to try their hand at what is a most demanding enterprise. The high point in the fashion for English sonnet sequences occurred between about 1592 and 1596 and as well as those of Drayton and Constable the major sequences of this period include Samuel Daniel's *Delia* (1592), Thomas Lodge's pastoral sequence *Phillis* (1593), and Spenser's *Amoretti* (1595).

The end of the century and the end of the sonnet (for now)

In sonnet 82 Shakespeare expresses the uncomfortable suspicion that he is losing touch with poetic fashion and that his own style has become outmoded,

> Finding thy worth a limit past my praise,
> And therefore art enforced to seek anew
> Some fresher stamp of the time-bettering days.
>
> (82:6–8)

This may involve some posturing by Shakespeare in regard to his patron and friend but it also depicts his sharp awareness of the competitive literary scene and of the constant need to produce fresh new work ahead of his eager rivals.

One of these pressing rivals was John Donne (1572–1631), the last major poet of the Elizabethan period, though his own sonnets were actually written during the reign of James I. His work also marks the summit of anti-Petrarchism: a reaction against what poets had come to regard as verse of stock emotional gestures, cooked up in a conventional formula of the recalcitrant mistress plus the inconsolable lover, garnished with a series of hackneyed emotional gestures and his 'majestic manner' of hyperbole and oxymoron. Characteristically, Donne recognises the fading idiom and recoils from it, injecting into love poetry fresh resources of imagery – a new poetics which is vital and robustly confrontational.

While appropriating the Shakespearean model, Donne's sonnets represent a new strain of individual intensity, narrower in the range of its experiences yet still brilliantly vivid in imagery, with the focus of the sonnet now shifted to the world of private ideas and spiritual ordeal.

Although writing relatively few sonnets, Donne at least opens up the form to new areas of experience and interest, and Milton (the pre-eminent English practitioner in the Petrarchan sonnet) refines it still further, exercising a great influence on the Romantics, particularly Wordsworth and Keats, in whose hands the sonnet undergoes a major renaissance.

The Court and courtly love

The two most common and related fictions in Elizabethan love poetry are the pastoral and courtly love conventions. In the pastoral, derived from Classical precedents, there is an idealised myth of a golden age, unfettered by worldly problems. If the poet-shepherd's suit to his shepherdess-lady is successful then nature blossoms but if he is rejected then usually the whole of creation shares his sadness. Successful love, such as that proposed in Marlowe's 'The Passionate Shepherd', is identified with a return to some Edenic paradise. Sometimes, however, as in Thomas Lodge's 'Melancholy', this custom is exploited to present a contrast between the lover and his world, pointing up the unnatural disjunction of his condition:

> The earth, late choked with showers,
>   Is now arrayed in green;
> Her bosom springs with flowers,
>   The air dissolves her teen;
> The heavens laugh at her glory,
> Yet bide I sad and sorry.

(lines 1–6)

The brooding Lodge is not just rejected but also alienated, set outside of nature's world (see also Spenser's sombre, political pastoral, *The Shepheardes Calendar*).

In the other major fiction, the poetic convention of courtly love, the woman is the lady of the court and her suitor adopts the role of servant. The origins of this genre (also known as *fin amors* and *amour courtois*) can be traced to the chivalrous lyrics of the troubadours of twelfth-century Languedoc in southern France, regularised and sharpened through Petrarch's adaptations (the origins of which go back even further to cultish worship of the Virgin Mary).

The rise of the sonnet as the major love lyric is very much bound in with the development of the complexities of the courtly-love myth, and it is important to remember that courtly love was probably only ever a literary feature. From the beginning of troubadours' songs of courtly love, subtle distinctions are made in the nature of *amors*. For example, the literature identifies two major forms of love: *agape*, a spiritual self less love, typical of the love of God for mankind or that of a parent for a child, a Platonic and non-physical love; *eros*, self-centred Ovidian lust and sensuality. A shrewd lover will of course protest to his lady that his love is more of *agape* than *eros*. Shakespeare's sonnets take up and explore these themes (*agape* in the 'begetting' sonnets and *eros* in the 'Dark Mistress' group) and their complex variations, as well as other forms of love.

In his *De amore* (*c.*1186), Andreas Capellanus codified conventional responses of aristocratic courtship. This code sets out to impose a system of social behaviour on the conduct of love, the dominating idea being the social and psychological control of sensual desire. At the heart of this code is the concept of the *domna* or courtly lady, who seeks to establish a distance between herself and her suitor, through which the latter is coerced into cultivating dignity and grace, by a process of patience and humility, and he is at length rewarded by some token of her favour. Courtly love or *fin amours* is the delight in intimate courtship arising from the subordination of promiscuous erotic love by rationality.

Influenced most notably by Aristotle's ideas on civilised aristocratic behaviour, Capellanus stresses a principle of conducting one's affairs according to moderation, with an awareness of one's own and others' needs, tempered by the exercise of reason. His thirty-one rules of chivalric manners address both male and female sides of courtship. The lady must be worthy of her suitor's praise (which ought not to be excessive) and must neither use unkind words nor deceive through false promises.

In early versions of *fin amours*, no physical contact was permitted, but later troubadour song allowed kissing and mild embracing. The central principle in all of this essentially literary convention is the idealisation of the woman: passive, she is adored from a distance and while the man cannot bear to be out of her sight he does not approach her directly, but displaces his feelings into composing love songs. Consequently the lovelorn fellow wastes away through sleepless nights, despair and illness. For the man in courtly love the true course is painful and frustrating (or 'tyrannous', as Shakespeare's sonnet 131 declares). Even sickness can overtake the suitor and he becomes subject to the mercy of the woman (sonnet 118 articulates this position while *Venus and Adonis* singularly reverses the scenario; for a fuller treatment of these elements see Chaucer's *The Knight's Tale* and his *Troilus and Criseyde, Books I and II*).

Courtly love is chiefly the domain of the young and is the love appropriate to aristocratic society. With its mannered process of love-making it is less a set of rules than a matter of decorum, and shares with Renaissance humanism the emphasis on reasoned behaviour towards other rational individuals. As a literary code its origins can be traced back through to Hispano-Arabic writings and Ovid (chiefly his lusty *Amores*), and back to ancient Greek elements. As a literary genre it reaches the Elizabethan poets via the influence of Petrarch and Dante (whose tormented sonnets explore his frustrated love for the famously unattainable Beatrice).

Most of the medieval traditions of courtly love were fervently taken up and given a personalised perspective by Petrarch in his intimate *Il Canzoniere*. His poetic style and ideological values, even if at first warmly embraced by English imitators, become in Shakespeare's *Sonnets* the object and instruments of his satire on love, particularly in the 'Dark Mistress' group of poems.

Although by the Elizabethan era the tradition of courtly love was effectively dead, even as an exclusively literary concept, poets still shared its elements with their readers as if it were extant. In the opening sonnet of *Astrophel and Stella* Sidney elucidates his motives in writing:

> Loving in truth, and faine in verse my love to show,
> That she (deare she) might take some pleasure of my pain;
> Pleasure might cause her reade, reading might make her know,
> Knowledge might pitie winne, and pitie grace obtaine.
>
> (lines 1–4)

To win her pity at least would be a start. She is distant, perhaps unapproachable and he composes a love song which can express his love and frustration, hoping to entice through the mind and the spirit.

Sidney's sequence, of the 1580's, attempts to re-enervate Petrarchism by injecting it with verve and tension. By 1596, with the popularity of the sonnet sequence on the wane and with it the Petrarchan 'principles', Sir John Davies publishes his parody of *fin amors* in *Orchestra: A Poem of Dancing*.

> The courtly love Antinous did make,
>   Antinous, that fresh and jolly knight,
> Which of the gallants, that did undertake
>   To win the widow, had most wealth and might
>   Wit to persuade, and beauty to delight:
>   The courtly love he made unto the queen,
>   Homer forgot, as if it had not been.
>
> (stanza 5)

Given that in Homer's *The Odyssey* the three suitors are trying to bed Penelope, paragon of marital chastity, this verges on a burlesque of courtly love. By contrast to what Davies understands as Homer's coarse and direct manner, his own style, in a poem about order and harmony, is both stately and decorous, thus in part sharing some of the original ideal.

Shakespeare has many examples of courtly love in his dramatic work, either affirmed or satirised; for example, *Love's Labour's Lost* is clearly a court play, in which Navarre and his friends undergo the vexing labour of teasing women; Ferdinand in *The Tempest* must convince Prospero of his worthiness for Miranda under ordeal (and respect her 'virgin-knot'); and Romeo and Juliet share a sonnet, each speaking a quatrain in the very familiar language of Petrarchan lovers, until symbolically their individual loves become unified when they share the third quatrain and the couplet (1.5.93–105). The wooing scene at the end of *Henry V* (5.1) closely mirrors the sparring of courtly love, even while Henry the warrior humbly excuses his soldierly clumsiness in the game of wooing. *Twelfth Night* exhibits strong elements of courtly love while *Hamlet*, *The Taming of the Shrew* and *Measure for Measure* all play against features of the tradition.

The Sonnets too are predicated on a full awareness of the courtly-love tradition, even though they rarely try seriously to sustain it. Most often Shakespeare makes use of the idealised codes of Petrarchism to undermine them, countering and subverting the social power embodied in their ideology. Although Petrarchism is ostensibly concerned with maintaining some ideal of the purity of love, Shakespeare often reveals that its concern with power, discipline and denial (or at least postponement) can be a powerful source of eroticism too.

But there are times when he writes even with some nostalgia for that 'antique pen', in the 'chronicle of wasted time':

> I see descriptions of the fairest wights,
> And beauty making beautiful old rhyme
> In praise of ladies dead, and lovely knights.
>
> (Sonnet 106:2–4)

On the other hand, this also proves technically valuable as a rod to beat those budding young rivals who 'lack tongues to praise'.

Although the concept of courtly love was obsolete well before the end of the sixteenth century – except as a sometimes useful device – it had a great impact on the theme and attitude of its love poetry and on its techniques, and some of these will be discussed in Chapter 7.

7

Humanism, Rhetoric and Poetry

> Let us conclude with the dignitie and excellency of knowledge and learning, in that whereunto mans nature doth most aspire; which is immortalitie or continuance . . . we see then howe farre the monuments of wit and learning, are more durable, than the monuments of power, or of the hands.
>
> (Francis Bacon, *The Advancement of Learning*, Book I.viii.6)

The sixteenth century, and the Elizabethan age in particular, constitutes an era of unprecedented cultural changes. As well as religious and political upheaval there were profound transformations in the English language as well as in poetics, both of which had an incisive effect on the production and reception of the literature of the period. And lurking behind all of this is the paradigm shift away from medievalism as the new spirit of humanism gradually pervaded western modes of thought. I would like to discuss the changing humanist context under the following headings:

Realism and rhetoric
Renaissance humanism and literature
The craft of poetry

205

(a) Realism and rhetoric

In his advice to aspirant authors the Elizabethan poet George Gascoigne advised that realism on its own was never going to be sufficient,

> if you do . . . never studie for some depth of devise in the Invention, and some figures also in the handling thereof, it will appear to the skilfull Reader but a tale of a tubbe. (*Certayne Notes of Instruction*, 1575)

In other words the slavish description of nature would mean nothing special to the Elizabethan reader: the poet was expected to embellish his work with an expert show of ornament, the 'depth of devise in the Invention'. This did not imply, of course, the abandonment of realism in his verse, but it did present a major rhetorical problem: achieving the exact balance between a natural depiction of subjects and the poet's personal style embracing that depiction. Decorum dictated that each should be appropriate to the other.

Gascoigne advised poets to make the essence of their subjects more significant by the use of some 'covert meane', namely rhetorical devices such as allegory or conceit, or the use of contrast to bring out the psychological realism of his subject or of the poet himself. Mere description would have seemed banal.

Intellectually difficult subjects would not have been a barrier to enjoyment in themselves – and indeed readers expected to be challenged in this way. Thus Shakespeare and other Elizabethan poets assiduously pursued the knotty metaphysical questions implicit in their subjects and also in the theory of their art. But art and elaboration ought to avoid confusion. Speaking for his fellow Elizabethans Sir Philip Sidney famously judged that a poet's task was to illuminate: the aim of poetry was to bring a man to a 'judicial understanding'.

Realism in art can begin with questions of perception and imitation but ultimately the artist is faced with the demands of poetic theory, which for the Elizabethan included didactic purpose and most importantly the need for ornament, or rhetoric.

Shakespeare would have studied formal rhetoric at his local school in Stratford-upon-Avon. The subject formed a central platform in the Elizabethan grammar school syllabus and was kneaded into the pupil's brain in countless lessons and exercises. Its twin objects were to change the reader by persuasion, while at the same time demonstrating one's own verbal fluency almost for its own sake. In rudimentary terms, rhetoric involved an attempt to persuade a specific audience towards a specific action.

Grammar school students in Shakespeare's day were rigorously drilled into debating 'questions' in the form of public exercises in logic and rhetoric. It was a forum for showing off cleverness in formalised arguments along prescribed lines. Such juvenile exercises can be seen as the precursors of the major soliloquies of Hamlet, Iago, and Mark Antony in *Julius Caesar*.

The teaching of rhetoric in schools derives from the old *trivium* (Latin, rhetoric and logic) of monastic schooling but its origins and aims are traced to the Classical world, interest in which had recently become re-awakened in England via the renaissance of Classical studies. The ancient authors had of course long been the subject of serious study in the medieval period but always through the religious straitjacket of scholasticism – the new sixteenth-century passion for Latin and Greek was crucially at the centre of the new humanism and its relatively free exploration of what it was to be a human individual.

For Renaissance scholars the study of Classical authors, along with The Bible, held out at least three principal inducements. The classics presented models of refinement or 'grace' in art as well as life; they offered obliquely the means to power (based on a rumour that Classical texts embodied some ancient secret of political power), and they offered a paradigm of order, especially in the social sphere, but spilling over into literary concepts of decorum and courtly love. Underpinning all three is a radical desire for order on all levels.

Rhetoric, as the art of persuasion, was dismissed by Plato as a tendency for falsehood, a glossy surface of deception, at the expense of truth, the only valid object for philosophers. Rhetoric for him was concerned only with the *appearance* of truth, not with the actual truth. Aristotle disagreed, believing that rhetoric in itself could be a valid source of truth, and the early Elizabethans tended to agree with him.

However, it was the Roman orator Cicero (106–43 BC) who was taken up most avidly by Elizabethan humanist educators. His treatise on the subject, *De Oratore*, is a very practical and highly system-atised guide to rhetoric and it catalogues the stages through which a speaker should achieve his objectives. Beginning with *inventio*, by which the speaker 'discovers' his or her subject matter, the presentation is next structured for optimum effect (*depositio*), before adornments of style are instilled (*elocutio*); the piece must be kept in memory (*memoria*) and then delivered to the public with charm and persuasion (*actio*).

Perhaps the most interesting of these from the point of view of poetic composition is *elocutio* since this deals with matters such as euphony (choice of alliteration, assonance, and so on) and elaboration (the adoption of figures including metaphor, metonymy, and simile). Critically important to the poet, however, is the speaker's *copia*, the command of a diverse range of stylistic resources and the fluency to move between them.

Conversely, too much *elocutio* can of course be detrimental. Over-embellishment can lead to ambiguity and it may cause the reader/listener to become aware of the persuasive element, leading to wariness about deception, a major theme in Shakespeare's Sonnets.

One of the reasons why Cicero emerged as such a strong influence in both rhetoric and poetics lies in the discovery by Petrarch of Cicero's original letters and speeches. This, plus the discovery of the texts of Quintillian's brilliant speeches, made clear to humanist scholars the ideals of Classical rhetoric: the fostering of the rounded virtuous man, eloquent in oratory but also experienced in life, with a knowledge of philosophy – in short, the statesman and orator. These ideals were taken up and embodied in the principles of early Renaissance thinkers such as Baldesar Castiglione and formed the backbone of his highly influential treatise on court manners, *The Book of the Courtier* (see especially, Book I).

In its bonding of style and subject matter, rhetoric came to be regarded as an essential element in the cultivation of the all-round individual, specifically male, the citizen, statesman and philosopher. By the early sixteenth century it also came to be considered not merely of an academic interest but as an essential aesthetic tool in literature and, in vividly hard-headed terms, as a pragmatic method in the life and advancement of the prince at Court.

Rhetoric was not, however, the invention of the Elizabethans and manuals on the subject had been regularly produced since the twelfth century. Accordingly, rhetorical culture was deeply entrenched, as much in Renaissance consciousness as in its school programmes. At the same time as his rigorous training in the ethos of rhetoric, Shakespeare would have been comprehensively schooled in rhetoric's cousin, the rules of logic, and in Latin culture, including the study of Classical texts and authors. All of which finds vivid expression in the writing. The techniques of comedic theatre, his Roman plays and the two major narrative poems are a lucid demonstration of, and a tribute to, his Classical learning.

Of Shakespeare's non-dramatic verse, *Venus and Adonis* and *Lucrece* are both calculated to appeal to the contemporary taste for Classics, and their composition can be seen as extended illustrations of the rules of rhetoric. Indeed, educated readers would expect to identify the formal rhetorical devices at work. In these narrative poems Shakespeare's use of language is conceived as the marriage of rhetoric and content, as both elocution and drama, representing an ideal decorum of technique. The sonnets too are often interpreted as small-scale soliloquies, miniature performances in the rhetoric of persuasion. Their structuring invariably exhibits the rules of logic (see, for example, sonnets 5 and 127, and their discussion in Chapters 2 and 5 above).

(b) Renaissance humanism and literature

The Renaissance, Michel Foucault has argued, is 'the privileged moment of *individualisation*', when the author came into being (Foucault, 1970, p. 71). But the Renaissance thinker would also recognise the concept of individualism in relation to God, as well as to other men. In considering their own view of 'humanism' the Elizabethans would eschew the modern concept of atheism, the complete abandonment of the possibility of God, but rather take on board a redefinition of man's relationship with God (*King Lear* is a sober warning about the desperate nihilistic chaos that a godless universe might lead to).

However, distinctly typical of Renaissance humanism is a mounting confidence in the power of human reason to comprehend man and Nature, in marked contrast to medieval scholasticism's faith in scriptural insights. In turn this confidence is predicated on a belief in the rationality of Nature, generating a new faith in the power of the human intellect, its capacity to span the arching heavens like a mighty demigod. Ambition, thus liberated, combines with a new emphasis on the individual and gives rise to the characteristic Elizabethan drive for personal advancement and fame.

But it is important to bear in mind that the balance of *mind* and *sense*, or feeling, is important here too. Elizabethan poetry aspires through music working on the feeling to raise the mind, while the poet assumes for himself the public role of spokesman and mentor of mankind as well as its moral adviser. At the same time he seeks to replace the preaching and admonition of the medievals with rhetorical grace, eloquence and wit.

G. K. Hunter identifies the principal change in philosophy between the medieval and Renaissance paradigms as one of pragmatism: where medieval scholars were interested in the contemplative life, Renaissance intellectuals are bent on action, putting ideas in the service of ambition, and chiefly at the Court (Hunter; p. 11). In pragmatic terms, how could the education rooted in the grammar school be implemented in action, in life, rather than limited to the contemplative cloisters of, for example, Alcuin, Anselm and Boethius? One answer was in the politics of public life, at the Court and in the diplomatic service: learning judged in strategic terms of action, promotion and power.

Erasmus of Rotterdam (*c.*1469–1536), quintessential humanist, also lays great store by the intellect and the personal moral accountability of the individual. In his eminently readable *Praise of Folly* (1511) he facetiously asserts that folly was given to mankind to enrich his life and to recognise that man is frail, with 'serious faults', but also that it is this, the essence of humanity, that makes life by turns tragic and appallingly absurd, painful but above all endlessly fascinating (Erasmus, p. 32). The inexorable focus of man's learning in the Renaissance is man himself.

In religious terms (but ultimately in cultural too) medieval Christians were marked out by an unequivocal belief in original sin. However, early sixteenth-century thinkers including Erasmus went some way towards moderating the problems implicit in this. Where the fifteenth century generally regarded human perfectibility to be largely extrinsic to human endeavour, Erasmus believed that the perfection of whatever it is to be human lay singularly *within* the scope of human endeavour.

And while the medievals may have striven with impossible ideals of spiritual perfection (in theory at least), the Renaissance confines man's perfectibility more reasonably within human limits. Man is seen to be by nature culpable but, crucially, he accepts individual responsibility for his hubris.

Erasmus's coming man stresses less his partaking of the divine (though grace and nobility are still strongly evident) than what it is to be the flawed master of his own more limited universe. This need not stop us striving to reach the stars even as we exercise our new-found powers of autonomy and self-determination, though all the time we would recognise that some things – 'fortuitous events' – still lay beyond any human power to change or prevent.

I have suggested above that writers and scholars in the English early modern period have a strong consciousness of a mythical Golden Age of Classical learning. There is an acute awareness of the long and heavy shadow cast by Classical authors and also by a broader image of medieval European culture. Early Elizabethan poets were abjectly stung by the knowledge that not since the time of Chaucer had there been an English poet of truly European stature. Roger Ascham described him as 'our English Homer' (*Toxophilus*, 1545) and Sir Philip Sidney complained 'either that he in that mistie time could see so clearly, or that wee in this clear age walke so stumblingly after him' (*Apologie for Poetrie*, 1581). Shakespeare in sonnet 106 voices a comparable veneration.

> I see their antique pen would have expressed
> Even such a beauty as you master now. . . .

> For we, which now behold these present days
> Have eyes to wonder, but lack tongues to praise.
>
> (lines 7–8 and 13–14)

One thing particularly admired in Chaucer was his ready intimacy with Continental literature, a central tenet of his enterprise being to refine and assimilate the English demotic with the French. English Renaissance writers again looked to the past for their literary models and inspiration – but they now looked specifically to the Continent.

The Italian Renaissance occurred much earlier than its English equivalent, its inspiration rooted in a rediscovery of the ancient Classical texts. Pre-Elizabethan poets such as Gower and Skelton, writing in English, tended to be self-conscious and apprehensive in their native dialects whereas Latin offered a safe, ostensibly permanent and universal channel. Spenser's headmaster recorded:

> There be two speciall considerations, which kepe the *Latin* and other learned tungs, tho' chieflie the *Latin* in great countenance among us, the one thereof is the knowledge which is registered in them, the other is the conference which the learned of *Europe* do commonlie use by them.   (Richard Mulcaster, *The Elementarie*, 1582)

This 'conference' or lingua franca dimension to Latin certainly held its traditional sway but other forces balked at its widespread adoption for popular literature in the sixteenth century. Rising nationalistic pride (Mulcaster: 'I love the *Latin*, but I worship the *English*') was certainly one factor. Another was commercial pressure to meet a massive increase in non-scholarly readers resulting from the spread of education and cheaper books in the wake of the new printing technology. Latin had also been long associated with the Roman Church while recently the vernacular had been established as the language of the new English Church and of the new English nation.

Unlike the Romantic view that poets were specially gifted individuals who could produce verse in some mysteriously intuitive and spontaneous way, ready formed, the Elizabethan view was that a gifted poet also needed to be a highly polished craftsman (the word 'poet' comes from the Greek for 'maker') and to write serious poetry entailed a long and meticulous apprenticeship. A poet was expected to learn his craft under a discipline which demanded the study of rhetoric and Classical principles of writing.

In the previous chapter we noted the debt to Italian poets felt by George Puttenham, Wyatt, Surrey and others – in terms of subject matter and the sonnet form in particular. But the Elizabethan poets also looked to Italy and the past for more specialised poetic features. At first there is a fairly inert and mechanical imitation of externals as the English poets remain dazzled by the charisma of foreign prototypes and the formidable standards implied in them. By 1570 the surge of Italian influence is running so deep that Ascham issues a warning against what he regards as the insidious corrupting influence of this foreign culture in creating the 'Italianate Englisman',

> a marvellous monster, which for filthiness of living, for dullness of learning to himself, for wiliness in dealing with others, for malice in hurting without cause, should carry at once in one body the belly of a swine. (*The Scholemaster*, 1570)

As a reaction to this nationalistic turnabout, new artistic developments emerge with Spenser's and Sidney's great efforts to formulate an indigenous poetical language and institute a quality literature in their own vernacular. It is a development that leads in the later Elizabethan period to anti-Petrarchism and ultimately to the decline in sonnet writing altogether.

(c) The craft of poetry

> Who hath nothing but langage only may be no more praised than a popinjay, a pye, or a stare, whan they speke featly. . . . They be moche abused that suppose eloquence to be only in wordes or coulours of Rhetoricke, for, as Tully saith, What is so furiouse or mad a thinge as a vaine sound of wordes of the best sort and most ornate contayning neither connynge nor sentence? (Sir Thomas Elyot, *The Boke Named the Governour*, 1531)

A writer who has 'language' but no cunning or opinions may be compared to a parrot. As we noted above, the pursuit of an exact mimicry of a subject would have seemed both futile and lame to an Elizabethan reader. Shakespeare's sonnet 103 refers to the bare facts as merely the 'argument' and sonnet 100 makes a distinction between 'skill and argument'. In sonnet 79 the speaker scorns his rival poet since what he calls 'invention' is actually merely a copy of their patron's beauty, not original stylistic ornament at all (79:8–9).

Sophisticated readers like Elyot and Gascoigne expected to find images designed to please by their formal beauty and wit rather than faithful depiction of the factual world. In other words the craftsmanship or 'ornament' of the poet was more valorised on the grounds that only the artificial heightening of a subject through wit will successfully approach reality (natural or psychological), while at the same time vaunting the skill of the writer. But, confusingly for us perhaps, this may not mean the same as 'invention'.

In the opening stanza of his sonnet sequence *Astrophel and Stella* (written about 1582), Sir Philip Sidney sets out his plan to use his text to win the 'pitie' of his lady. He starts not by seeking some original idea or approach but, by

> Studying inventions fine her wits to entertaine;
> Oft turning others' leaves, to see if thence would flow
> Some fresh and fruitfull showers upon my sunne-burn'd braine.
>
> (1:6–9)

It may seem odd to us that invention could involve 'turning others' leaves', looking through the work of others as the starting point. But in Elizabethan poetic composition 'invention' covers a diversity of ideas. In formal rhetoric, *inventio* (from the Latin 'to find out') referred to the selection of the subject matter, discovering what it was the orator/poet was to say, finding the appropriate matter to be brought forth ('bring forth' is a recurring theme in Shakespeare's sonnets). In addition to 'fabricate', invention can also mean to 'discover', to 'come upon by chance'.

By the end of the sixteenth century, attitudes to formal rhetoric had considerably slackened and Shakespeare himself uses the term 'invention' inconsistently. His sonnet 59 directly confronts the possibility of truly original composition:

> If there be nothing new, but that which is
> Hath been before, how are our brains beguiled,
> Which, labouring for invention, bear amiss
> The second burden of a former child?
>
> (lines 1–4)

Sonnet 79 seems to say that the poet does not truly create in the sense of an original work, though sonnet 84 appears to remind the reader that what is to be prized in invention is a strong embellishment of style.

In effect, the depiction of realism in Elizabethan literature is complicated and negotiated by the demands of contemporary aesthetics, and in particular strategies of decorum and verbal ornament (as well as the didactic purpose of the text). To close this chapter we can examine both of these features and their implications for a reading of Shakespeare's sonnets.

(i) Decorum

Imitation was largely concerned with adopting the respected models offered by classical authors, the well-tried and proven sources of rhetoric and moral strength. The principles of rhetoric and their practice in the writings of Classical authors also dictated that the Elizabethan poet should pay close attention to 'keeping decorum', both literary and moral. This is connected with the ideas of sensual control and moral propriety implicit in courtly love. And both of these elements necessarily imply the use of 'indirect' poetics, such as understatement, allegory, conceit, imagery and symbol to conceal and hint, as the exercise of the poet's wit.

For Elizabethan poets decorum also has its more specialised, literary meaning: in line with Classical forebears, writers held that rhetoric could lead to truth only if there was a balance between style and substance, Which contrasts with the modern view that rhetoric equates to gloss or spin, or that politics is all about presentation, as if the subject matter was less important than flattering and bamboozling the audience. Decorum for the Elizabethans meant matching ornamentation with the subject, adopting a style to suit the poem's subject:

> Ye know not what hurt ye do to learning, that care not for wordes but for matter, and so make a diverse betwixt the tongue and the heart.
> (Roger Ascham, *The Scholemaster*, 1570)

The Fool in *King Lear* warns of the great confusion that will come if, among other things, 'priests are more in words than matter' (3.2.81), while at a different extreme, in *Love's Labour's Lost* Shakespeare parodies euphuism, an elaborate and highly artificial style which in many ways takes decorum to such an extreme that itself becomes, ironically, overbalanced.

Sometimes this was taken literally, as in, say, deploying English words in a Greek or Latin syntax for a Classical translation (for example, in Richard Stanyhirst's translation of Virgil). Indeed, Erasmus believed that decorum extended beyond artistic matters into life in general, 'for the importance of decorum extends beyond mere skill and covers every action' (Erasmus, p. 36).

In practical literary terms it could entail a suitor trying to charm his mistress using all the appropriate tricks of wit, ornament and dissimulation, not to mention quibbling deception. Devotional work would naturally require a flatter, plainer style, equally persuasive perhaps but less energetically ornate. A similar decorum is usually at work in Shakespeare's plays; for instance, in the apportioning of prose and verse to different social classes in *Much Ado*, and in his differential use of 'thee' and 'you' in *Othello* and *The Tempest*. In his guide to the topic, *The Arte of English Poesie* (1589), George Puttenham firmly prescribes for prospective authors

> which matters be high and lofty, and which be but mean, and which be low and base, to the intent that styles may be fashioned to the matters, and keep their decorum and good proportion.

In a turbulent age of political upheaval and major developments in poetic form, decorum, as canon of proper style, acted as a curb on literary style, keeping all matters in 'good proportion' (and most of Shakespeare's sonnets are suffused with themes and anxieties of mutability and uncertainty). Literary decorum can be seen as a drive towards applying organic unity to a text – stabilising its divisions and tensions. In the formal restraint of its compact fourteen-line format, and its internal discipline of form, rhyme and rhythm, the sonnet itself comes to stand as an allegory of decorum.

Yet Elizabethan insistence on unified and coherent meaning does not in itself necessarily impose moral orthodoxy on the poet. The fusing of the poet's didactic purpose with an appropriate style was in itself a moral as well as aesthetic injunction but it did not logically imply a type of subject matter, only its treatment (for example, there was lively controversy about the right means to deal with the theme of pleasure). Taste and the forces of Elizabethan autocratic censorship might do the rest. But the crucial point for us is that the principle of decorum naturally rules out any idea that a poem can be reducible to a comfortable paraphrase.

Decorum then could lead to a sense of poetic artifice, as authors strove to imitate not the particulars of their subject but its generality. A modern reader's notion of truth is likely to be naturalistic, particular, relative, subjective and 'literal'. But Elizabethan poets offer an interpretation of nature, relying strongly on rigorous selectivity and careful reordering, to allow the subject to cohere with its decorous pattern. The Elizabethan poet is likely to argue that it is not *my* woman or even *this* particular woman but the *idea* of woman, general and formal rather than particular (and this is clearly evident in many of the 'Dark Mistress' sonnets).

(ii) Ornament

Ornament in all things was a defining characteristic of Elizabethan elite society, in the Court as in the verse of the period. That said, rigorous standards of taste did apply while exaggeration, for example in excessive hyperbole, was abhorred.

Puttenham again:

> Ornament . . . is of two sorts, one to satisfie & delight th'eare onely by a goodly outward shew set upon the matter with wordes and speaches

smoothly and tunably running, another by certaine intendments or
sence of such wordes and speaches inwardly working a stir to the mind.
(*The Arte of English Poesie*)

One type of ornament to please the senses, the other to satisfy the
mind. And he adds, 'But generally to have the style decent and
comelye it behoveth the Poete to follow the nature of his subject. . .'.

In terms of literature, refinement and grace were highly valued,
sharing a community of outlook and expectation with a learned
audience. Accordingly poets aspired to elaboration in style, involving
virtuoso techniques such as sophisticated wit and elegance, sometimes
explored for its own sake or to exceed a rival. Again, models of
ornamental style could be derived from Classical models, such as
Cicero's oratory, when it was thought that these might also imbue
a sense of order. Ornament was intended to appeal as much to the
intellect as to the eye or ear.

In sonnet 70 ornament is viewed as a slight thing, supeficial and
distracting while 'ornament of beauty is suspect' (line 3), since ornament could adorn superficially what was in essence something ugly or
even 'canker vice'. Here and in sonnets 67 and 68 Shakespeare makes
a distinction between beauty which is true and deep-rooted or integral
and that which is merely a superficial embellishment, or outward
show. In sonnet 68, he thus equates ornament with deception, the
concealment of age through artificial aids (and see 66 and 67).

Sonnet 82 also refers to the 'strained touches rhetoric can lend'.
Yet by warning the reader that ornament can lead to deception he
opens up the minefield of truth versus falsehood, substance versus
shadow, in which he himself resorts to deception. As such, ornament
inexorably encompasses flattery too, a very valid tool in the art of
persuasion, seduction and advertisement, manifested chiefly through
figures such as hyperbole. The Sonnets are no stranger to this idea, but
as part of the shifting politics and moods of the Sonnets Shakespeare
even dismisses flattery in his attempt to first undermine truth and
then claim it for himself ('my adder's sense / To critic and to flatterer
stopped are'; 112:10–11). Gabriel Harvey (1545–1630), humanist
scholar and teacher of rhetoric, sought to adjudicate between the good
and the bad in ornament, 'visible flattery is abject and unworthy of

a gentleman; invisible flattery is a matter of skill and suited for men of affairs' (*Marginalia*). So long as it was done well it was well done.

The excesses of euphuism apart, the inclusion of ornament into a text was still expected to conform to the requirements of decorum, at first anyway (Berowne in *Love's Labour's Lost* also disparages excess, 'Fie painted rhetoric!'; 4.3.235). The very process of rhetoric involves artifice and we have noted how naturalism was not a poet's primary concern. In the later decades of the sixteenth century, the most approved language was that which was artificially enriched. Two factors which enhanced this current were the great enlargement in the wordstock of the language during the century and the popular fashion for a range of wordplay tricks such as quibbling and punning, which could exercise a poet's drive for ornament.

Although Elizabethan verse springs from the subjective reality of the poet, the world of the individual work depends upon the public language it uses. Given the scrupulously conventionalised nature of Elizabethan poetry it is hardly surprising that it employed such a rich set of culturally coded images with fixed or conventional significances. These included myth, symbol, conceit, allegory, cultural metaphor, and recognisable stock characters. Iconic images too were a pervasive feature of Elizabethan culture.

Allegory was highly important – particularly so, given the political and religious censorship and prevailing inhibitions on sexual matter imposed by taste (matters which also challenged and exercised a writer's capacity for wit to encode an allegory while alerting the reader to its importance). The sixteenth century could recognise in a metaphor the allegory of even a single word. Some of Shakespeare's sonnets are so much extended as metaphors (or are so far removed from their physical sources of inspiration) that they too border on allegory.

Because they are so essentially an element of the Comedies, quibbling puns now seem to be the very soul of courtly Elizabethan love language. Accordingly, although the simplicity of iambic pentameter contrasts with the great weight of quibbling word play borne by it, quibbles encapsulate both ornament and decorum for sixteenth-century verse. Indeed a lover's prowess may be measured in direct proportion to the quality of his puns as a pointer of his skill in seduction. Quibbles and word-wrangling constitute the epitome of wit, by paradoxical turns both concealing and revealing, and Shakespeare is the grandmaster of the game.

Wit intellectualises, conceals, makes curious, heralds an original attitude on a familiar range of themes and symbols ('Our erected wit maketh us to know what perfection is'; Sir Philip Sidney, *The Defence of Poesy*). Wit is the soul of both the Comedies and the Sonnets, clarifying and concealing. Wit is ornament in eloquent action, drawing the moment(s) to the edge of chaos, intimating confusion through apparent illogicality, but reassuring of control without actually dispelling danger. Ultimately wit leaves the original questions teasingly unanswered.

Over the course of the sixteenth century rhetoric gradually became devalued as an ideology and a literary competence and by the 1590s it had declined to the level of a hollow convention, mere glossy spin adopted less for truth than for deception. In a crisis of cultural scepticism during the final decade of the century, a crisis as much about the past as about the ideals of the Renaissance, the practice of formal rhetoric as a route to truth fell into disuse among authors. In the Sonnets and when it suits his argument, Shakespeare frequently looks upon rhetoric as little more than a form of sophistry or deception glossing over and presenting an acceptable outward image in order to persuade or flatter (see sonnets 82 and 83). Yet he never shrinks from the challenge of wit and ornament in his poetry, as the rich catalogue of his tropes dazzlingly reveals.

The following list traces some good examples of the many rhetorical figures adopted by Shakespeare in the Sonnets:

allegory (5), anaphora (86), antiblazon (130), antistasis (152), blazon (106), chiasmus (79 and 152), *epanorthosis* (116), hendiadys (23 and 144), hyperbole (78), hypotyposis (12), litotes (22), extended metaphors (116), metonymy (78), mimesis (116), *occupatio* (82 and 85), parataxis (100), personification (127), pleonasm (20), psychomachy (144), synecdoche (86 and 138)

8

Some Critical Responses to the *Sonnets*

> in your perusal you shall finde them Serene, cleere and eligantly
> plaine, such gentle straines as shall recreate and not perplex your
> braine, no intricate or cloudy stuffe to puzzell intellect, but perfect
> eloquence.
>
> (John Benson, *Poems: Written by*
> *Wil. Shake-speare* (1640), Preface)

Many critics believe that Shakespeare's Sonnets was published
without the sanction of the author, and if so he must have been
surprised and infuriated to find verse published that he had carefully
protected from public scrutiny. If this is the case, then Shakespare
himself was also one of their earliest and severest critics.

The second vogue in Elizabethan sonnets ended a decade or more
before Shakespeare's collection was published in 1609. At the time of
its publication the 1609 Quarto seems to have been received largely
in an ominous silence. I have already cited Francis Meres's honey-
tongued praise of 'his sugred Sonnets' in manuscript, but there are no
existing contemporary discussions of them. Whether or not they were
seen through the press by Shakespeare himself, they proved strikingly
less popular in terms of printings than his two long narrative poems
since both *Venus and Adonis* and *Lucrece* went through multiple

reprintings during and after Shakespeare's lifetime. From Jonson, Donne and Herbert there is no word, though all of them must have studied Shakespeare's sonnets at some time and seem to have been spurred by them into composing their own.

After its first publication in 1609, *Sonnets* did not appear in print again until 1640 in John Benson's muddled and bowdlerised edition, while by 1675 *Venus and Adonis* had gone through seventeen reprints. Benson was perhaps attempting to do for the poems what the 1623 Folio had done for the plays, to establish and perpetuate the reputation of Shakespeare as a poet, but decidedly not as one who addressed love poems to other men.

This great disregard of a collection released at the height of Shakespeare's fame has sometimes been attributed to deliberate suppression. One common theory is that some of the poems were interpreted as immoral revelations of a public figure, perhaps the Earl of Southampton, and consequently proscribed. Yet, by 1609 the sonnet form itself had fallen out of favour and even in Benson's preface to his edition the term 'sonnet' barely figures at all, suggesting a continued lapse in popularity (Benson brashly implies that his is actually the first edition of these sonnets).

Although Milton revives the form with his sonnets of about the middle of the seventeenth century he seems not to have been aware of Shakespeare's. The turning point in the critical progress of the collection comes in 1780 when Edward Malone edited them as the *Supplement* to George Steevens's publication of the collected plays. However, it was not until the Romantic period that commentators began to treat them with any critical esteem in their own right. Byron disparaged the sonnet form *per se* and Coleridge virtually ignored Shakespeare's completely. Wordsworth ('Scorn not the sonnet...') and Keats were especially instrumental in rejuvenating it, particularly as a result of their sympathetic study of Shakespeare's sonnets. In a letter to his friend and fellow author John Reynolds, Keats enthused but with mixed feelings:

> I neer found so many beauties in the Sonnets – they seem to be full of fine things said unintentionally... (November 1817)

Through the nineteenth century the Sonnets were highly celebrated as romantic lyrics and investigated chiefly as biographical documents, inspite of the fact that since Malone's edition it had been customary for editions of the Sonnets to appear only in the form of selections. The ground-breaking edition which set them up as serious objects of critical study, pioneering the way for their great popularity in the twentieth century, came in 1832 with Alexander Dyce's publication of the whole set, at last presenting readers with a text worthy of serious scholarship.

Until the early twentieth century, criticism of the Sonnets tended towards a vague, generalised rambling akin to reflecting on fine wines sipped in a gentleman's club. Such *belles-lettres* criticism was emphatically subjective, being based on a shared upper middle-class moral and cultural ideology. Written reviews frequently adopted a casual haughtiness, handing down judgements usually limited to tropes of irony, paradox, complexity, and using methods derived from classical or biblical studies.

Subjectivist and elitist, it inclined towards ascribing 'greatness' to writers whose work was elevated into an exclusive literary canon founded on approved qualities and values. Inevitably, given their cultural origins, these values tended to reflect their own narrow circumstances, typically male, white, middle-class, heterosexual and Protestant. In spite of efforts to enlist Shakespeare as a kind of honorary Edwardian gentleman his values are often fugitive and equivocal, interested in the outsider, frequently subversive.

Before 1950 the issues that perennially occupied critics of the Sonnets were largely biographical in nature. These derived momentum from the growing myth of Shakespeare as the national genius, and the mysteries surrounding the man and the Sonnets have meant that they have attracted more than their fair share of madcap theories.

Discussion centred on a range of intensely controversial issues: fixing their dates of composition, authorship, the identities of the main characters (the 'sweet youth', the Dark Mistress, W. H., and the Rival Poet), the 'proper' order of the poems, and assessing whether the collection represented a sequence based on Shakespeare's private life. John Middleton Murry and L. C. Knights, two influential literary academics of the early half of the twentieth century, are fairly typical of this sort of approach.

In a wide-ranging study, *Shakespeare* (1936), Murry accepts the whole of the sonnets as chronologically narrating one long complex tale in five phases, closely recounting events in Shakespeare's own life in the period 1593–5. He concludes that the Earl of Southampton himself was responsible 'directly or indirectly' for handing over the poems to Thomas Thorpe for printing, with himself as the dedicatee.

Likewise, L. C. Knights considers the collection as homogeneous and continuous, though in his 1934 essay 'Shakespeare's Sonnets' published in the journal *Scrutiny*, he criticises them as lacking in the subtleties found in the dramas. On the other hand he warns against a too easy biographical reading of the text on the grounds that the writer firmly establishes a critical detachment towards both his subjects and himself. The main interest of the poems lies 'not in any general theme or situation... but in various accretions of thought and feeling' (pp. 78–9). He focuses most closely on their technique:

> The most profitable approach to the Sonnets is... to consider them in relation to the development of Shakespeare's blank verse. (p. 79)

Hence Knights treats the Sonnets less in their own right and on their own terms than as an adjunct to and secondary to the plays. While he admires the precision of their imagery he feels that their author had not yet fully mastered that technique of complex phrasing achieved in the 'mature plays'. He concludes,

> The Sonnets yield their proper significance only when seen in the context of Shakespeare's development as a dramatist. (p. 101)

The development of the Anglo-American 'school' of Practical Criticism which emerged just before the Second World War was a significant factor both in the reaction against *belles lettrism* and in insisting on close and detailed verbal analysis, preparing the way to serious study of the Sonnets. Among its early practitioners were I. A. Richards, F. R. Leavis, William Empson, T. S. Eliot and Yvor Winters.

William Empson's work is exemplary of this style of criticism and his essays collected in works such *Seven Types of Ambiguity* (1930; revised 1947 and 1961) and *Some Versions of Pastoral* (1935) are paradigms of practical criticism still remarkably stimulating today. In his earlier study Empson presents some highly polished analyses of individual Shakespeare sonnets and in particular numbers 81 and 83, where he tries to show how the choice and position of individual lexical items can radically affect a reading of a poem. In discussing the 'fluid unities' of the Sonnets he also shows how modern systematic punctuation can compromise the syntactic plasticity of Shakespeare's sentences. He demonstrates how Shakespeare's careful word-craft can generate richly ambiguous, indeterminate and even contradictory readings but that these can sometimes be resolved by reference to other sonnets within the collection, thus seeing the whole work as a network of interconnected meanings.

The meticulous work of Empson and other practical critics on Shakespeare had the crucial effect of accelerating the end of the vague, romanticised approach of the previous century. But, more significantly for the *Sonnets*, it helped to establish Shakespeare's verse as texts which are highly significant in their own right, autonomous of the plays, and this has been the governing attitude since the middle of the twentieth century.

I have chosen to look in detail at four critics, all writing in the period since the 1950s: G. Wilson Knight, Stephen Booth, A. D. Cousins, and Peter Hyland.

G. Wilson Knight

The Mutual Flame: on Shakespeare's Sonnets *and* The Phoenix and the Turtle (1955)

G. Wilson Knight (1897–1984) was both an actor and a theatrical producer but was best known as an academic, lecturing first at Toronto University, and later as a professor at the University of Leeds. He was a pioneer in the symbolic 'school' of textual interpretation. This approach employs a technique of close examination of

Shakespeare's texts in terms of its clusters of images, precisely tracing complex symbolic patterns and devoting special attention to imagistic oppositions, most commonly for Knight the antithesis of 'tempest' and 'music'.

Knight is acclaimed for his holistic attitude towards Shakespeare's opus, reading the plays as a coherent unity, a whole poetic experience. Although he worked independently of any formal academic circle or movement, Knight's research, along with that of John Middleton Murry, signifies the foundation of a more rigorously systematic approach in the study of literature. His work builds on Caroline Spurgeon's highly seminal *Shakespeare's Imagery* (1935) and Murry's own *The Problem of Style* (1922) and at several points it anticipates many of the values and methodologies of Practical Criticism.

Typically, Knight draws out the spatiality inherent in Shakespeare's work so that, paradoxically, while recognising some narrative sequencing within the Sonnets and the plays, he comes to regard their diverse elements as forming a sort of simultaneity, a hovering stasis that he terms 'atmosphere'. Both ideas are evident in *The Mutual Flame*.

Knight's detailed examination of the *Sonnets* appears in the first part of his book, opening with a survey of the perennial problems and theories with which critics had laboured. He finds that these have been almost exclusively biographical – the true identities and relationships of the chief players, the dates and order of the lyrics, and so on. He sets out to give an account of the 'narrative' that he finds woven through the 154 poems, for 'The poems, as they stand, tell us rightly or wrongly, a story' (12). Apart from Shakespeare himself Knight finds only two other characters, the Fair Youth and the Dark Mistress, while the significant difference in their respective relationships with the poet is that only the latter involves any lustful intimacy and sensuality.

Knight's study is ground-breaking in being among the first of academic critics to openly recognise and explore the homoerotic dimension to the Sonnets. However, he tends to do this in symbolic terms, consistent with his own general literary approach. Subsequently, the Youth and the Dark Mistress emerge less as real and biographical individuals than as allegories for homosexual and heterosexual predispositions.

Knight construes the 'great problem of love' which Shakespeare set himself in the Sonnets as merging the homosexual and heterosexual sides of his nature. Shakespeare's depiction of the 'fair youth' is so intense that, agreeing with Masefield and Wilde, he concludes that the boy was probably a fellow actor in the Chamberlain's company. He understands the youth as starting out as a 'real presence in the poet's mind' (106) but sees that eventually the poems depict a composite figure made up of many of Shakespeare's friends.

As we might expect, Knight himself acknowledges this, conceding that 'The young man has been idealised: he is not exactly the poet's self, but rather his higher self' (43). Knight's strategy here, however, is to retrench or qualify his remarks on the Youth's sexuality. While he is unafraid to see that Shakespeare expresses his own strong homosexual feelings through this Youth he hedges this in by adding that they are non-physical, and in any case identifies them as 'abnormal', better seen as 'presexual'. The relationship between the Youth and England's pre-eminent poet is thus redeemed as a spiritual one.

> The Fair Youth, possessing the lower integration of youthful, and therefore in a sense bisexual, charm and grace, has been pointing the poet, through experiences of unity, towards the higher, spiritual integration. (44)

This succinctly encapsulates the main theme of Wilson Knight's second chapter. Bodily sexuality, though unexpressed in physical terms, is the portal to a higher spiritual purity that represents the womb of creativity.

Having set out the narrative of the Sonnets and their central themes, Knight now, in chapter III, tries to show how certain key symbolic images operate to penetrate the mystery (or 'superthought') underlying these themes

> We have seen how certain supposed 'conceits' or 'fancies' may be in reality attempts to grapple with some superthought which baffles expression. The most usual medium for such intuitions is poetic symbolism, and the Sonnets show a rich use of it. Indeed, the weighty

realisation of these imaginative solidities sets them apart from the poetry of Donne and Marvell. (p. 58)

Knight's approach, especially in suggesting that the Sonnets are the intellectual equal of the work of the Metaphysical poets, is daring and original and one not generally taken up by other major commentators.

But Knight is here more interested in pursuing the relationship between the surface tropes and 'superthoughts'. This comes about through the poet's recurrent use of symbolic associations. These associations in turn function as the chief structuring figures within the text by creating a verbal connection with the mysterious 'superthoughts'. Knight lists these for the Sonnets as: flowers – especially the rose - the sun, moon, jewels, heart, gold, and king. For example, king and gold come together in 55:1–2 and sun and gold converge at 18:6. Knight argues that in the Sonnets homosexual love is associated with the sun and heterosexual with the moon (64).

Chapter IV is taken up by an examination of the subject of time. As with other themes, time has a enigmatic quality which rationalistic literary criticism cannot fully penetrate and explain. Knight later concludes that at the back of the Sonnets there hovers a great numinous presence, what he calls the 'mysterious continuum', something existing beyond human comprehension. This has particular application to the Youth, who enjoys a mysterious existence partly outside of time as well as partly within it, consistent with Shakespeare's perceived religious attitude to time in the Sonnets.

While this has a grand-sounding transcendence about it (akin to Nietzsche's theory of intuitive epistemology) it tends to undermine the rationalistic groundwork that the critic has carefully toiled to erect in earlier chapters. And as if anticipating the obvious objections, Knight retorts that it is not always possible to 'prove' an interpretation.

The book's chapter V is the final one on the Sonnets and in it he expands his discussion to include individual poems in more detail (namely sonnets 113 and 114, 117 and 118, 124 and 125). These are set in the wider context of a discussion of some of the plays, taken across the whole of Shakespeare's theatre career, in the process exploring especially the themes of love, jealousy, truth and ingratitude. Knight's aim here is to trace parallels between the 'Fair Youth' and some of the characters from the plays, because 'The Sonnets define the spiritual principle behind all of Shakespeare's work' (for instance, he compares the Youth with Ariel from *The Tempest*). He justly points out that 'We must see the Sonnets not as *antedating* Shakespeare's drama, but rather as *central* to it' (109). Thus, there is clearly no useful point in dating the Sonnets since they are not bibliographically specific.

In many ways G. Wilson Knight prepares the way for recent attitudes in literary studies, especially in his stress on the close scrutiny of the texts under consideration. At the same time his is a mostly descriptive order of holistic criticism, tracing patterns of imagery, motif and symbolism to discover deeper consciousnesses and intertextualities, rather than following an evaluative route based on aesthetic or ethical precepts as his predecessors had done.

Against this a major criticism is that his discursive style is somewhat archaic and heavy-going, often involving a distracting relish for obscurely private introspection. His subjective non-historical perspective would be at odds with recent post-structural poetics.

In terms of the Sonnets' sexual themes Knight is, for his time, relatively bold and liberal-minded. Even referring at all to the 'love that dare not speak its name' was comparatively daring, especially since in 1955 homosexual love was legally classified as an act of 'gross indecency'. And it is perhaps for this reason that he repeatedly modifies his view of the homoeroticism that he sets out to confront, often transmuting it into a discussion of obscure metaphysics. We find him making assertions such as:

> The Sonnets record a progress through bisexual adoration and integration to an eternal insight, or intuition. And from such an intuition, creation inevitably proceeds.   (104)

But he is of his time and feels the need to shield himself by interpolating more guarded comments. So, behind the Sonnets lies what he describes as a 'perverted' love, 'a non-sexual, yet sexually impregnated, adoration for a boy', adding that in the end this amounts to a 'psychological illness' (127).

Stephen Booth

An Essay on Shakespeare's Sonnets (1969)

Stephen Booth is professor of English at Berkeley University, California, whose principal area of academic interest is English Renaissance poetry and drama. He has published extensively on Shakespeare but is perhaps most widely distinguished for his 1977 edition of Shakespeare's *Sonnets* (revised 2000).

At the very beginning of his essay Stephen Booth disarmingly admits to the reader, 'Shakespeare's sonnets are hard to think about' (p. 1). He later repeats this admission as if to sympathise with readers who might find support or solace in this consideration. But what he really means by his statement is that it is hard to think of the sonnets as they appear in 1609 Q, that is as a coherent whole, particularly if we try to connect them by seeking only one or two common strands, and especially thematic ones.

His Preface sets out some of the things his study will steer clear of, and like Knight he avoids resolving those old chestnuts about the dates of composition of the poems, or the identities of the putative characters, or the 'correct' order of the poems. Also like Knight he sets out on a 'line-to-line experience of reading them', which he believes is the true source of pleasure in studying the text. He gives us a clear overall idea of his aim and emphasis in this 'Essay':

> I have tried to demonstrate that a Shakespeare sonnet is organised in a multitude of different coexistent and conflicting patterns – formal, logical, ideological, syntactic, rhythmic and phonetic.   (p. ix)

The book is written in seven chapters, the first four devoted to examining these 'coexistent and conflicting patterns', followed by detailed analysis and data relating to patterning.

He lets us know early on that he has no intention of offering an exegesis, though some uninvited interpretations do slip in under the radar. His eyes are fixed firmly on the 'reading experience', with an almost scientific analysis of this.

The phrase 'reading experience' itself can be a bit vague of course and in chapter 1 Booth launches into a definition. This really comes towards the middle of the chapter under the heading 'Finding a structural principle for the sequence',

> Perhaps the happiest moment the human mind ever knows is the moment when it senses the presence of order and coherence.   (14)

Booth feels this is axiomatic not just for reading literature but, by extension, for life itself, and, not unnaturally, this is his ruling principle in the essay. In other words it is the job of the literary critic to seek unity in the text and to determine the patterns that give rise to this unity.

On page 2 he sets out three extraneous reasons why readers would want to find order in the Sonnets: the first is that by analogy with the ordered sequences of Dante and Petrarch we would expect to find the same in Shakespeare; the second is that there are traces of sequencing in the collection already (for example, in numbers 1 to 17); and the third, is that, given the widespread assumption that printer Thorpe rather than writer Shakespeare probably arranged the poems, anyone else is authorised to impose his or her arrangement on them. He suspects that even had Thorpe or others arranged the Sonnets differently our reactions to them might not have been all that different.

Then Booth throws in something highly apposite to his thesis: as we read the text we are aware 'that Shakespeare is saying something in the collection as a whole that the reader can almost but never quite hear' (2). This hidden 'something' will be the subterranean patterning that imparts wholeness to the collection. He finds that

> There is indeed a pervading sense of relationship among the poems, but no consistent sense of progress.   (3)

Taking as a sample the sonnets 33–37, he argues that many readers make a mistake in assuming the poems relate to each other only in a single or narrow range of common themes. He sets out to demonstrate here and in the remainder of the essay that they are connected with each other and the rest of the collection through 'multitudinous frames of reference and systems of interrelation', involving subject-matter, figures, voices, motifs and so on. (5–14).

Turning his attention to the internal structure of the sonnets, Booth hints that the same broad ordering principles are at work on the microcosmic scale. At the heart of this, the most inter-esting part of the analysis, is the long-held realisation that the formal structure of Shakespeare's sonnets (based on their rhyme scheme) rarely corresponds with their logical structure (based on their 'argument').

He makes it known at the end of the first chapter that the main body of his essay is an effort to demonstrate the various kinds of structural patterns at work within the poems and the effect of their interaction, and he begins, in chapter 2, by wryly pointing out how important the sonnet form is to the sonnet.

The most important thing about a sonnet is that it is a sonnet.   (28)

What is likely to strike us on first encountering a sonnet is its compact sense of unity. It looks on the page like a 'tight little block'. We see the whole poem at once and it takes less than a minute to read. Yet, the rhyme pattern that distinguishes it from any other 14-line poem also makes us aware of its internal division. And it is this latter point that has proved such a challenge as well as an opportunity for the best sonneteers.

What Booth brilliantly makes us aware of in this chapter is just how infinitely versatile the sonnet form is. He nimbly draws out the formal and thematic potential of the form together with the complications and tensions inherent in that form. For example, beginning with the Petrarchan sonnet,

The logical and syntactical reinforcement of the division between the two physically dissimilar parts of the sonnet centres the energy of the poem inside it.   (30)

But Shakespeare makes life even more difficult for himself by using three quatrains and a couplet: four blocks using seven rhymes (where the Italian has only two blocks and only five rhymes). The problem that Booth lights on is how to overcome the sense of internal division between the three quatrains in such a way as to maintain the forward thrust of the poem (33).

He shows that the division between the quatrains can be muted by adopting cross-patterning devices as a counter to the formal phonetic (or rhyme) patterning in the poem. These include thematic (or what Booth calls 'rational'), metrical and syntactical patterns. Sir Philip Sidney's simple solution was to run the syntax of the final quatrain into the couplet but very few followed this route (Shakespeare does so only in sonnets 35 and 154).

Translating this to the rest of the sonnet cycle, the multiplicity of cross-patterning devices (especially syntactic disruption) has the major result of unsettling the reader through a series of false starts. The reader's expectations become disrupted and dislocated through logical and syntactical patterning, for instance confusions brought about by puns and objective genitives. Ultimately the chief effect of all this is to make readings of the text highly tentative and provisional.

In chapter 3, 'Multiple Patterns', Booth takes as his starting point and inspiration some highly charged remarks by C. S. Lewis in his *English Literature in the Sixteenth Century*. Acknowledging Lewis's strong influence on his own ideas ('the best work that has been done on the structure of the sonnets'; 64), he sets out to extend rather than challenge Lewis's findings, which were focused on sonnet 12.

His working thesis is that where his precursor talked in terms of a single patterning device at work in this sonnet, Booth uncovers a multiplicity of devices sharing in the effect. None of these dominate but each of them 'participates simultaneously in several separate schemes of organisation' (p. 83). His analysis of sonnet 12 is a scintillating demonstration of the interrelatedness of sounds, diction, and syntax and their bearing on the poem's theme of mutability,

> everything mentioned [in the sonnet] is thus appropriate to everything else and to the poem.   (p. 84)

Perhaps most significantly, this 'everything else' is expanded to take in the whole of the Sonnets, so that this multiplicity of patterning can be found in the total collection and we are struck not by disorder in 1609 Q but by the great sense of order as a 'single work of art' (84).

Thus far Booth has focused most closely on technical elements of unity in the sonnets. In chapter 4, 'Unity and Division, Likeness and Difference', he gives some attention to thematic features to propose another principle at work in the sonnets, that of simultaneous similitude and dissimilitude. In this chapter he investigates the devices by which Shakespeare produces a pulsation effect through simultaneous unity and division, likeness and difference, which he believes informs the Sonnets 'at every level', from the smallest phonetic to the broadest thematic scale.

Over the next two chapters Booth continues in what he finds most fascinating, namely a highly receptive analysis and description of particular texts, here sonnets 60, 73 and 94. Applying his thesis from earlier chapters, he cites Arthur Mizener as another of the important pioneers in this field of close study, 'describing the effects of a sonnet as it is read', or in Booth's own words, following the 'motion of the reading mind'. Both authors point up the importance of the active mind of the reader in making sense by connecting the 'blocks' or components of a text, led by the almost subliminal operation of the text's system of patterning.

In his final chapter Booth uses sonnet 15 to try to pull together and summarise his thesis on patterning in the sonnets. He concludes that a work of art must still relate the reader to the real world (in other words the internal patterning must not be an end in itself, like the dead end of art simply for the sake of art). Art should relate to the truth of experience and the reader prefers it if it does so without manifest artifice, in order to give something of the randomness of experience itself. However, art can never be perfectly successful at this because the ordering principles behind art and those behind life are different in kind. Shakespeare, he argues, 'comes closest to success' because he marshals such a multiplicity and diversity of ordering principles, systems of organisation and frames of reference.

Stephen Booth's essay shows the marked influence of the structuralist approach to textual criticism' an approach that flourished during the 1960s. As its title implies, it is concerned with examining structures within a text and, in general, with trying to define the principles by which these structures function. At the heart of structuralism is the belief that the individual parts of a text derive their meanings only by virtue of their relationships to each other, and have no intrinsic meaning. By the same token a structuralist might compare the systems at work in two or more sonnets, say, and discuss the different effects created by each. Structuralism would argue that the form of a literary text *is* its content and Stephen Booth concurs with this view when he suggests in chapter 2 that the unsettling effect of a sonnet's patterning acts as a parallel or correlative to the uneasy relationships experienced by the poet.

Booth's outstanding yet largely understated treatise has two chief aims. His most explicit aim is to locate and describe systems of order, or structures, at work in the Sonnets; the second and most exciting seems almost a by-product of this, to describe the detailed, shifting reactions to the texts in the reader's mind, word by word in a continuum, as he or she reads.

Under the first aim, Booth's thesis is keen to link his technical findings in two related areas: the effects of the multiplicity of *internal* patterning techniques on the way the reader participates in them, and their effects on the way we view the wider picture, the Sonnets as a whole. As a structuralist he is naturally eager to convince us that the Sonnets are a unified sequence.

While Booth is dazzlingly good on the former area he is much less so on the latter. Most readers would judge the unity of the Sonnets as a sequence on the level of their *content*, especially narrative, theme and character, as well as a seriality. What Booth does is convince us of their unity in terms of what they have in common technically, as sonnets *per se*. We might go further and say that the poems cohere through the uniting creative mind behind them, revealed in the multiple patterning. But this would not necessarily qualify them as a 'sequence'.

One of the great attractions of this study is the author's work on the 'motion of the mind' in reading. In common with Knight's general scientific approach this necessitates a very close analysis of the minutiae of the poems in order to monitor the dynamic inter-relatedness of poetic devices. His work borders very closely on a study of the psychology of reading, though a full treatment is clearly beyond the scope of an essay. At times Booth also skirts the realm of reader-response theory but always his emphasis remains on the reader reacting to a governing text.

On the down side, his interpretation is often presented as *the* inter-pretation, where we now might prefer to acknowledge the openness of a text. Perhaps more significantly, Booth is convinced from the outset that there is a narrative order within the Sonnets where clearly this is not necessarily so. He also has an unflinching faith in the stability of language as a given. However, as I have tried to show, for instance in the 'Dark Mistress' sonnets, the language itself is a major source of conflict and dis-organisation.

Stephen Booth starts out by stating that 'Shakespeare's sonnets are hard to think about'. In the course of his essay he more than adequately proves this, and they are no less hard by the end. But what he gives us is a very satisfying appreciation of what makes them so.

A. D. Cousins

Shakespeare's Sonnets and Narrative Poems (2000)

A. D. Cousins is professor of English at Macquarie University in New South Wales. His *Shakespeare's Sonnets and Narrative Poems* is a volume in Longman's Medieval and Renaissance Library and although it is described by its publishers as a 'critical introduction' it is not an entry-level book, the main thesis being densely argued, and it presupposes a sound familiarity with the intellectual and cultural context of Shakespeare's poems.

Cousins's study appeared at a time when the movement known as New Historicism was becoming established in literary studies. This Postmodernist movement examines the ways in which liter-ature reflects, shapes and represents the cultural forces of history. In particular it reads literary texts as material products inseparable from specific historical conditions. History is viewed not as a separate background, informing literary composition or criticism, but as an integral constituent, shaping and being shaped by the ideological forces at work in any period. In its most radical form, New Historicism sees literary texts as inevitably created less by discrete authors *per se* than by their specific cultural context. It opposes a-historical readings which treat texts as autonomous artefacts (such as the above studies by Knight and Booth): poetry is to be understood in relation to a nexus of ideological values.

New Historicism is, of course, a product of its own time too and has been heavily influenced by cultural philosophers such as Michel Foucault and Claude Lévi-Strauss. Acclaimed among literary critics influenced by New Historicism are Stephen Greenblatt and Louis A. Montrose.

However, it would not be accurate to describe Cousins's essay as an out-and-out New Historicist study. It is less interested in situating Shakespeare's verse within the social conditions of the English early modern period than in placing it within its artistic frame of reference, siting the *Sonnets*, for instance, alongside Petrarch's *Rime* and Sidney's *Astrophel and Stella*, as well as examining the influence of Classical texts such as Ovid.

The Introduction outlines the main thrust of the study as focusing on Shakespeare's non-dramatic writings,

> in particular on their variously manifested scepticism, their concern both with what wisdom might be in human conduct and with the extent to which human conduct might be directed by wisdom.   (p. 1)

Cousins looks closely at the verse's 'preoccupation with knowing, inventing, or reinventing the past' (p. 1). His philosophical starting point is with the form of epistemological scepticism known as 'Pyrrhonism', which while accepting a deep uncertainty about knowledge, says that the only safe way to deal with this is to accept and live by the reality of appearances. Cousins argues that the sonnets exhibit this form of scepticism but they also try to resolve this problematic through a pragmatic form of wisdom known as *prudentia*.

The work on the Sonnets begins in earnest in chapter 3, 'Shakespeare's Sonnets 1–19', and after dismissing speculation on the overall order Cousins wonders how they fitted into the contemporary fashion for sonnets and sonnet sequences. To expand this theme he examines the influence of court poetry, especially that of Petrarch on Sidney's *Astrophel and Stella* and on the 1609 Q.

Petrarch's treatment of love, sexuality and rhetoric casts a long shadow over English sonneteers who adopted the persona of Laura as a paradigm of the chaste and unattainable object of love. As a virgin, Laura has a virtuous, ennobling effect, but essentially she epitomises the very root of sexuality and thus, in contrast to that of the Virgin Mary, the love she generates is profane or *cupiditas.*

Cousins finds the strong influence of both Petrarch and Sidney in 1 to 19 of Shakespeare's Sonnets:

> In the first four of Shakespeare's Sonnets ... the reader sees a different if not wholly dissimilar evocation of the Narcissus myth, one that will dominate the initial nineteen poems and thereby form a prelude to use of the myth in sonnets 20–126.   (p. 123)

But Cousins is at pains to insist that the myth is not used to imply a relationship akin to that of a lover and the idealised object of desire. The older man's tone is that of a 'benign counsellor'. However, the young man's narcissism offends the basis of the older man's advice both in the moral duty to prolong the family's line and in the Old Testament fiat that a man has a duty to marry and beget children.

Time is the dominant force in these early sonnets, represented as an artist with the power to transform and deface. This image of time also becomes for the speaker a sort of artistic rival since he believes that his own literary art may also defy time.

The role of counsellor reveals the pre-eminent role of wisdom as prudence. As well as reminding or educating the youth into the nature of time, prudence is a means of revealing the speaker's relationship to the young man. Wit is important here too, and as a wise counsellor he uses his courtly wit to mediate wisdom to his protégé. Wit is a function of the respectful distance the counsellor must observe in his advice, and Cousins traces this feature back to Petrarch's attitude to

Laura, a species of inequality, not unlike that of the author in pursuit of patronage.

Whereas in sonnets 1–19 narcissism is the accusation levelled against the young man, this later becomes a feature of the speaker himself. In other words the youth becomes a mirror up to the speaker, a means of exploring his own experiences in love, his personal ideals and the power of his art. Chapter 4 compares Petrarch's persona and Sidney's Astrophel on these terms, the youth of the early poems ceasing to exist as anything like a real character, while the mature speaker imposes an accumulation of fictions on the image of the youth that will 'dominate the rest of the poems'. To illustrate this view, Cousins analyses sonnets 22 and 31 in detail. For example, one of these fictions is that the young man becomes the embodiment and therefore the perpetuation of his dead friends; so,

> On the youth, that is to say, the speaker imposes an idealising and self-consolatory fiction which functions at the same time as a fable of identity, a fable of spiritual union in love, and so allows the speaker to meditate on his experience of loving. (p. 146)

Cousins continues his essay through close analysis of sonnets 83 and 116. In 83 the speaker acknowledges and confronts his doubts, contrasting wise doubt against naive belief. He reaches a better understanding of himself by understanding the object of his devotion. Analysis of 116 draws attention to its persistent idealism and its use of negatives, by which the speaker approaches a definition and a sense of certainty about the possibility of love through saying what it is not.

Chapter 5 develops what Cousins terms 'Petrarch's drama of the divided self' (p. 188). This theme is seen as the dominant concern of the sonnet range 127–54 and is fleshed out in the speaker's devotion to two objects of desire: the youth again, and now the Dark Mistress, desire for whom holds both the speaker and the youth in thrall as her prisoner. The sonnets in this section are characterised by conflict, insecurity, uncertainty and unstable fluctuations. As elsewhere in the Sonnets, the speaker sets up fictions and histories, here the fiction of beauty.

Cousins concludes that one of the worldly preoccupations of Shakespeare's Sonnets (and of his other non-dramatic verse) is wisdom. This is the baulk against the scepticism he construes as endemic in them and in Elizabethan verse as a whole. He reiterates his judgement that the wisdom of the Sonnets is prudence rather than sapience or contemplative wisdom, and prudence is associated in the Sonnets and elsewhere with gaining control over time. All the Sonnets express a sensitivity to the movement of time, and prudence is concerned not only with caution and discretion but with the seizing of an opportunity at the best possible moment rather than wasting it.

The chief fascination of Cousins's approach lies in its close attention to the details of Shakespeare's texts. The discussion also reveals the writer's masterly facility with the details of the Classical and Renaissance sources that are marshalled alongside the poems under consideration. So detailed and densely argued are the discussions of individual sonnets that the scope of the essay allows little margin for an analysis of the wider aspects of the Sonnets even though the expansive-tending discussion demands and deserves a wider perspective. So, there is no scope for discussion of textual issues; for instance, although he does not interpret the Sonnets as intently auto-biographical, he takes their order as read, and appears to presume their coherence, at least for a discussion of the narratives that he traces within them.

Particularly interesting is Cousins's commentary on what he describes as the 'fictions and histories' at work on different levels and at different stages in the Sonnets. The impression distinctly conveyed is that within the outward unity of the collection there are at work divisions and tensions that threaten to subvert the poet's tenacious desire for stability and wholeness.

Although this essay sets out with a strong idea of imaging Shakespeare's Sonnets and other non-dramatic verse within a perspective of humanist themes of scepticism and *prudentia* this is not fully realised. The primary attraction here actually lies in the closely detailed analysis of individual sonnets but also in the way that Cousins brings out their intertextual dialogues within the humanist paradigm. Unlike Booth's study there is no clearly defined thesis motoring the discussion, which in effect defers to a densely argued study of the multiple discourses that animate the verse. It is on this level that Cousins's critique is to be most prized.

Peter Hyland

An Introduction to Shakespeare's Poems (2003)

Peter Hyland's study of Shakespeare's non-dramatic verse sets out to position the poet's voice firmly in its own social and cultural context. In broad terms, the core of his thesis is that as an ambitious poet and dramatist Shakespeare found himself precariously on the margins of aristocratic social circles. Moreover, he argues that the insecurity associated with writing and the patronage system induced a voice that was sceptical both about the elite values of his time and about the conventions of the Petrarchan sonnet. Crucial to this thesis, Hyland is keen to stress that Shakespeare was primarily interested less in producing high art from his pen than in the hard realities of making a livelihood in a literary marketplace that was highly unstable and prone to the fickle tides of fashion.

Hyland signals his generally New Historicist approach early on,

> I want to focus on these non-dramatic poems, setting them in their original context, a dynamic and often dangerous milieu where poetry performed important social and cultural work. Shakespeare is often represented as a defender of the narrow conservative interests of an elite establishment, but that is too simple a characterisation. He was a child of his time. (3)

Hyland goes out of his way to argue against the grain, maintaining Shakespeare was no aristo toady, at least not out of choice, and like Cousins, finds him fiercely sceptical about these interests and ultimately disillusioned.

Chapter 1 reads Shakespeare as an ambitious poet arriving in London and having no choice but to accept the prevailing social and cultural system with all its ruthless vicissitudes. He encounters men from similar social circumstances harbouring similar literary aspirations but often thwarted. Hyland regards this artistic disenchantment as the basis of the 'malcontent' character in contemporary drama, metaphor of the ambitious lower-class writer shut out by an exclusive gentry. Even as an established author Shakespeare found himself having to balance the need to please his readers with the desire to interrogate established values – and he resorted to covert and ironic means of doing this.

Hyland believes that Shakespeare probably began writing the sonnets in about 1592 and that the publication of 1609 Q was probably authorised. Yet like a great many before him he is at a loss to explain why it was put into print so long after the vogue for sonnets had passed (on page 138 he posits that by 1609 the weight of Shakespeare's reputation made the commercial risk viable).

In 'Shakespeare and the Literary Marketplace' Hyland expands on his treatise that the poet's fundamental task had been to make a living rather than a reputation from his pen. He also introduces the crucial political position of literature as a means 'both of transmission and of control of the ideas, beliefs and attitudes, the aesthetic and ideological positions' of the elite court group (23). He is at pains to establish that poetry, especially in manuscript transmission, was far from being a peripheral or insignificant matter but represented a highly valuable commodity, even though its elite consumers held the professional writer and common reader in contempt. Literature, Hyland claims, was central to the Elizabethan power hierarchy.

Encouraging though this sounds, it is not a convincing argument and Hyland does not pursue it. Rather, it is a useful predicate for the author's central theme that Shakespeare was neither at ease with nor an apologist for conservative court dogma. This theme is also used to explain why the Earl of Southampton's valuable patronage did not extend (explicitly at least) beyond the two narrative poems dedicated to him. Examining the dedications to *Venus and Adonis* and *The Rape of Lucrece*, Hyland finds in addition to deference to his socially superior benefactor a deep sense of Shakespeare's self-assurance in the value of his work. There is some intimacy there too but, like the deference, this sounds conventionally so: Shakespeare was well aware of what exactly was expected of him and what was likely to gain the favour of a wealthy patron.

The question of why Shakespeare ceased to enjoy the patronage of Southampton is extended through a discussion of the image of the 'poet' presented in the plays. The second chapter concludes with the verdict that Shakespeare was repelled by the patronage system with its concomitant aristocratic values, and instead hastened back to the theatre where 'the comparative freedom of the public stage also allowed for a comparative honesty of self-expression' (41).

In chapter 3 the essay turns to consider the aesthetic as opposed to the material value of poetry. Hyland sets out very lucidly the Continental precursors of Tudor humanism as well as the later efforts of Sir Philip Sidney and George Puttenham in raising the status of poetry and establishing an independent domestic literature in the vernacular. It is at this point that Hyland crucially demonstrates Shakespeare's awareness of the dangers inherent in rhetoric as taught in Elizabethan grammar schools: namely, that in literature it privileged 'delightful' presentation over truth. Shakespeare expresses his distaste for such excess in his satirical treatment of 'euphuism' in *Love's Labour's Lost*.

After rehearsing the printing history of the 1609 Quarto edition, Hyland ponders the usual insolubles such as the dating of individual sonnets and the likely biographical dimension to them. His own view on the latter is a warning that we should not take the sonnets as closely autobiographical, with the reminder that Shakespeare is not after all to be closely identified with his dramatic creations such as Hamlet.

But does the collection of 154 sonnets constitute a sonnet sequence? His answer to this is not very clear but he appears to regard it as made up of two fairly baggy sequences: sonnets 1–126 addressed to a young man, and 127–54 concerning an older woman, and these two units form the basis of the discussions in chapters 8 and 9 respectively.

In these chapters he gets down to what he calls the 'real creative significance' of the verse. He sets out his stall by arguing that any individual sonnet works less well when examined in isolation the sequence, thus committing himself to the idea that there really are two strong sequences at work. However, the sonnet he chooses to support this view is 18, which does come at the end of Quarto's most coherent sequence, the 'begetting' sonnets, and so is not characteristic of the norm.

Yet, Hyland's brisk analysis of the poems under scrutiny (especially sonnets 29, 116 and 144) does effectively support his argument that meanings planted in early sonnets are expanded and developed throughout the 'sequence'. He follows up Arthur Marotti's suggestion that we draw a parallel between a lover petitioning his object and a poet seeking to secure patronage. In this way 'love' in a poem may in fact be code for 'commercial loyalty'.

Hyland is on much sounder ground when he turns to examine the 'Dark Mistress' poems and exposes the paradoxes, deceptions and equivocations that 'deny and perplex' the reader. Reiterating his belief that the speaker of these poems is not directly identifiable with their author, he asserts that the vital relationship is not that between the poet and his subject, here the mistress, but between the poet's voice and the reader (p. 175). And he adroitly contends that Shakespeare, in the Sonnets,

> has created a voice that can express a new and complex range of experiences …a voice that is like those of the narrative poems in that it should be listened through as well as listened to. (175)

Ultimately, however, Hyland believes that this voice is far from secure and he returns at the end to insist that its scepticism and instability are indicative of the poet's own sense of insecurity.

A Glossary of Some Rhetorical and Literary Terms

For a general discussion of rhetoric in literature and learning in the sixteenth century, see Chapters 6 and 7. For a list of examples of some of the rhetorical figures used in the sonnets, refer to Chapter 7 and the Index.

anaphora   The repetition of a word or words at the beginning of successive lines or sentences (e.g. sonnets 129:6–7 and 130:3–4).

antanaclasis or antistasis   The repetition of a word in its different senses – a species of pun (e.g. sonnet 106, lines 2 and 7, or sonnet 127, lines 10, 13, 14).

blazon   A list detailing and extolling the attributes of the loved one (see sonnet 106:5–6; and see the **antiblazon** in sonnet 130).

chiasmus   The reversal of syntax in successive clauses or phrases to produce a cross-over effect (e.g. sonnet 23:12).

decorum   The writer's matching of style and form appropriate to the subject matter of a text (see Chapter 7 and the analysis of sonnet 23 in Chapter 3).

the *douzaine*   The first twelve lines of a sonnet working as a structural unit (see sonnets 55 and 129).

elocutio   The finesse of a writer in structuring an argument and selecting the appropriate style(s) to convey it.

epanorthosis   A figure in which the poet replies to or corrects a previous statement (e.g. sonnet 116:5).

euphuism   An exaggeratedly ornate style of writing named after John Lyly's 1578 novel *Euphues: The Anatomy of Wit* (this style is parodied by Shakespeare in *Love's Labour's Lost* in the flamboyant language of Armado and Holofernes).

hendiadys   A figure using two separate nouns, verbs, adjectives etc., joined by a conjunction to spell out a complex idea, as in 'try and do better' (= 'try to do better'; see sonnets 23:9–10 and 152:10–11).

hypermetric line   A line of verse with extra syllable(s) (e.g. in sonnet 20 every line is hypermetric, 'adding one thing'!); a **catalectic** line has missing syllable(s).

hypotyposis   A figure in which something absent is expressed as though it were present (e.g. sonnet 12:2–4).

litotes   An understatement, used to create emphasis (e.g. sonnet 23:7).

metonymy   A figure in which the name or attribute of something is used to represent it; in 'The ring is a tough career', the 'ring' stands for boxing in general. (See sonnet 55:5; compare **synecdoche**).

objective genitive   An ambiguous construction typically using the possessive form, as in 'Tom's assault', which could mean 'the assault carried out *by* Tom' or 'the assault done *to* Tom' (see sonnet 55:10).

occupatio   An ironic figure where, in the act of denying something, the author actually affirms it; so in sonnet 106 the poet eloquently denies that he has any eloquence.

oxymoron   A phrase combining incongruous or seemingly contradictory elements for special effect (e.g. sonnet 20:2).

Petrarchan form   The sonnet form popularised by Petrarch, dividing a poem into octave (*rhyming abbaabba*) and sestet (often *cdecde*); see Chapter 6.

Petrarchism   Imitation of Petrarch's style and subject matter, especially in his use of courtly-love conventions such as the adulation and idealisation of the woman's physical and moral beauty.

pleonasm   Using more words than necessary to express the meaning, often resulting in tautology (see sonnet 23:12 and the ironic use of pleonasm in 137:1–3).

polysyndeton   The repetition of conjunctions (e.g. sonnet 5:6–8).

psychomachy   A dramatic scenario in which two opposing forces (conventionally, good and evil) compete for the mind or soul of a character (see sonnet 144). It is possible to interpret the whole of the *Sonnets* as a larger psychomachy – the contest for Shakespeare's sexual soul between the young man (sonnets 1–126) and the Dark Lady (127–52).

synaesthesia   Mixing sensory perceptions, such as in 'To hear with eyes' (sonnet 23:14).

synecdoche   A figure in which a part stands for the whole; e.g. 'gaze' in sonnet 5:2 stands for the youth himself (compare **metonymy**).

The following contain useful and interesting details or offer a fuller discussion of the above and other relevant terms.

J. Biester, *Lyric Wonder: Rhetoric and Wit in Renaissance English Poetry* (Ithaca, NY: Cornell University Press, 1997).

J. A. Cuddon, *The Penguin Dictionary of Literary Terms and Literary Theory*, 4th edn (Harmondsworth: Penguin, 1998).

R. A. Lanham, *A Handlist of Rhetorical Terms*, 2nd edn (Berkeley, Los Angeles: University of California Press, 1991).

Tom Lennard, *The Poetry Handbook*, 2nd edn (Oxford: Oxford University Press, 2005).

L. A. Sonnino, *A Handbook to Sixteenth-Century Rhetoric* (London: Routledge, 1968).

Further Reading

Editions of the Sonnets

Booth, Stephen (ed.), *Shakespeare's Sonnets* (New Haven, CT: Yale University Press, 1977, revised 2000).

Burrow, Colin (ed.), *William Shakespeare: The Complete Sonnets and Poems* (Oxford: Oxford University Press, 2002).

Burto, William (ed.), *Sonnets*, Introduction by W. H. Auden (New York: Signet Editions, 1964).

Duncan-Jones, Katherine (ed.), *Shakespeare's Sonnets* (London: Thomson Learning/Arden, 1997).

Kerrigan, John (ed.), *William Shakespeare: The Sonnets and A Lover's Complaint* (London: Penguin Books, 1986).

Rollins, Hyder Edward (ed.), *New Variorum Edition of Shakespeare: The Sonnets* (Philadelphia: J. P. Lippincott, 1944).

Critical Studies and Secondary Sources

Bate, Jonathan, 'Ovid and the Sonnets', in *Shakespeare Survey*, 42 (1990).

Bate, Jonathan, *The Genius of Shakespeare* (London: Macmillan, 1997).

Booth, Stephen, *An Essay on Shakespeare's Sonnets* (New Haven, CT: Yale University Press, 1969).

Booth, Wayne C., *The Rhetoric of Fiction* (Chicago: University of Chicago Press, 1961).

Bray, Alan, *Homosexuality in Renaissance England* (London: Gay Men's Press, 1982).

Burton, Robert, *The Anatomy of Melancholy: A Selection*, ed. Kevin Jackson (Manchester: Carcanet Press, 2004).

Castiglione, Baldesar, *The Book of the Courtier*, trans. George Bull (London: Penguin Books, 1967).

Cousins, A. D., *Shakespeare's Sonnets and Narrative Poems* (Harlow: Pearson Education, 2000).

Crystal, David and Ben Crystal, *Shakespeare's Words* (London: Penguin Books, 2002).

De Grazia, Margreta, 'The Scandal of Shakespeare's Sonnets', in *Shakespeare Survey*, 46 (1994).

Duncan-Jones, Katherine, 'Was the 1609 *Shakespeare's Sonnets* Really Unauthorised?' *Review of English Studies*, XXXIV, 134 (1983): 151–71.

Edmundson, Paul and Stanley Wells, *Shakespeare's Sonnets* (Oxford: Oxford University Press, 2004).

Empson, William, *Seven Types of Ambiguity* (Harmondsworth: Penguin Books, 1961).

Erasmus, *Praise of Folly*, trans. Betty Radice (London: Penguin Books, 1971).

Foucault, Michel, *The Order of Things: An Archaeology of the Human Sciences*, trans. Alan Sheridan (London: Routledge, 1970).

Foucault, Michel, 'What is an Author?' in *Textual Strategies: Perspectives in Post-structuralist Criticism*, ed. Josué V. Harari (London: Methuen, 1979).

Graves, Robert and Laura Riding, 'A Study in Original Punctuation and Spelling' (1926; reprinted in Jones, 1977).

Gurr, Andrew, 'You and Thou in Shakespeare's Sonnets', *Essays in Criticism*, XXXII, 1 (1982): 9–25.

Hattaway, Michael (ed.), *A Companion to English Renaissance Literature and Culture* (Oxford: Blackwell, 2000).

Hunter, G. K., 'Humanism and Courtship', in *Elizabethan Poetry: Modern Essays in Criticism*, ed. Paul J. Alpers (Oxford: Oxford University Press, 1967).

Hyland, Peter, *An Introduction to Shakespeare's Poems* (Basingstoke: Palgrave Macmillan, 2003).

Jones, Peter, *Shakespeare, The Sonnets: A Casebook* (Basingstoke: Macmillan, 1977).

Kastan, David Scott (ed.), *A Companion to Shakespeare* (Oxford: Blackwell, 1999).

Knight, G. Wilson, *The Mutual Flame* (London: Methuen, 1955).

Knights, L. C., 'Shakespeare's Sonnets', in *Scrutiny* 3 (1934), pp. 133–60.

Leishman, J. B., *Themes and Variations in Shakespeare's Sonnets*, 2nd edn (London: Hutchinson, 1963).

Mahood, M. M., *Shakespeare's Wordplay* (London: Methuen, 1957).

Martin, Philip, *Shakespeare's Sonnets: Self, Love and Art* (Cambridge: Cambridge University Press, 1972).

Miller, E. H., *The Professional Writer in Elizabethan England* (Cambridge, MA: Harvard University Press, 1959).

More, Thomas, *Utopia*, trans. Paul Turner (London: Penguin Books, 1965).

Ovid, *Shakespeare's Ovid being Arthur Golding's Translation of the Metamorphoses*, ed. W. H. D. Rouse (London: Centaur Press, 1961).

Prince, F. T., 'The Sonnet from Wyatt to Shakespeare', in *Elizabethan Poetry*, ed. John Russell Brown (London: Edward Arnold, 1960).

Shapiro, James, *1599: A Year in the Life of William Shakespeare* (London: Faber, 2005).

Sheavyn, Phoebe, *The Literary Profession in the Elizabethan Age* (Manchester: University of Manchester Press, 1909; rev. edn. 1967).

Smith, Bruce R., *Homosexual Desire in Shakespeare's England* (Chicago: University of Chicago Press, 1991).

Taylor, Gary, 'Some Manuscripts of Shakespeare's Sonnets', *Bulletin of the John Rylands University Library of Manchester*, 68/1 (1985): 210–46.

Vendler, Helen, *The Art of Shakespeare's Sonnets* (Cambridge, MA: Harvard University Press, 1997).

Wait, R. J. C., *The Background to Shakespeare's Sonnets* (London: Chatto and Windus, 1972).

Waller, Gary, *English Poetry of the Sixteenth Century*, 2nd edn (Harlow: Longman, 1993).

Wells, Stanley, *Shakespeare: For All Time* (Oxford: Oxford University Press, 2003).

Wilson, Katharine M., *Shakespeare's Sugared Sonnets* (London: Allen & Unwin, 1974).

Wraight, A. D. and Virginia Stern, *In Search of Christopher Marlowe*, 2nd edn (Chichester: Adam Hart, 1993).

Compact Disc Spoken Recordings

RADA (various artists), *When Love Speaks* (CD), EMI.

Alex Jennings, *Shakespeare: The Sonnets* (CD), NAXOS.

Website

www.shakespeares-sonnets.com/

Index